THE NEW URBAN R

Urban Policy, Planning and the Built Environment

Series Editors:

Nick Gallent, Bartlett School of Planning, University College London, UK

Pierre Filion, University of Waterloo, Canada

Nicole Gurran, University of Sydney, Australia

This international series embraces the interdisciplinary dimensions of urbanism and the built environment – extending from urban policy and governance to urban planning, management, housing, transport, infrastructure, landscape, heritage and design. It aims to provide critical analyses of the challenges confronting cities around the world at the intersection between markets, public policy and the built environment, as well as the responses emerging from these challenges.

The series looks in particular at the contested nature of government intervention in the urban land and housing market and how urban governance, planning and design processes respond to increasing social complexity, social-spatial diversity and the goal of democratic renewal.

Urban Policy, Planning and the Built Environment

Out now in the series:

The Self-Build Experience edited by **Willem Salet, Camila D'Ottaviano, Stan Majoor** and **Daniël Bossuyt**

Rescaling Urban Governance by **John Sturzaker** and **Alexander Nurse**

Find out more at
https://policy.bristoluniversitypress.co.uk/urban-policy-planning-and-the-built-environment

THE NEW URBAN RUINS

Vacancy, Urban Politics and
International Experiments in the
Post-crisis City

Edited by
Cian O'Callaghan and Cesare Di Feliciantonio

First published in Great Britain in 2023 by

Policy Press, an imprint of
Bristol University Press
University of Bristol
1-9 Old Park Hill
Bristol
BS2 8BB
UK
t: +44 (0)117 374 6645
e: bup-info@bristol.ac.uk

Details of international sales and distribution partners are available at
policy.bristoluniversitypress.co.uk

British Library Cataloguing in Publication Data
A catalogue record for this book is available from the British Library

ISBN 978-1-4473-5687-5 hardcover
ISBN 978-1-4473-5688-2 paperback
ISBN 978-1-4473-5690-5 ePub
ISBN 978-1-4473-5689-9 ePdf

Cover design: Andrew Corbett
Front cover image: Cian O'Callaghan

Contents

List of figures and tables   ix
Notes on contributors   xi
Acknowledgements   xiv

Introduction   1
Cian O'Callaghan and Cesare Di Feliciantonio

PART I   Rethinking ruination in the post-crisis context
1   Rem(a)inders of loss: a Lacanian approach to new urban ruins   21
     Lucas Pohl
2   Dignifying the ruins: a former Jewish girls' school   35
     in Berlin
     Karen E. Till
3   Traversing wastelands: reflections on an abandoned   53
     railway yard
     Sandra Jasper
4   Building the new urban ruin: the ghost city of Ordos   73
     Kangbashi, Inner Mongolia
     Christina Lee

PART II   The political economy of urban vacant space
5   *Nullius* no more? Valorising vacancy through urban   91
     agriculture in the settler-colonial 'green city'
     Nathan McClintock
6   Conflicting rationalities and messy actualities of dealing   109
     with vacant housing in Halle/Saale, East Germany
     Nina Gribat
7   Post-disaster ruins: the old, the new and the temporary   125
     Sara Caramaschi and Alessandro Coppola
8   The post-crisis properties of demolishing Detroit, Michigan   145
     Michael R.J. Koscielniak
9   Guarding presence: absent owners and the labour of   163
     managing vacancy
     Lauren Wagner

PART III   Reappropriating urban vacant spaces
10   Politicising vacancy and commoning housing in   181
     municipalist Barcelona
     Mara Ferreri

11   Spatio-legal world-making in vacant buildings: property   197
      politics and squatting movements in the city of São Paulo
      Matthew Caulkins

12   (Im)Material infrastructures and the reproduction of   211
      alternative social projects in urban vacant spaces
      Cesare Di Feliciantonio and Cian O'Callaghan

13   Tracing the role of material and immaterial   229
      infrastructures in imagining diverse urban
      futures: Dublin's Bolt Hostel and Apollo House
      Rachel McArdle

Conclusion: Centring vacancy – towards a research agenda   243
Cian O'Callaghan and Cesare Di Feliciantonio

Index   251

List of figures and tables

Figures

2.1	Detail of Ram Katzir's 'Milk Teeth', 2006	43
2.2	Detail of Martha Roseler's 'Reading Hannah Arendt (Politically)', 2006	45
3.1	Assemblages of plants flourishing in the abandoned Schöneweide railway yard, Berlin, May 2020	56
3.2	The abandoned tracks of the Schöneweide railway yard, Berlin, provide habitats for the sand lizard and various ground-breeding birds, May 2020	57
3.3	A newly paved road with street trees and bike racks cutting through the Schöneweide railway wasteland, May 2020	62
4.1	New residential complexes, Kangbashi	77
4.2	Genghis Khan Square, Kangbashi	79
4.3	Abandoned construction site, Dongsheng	80
4.4	Man asleep in the Cultural and Art Centre, Kangbashi	83
4.5	Makeshift dwelling in a commercial building, Kangbashi	83
7.1	Post-emergency solutions in L'Aquila	128
7.2	Taxonomy of the conditions, the actors involved and the factors and impacts that result in different forms of vacancy, abandonment, underoccupancy and ruination of the stock	131
7.3	Case studies and location map	132
9.1	View of houses across a field, near Tangier Boukhalef, 2015	164
9.2	On-site advertising for an apartment complex under construction, Tangier 2015	168
9.3	The post of guardian, Tangier 2015	171
9.4	Being shown around an apartment complex by a security guard, Tangier 2012	174
10.1	Stencil graffiti on a wall, District Sants-Montjuic, May 2019	188
10.2	Banner drop at Bloc Llavors, District Sants-Montjuic, May 2019	191

Tables

8.1	Reimbursement sought by Adamo after demolishing the structure at 18410 Stout Street	152
8.2	Hardest Hit Fund lien annual discount	153
8.3	Backfill source sites by category	155

Notes on contributors

Sara Caramaschi is a postdoctoral research fellow in urban studies at the Gran Sasso Science Institute, Italy. Her research focuses mainly on the evolution, uses and meanings of the built environment, with particular reference to processes of emptiness in contexts of urban contraction and post-crises cities.

Mathew Caulkins studied architecture in Sao Paulo, a master's in urban planning in Santiago de Chile and a PhD in urban studies in Melbourne. He is currently organising a laboratory at the Universidad de Concepción, Chile, focused on analysing property expressions in Indigenous spaces in various cities of the region of Biobio.

Alessandro Coppola is Assistant Professor at the Department of Architecture and Urban Planning at Politecnico di Milano, Italy. He has had research, teaching and visiting appointments at several institutions. His research interests include urban policies and governance, resilience, and urban informality. His work has featured in journals such as *Urban Geography*, *Urban Studies* and *European Planning Studies*.

Cesare Di Feliciantonio holds a double PhD in geography from Sapienza University of Rome and KU Leuven. He is Lecturer in Human Geography at Manchester Metropolitan University, UK. His work has been published in, among others, *Antipode*, *European Urban and Regional Studies*, *Gender, Place & Culture*, *Geoforum*, *International Journal of Urban and Regional Research* and *Urban Geography*.

Mara Ferreri is Vice-Chancellor Research Fellow in the Department of Geography and Environmental Sciences at Northumbria University, UK. Her research interests include urban precarity, temporary and platform urbanism, and housing commons. She is the author of *The Permanence of Temporary Urbanism: Normalising Precarity in Austerity London* (AUP, 2021).

Nina Gribat is Professor of Urban Planning at B-TU Cottbus, Germany. Her research focuses on urban restructuring processes and conflicts in the context of planning in the Global North and South, as well as study reforms in architecture and planning since the 1960s and 1970s.

Sandra Jasper is Junior Professor of Geography at the Humboldt-Universität zu Berlin. Her research interests are in urban nature, soundscapes and feminist theory. She is co-editor of *The Botanical City* (Jovis, 2020) and co-producer of *Natura Urbana: The Brachen of Berlin* (2017, UK/Germany, 72 mins). She is currently completing her first monograph on the experimental spaces of West Berlin supported by a Graham Foundation grant.

Michael R.J. Koscielniak studies decline as an urbanisation process of racial capitalism. He focuses on policies, pathways and pipelines that extract value from built environments. By concentrating on logistical and environmental operations, he contributes to renewed approaches to rentiership and disinvestment. He is Assistant Professor at Eastern Michigan University, US.

Christina Lee is Senior Lecturer in English and Cultural Studies at Curtin University, Australia. She is the author of *Screening Generation X: The Politics and Popular Memory of Youth in Contemporary Cinema* (Routledge, 2010) and the editor of *Spectral Spaces and Hauntings: The Affects of Absence* (Routledge, 2017) and *Violating Time: History, Memory, and Nostalgia in Cinema* (Bloomsbury, 2008).

Rachel McArdle is an urban geographer and Lecturer based at Maynooth University, Ireland. She is interested in the way people make spaces and places in the city, and past research has focused on creative cities, festivals, autonomous spaces, squats and other provisional uses of the urban.

Nathan McClintock is Associate Professor of Urban Studies at the Institut national de la recherche scientifique (INRS) in Montréal, Québec. He received his PhD in geography from UC Berkeley, and has published on urban political ecology, urban agriculture and environmental justice in a wide range of journals and edited volumes.

Cian O'Callaghan is Assistant Professor in Geography at Trinity College Dublin. Working in the area of urban and cultural geography, his recent Irish Research Council-funded research was broadly concerned with the impacts of Ireland's property bubble and associated crisis, with a particular focus on housing, urban vacancy and spatial justice.

Lucas Pohl is a postdoctoral researcher at the Department of Geography of Humboldt-University Berlin, Germany. He received his

PhD with a dissertation on a psychoanalytic approach to urban ruins. He works on the interstices between human geography, psychoanalysis and philosophy, with a focus on spatial theory, built environments and politics.

Karen E. Till is Professor of Cultural Geography at Maynooth University, Ireland. She directs the MA in Spatial Justice and the Space & Place Research Collaborative, and is co-convener of the Mapping Spectral Traces international network. Her numerous publications include *The New Berlin: Memory, Politics, Place* (University of Minnesota Press, 2005). Her book in progress, *Wounded Cities*, highlights the significance of place-based memory-work and ethical forms of care.

Lauren Wagner is a sociolinguist and human geographer, and Assistant Professor in Globalisation and Development at Maastricht University, the Netherlands. She uses microanalysis of everyday encounters, compiling interactional, observational and experiential data, to investigate issues around diasporic mobilities and belongings between Morocco and Europe. More of her work is available at: www.drlaru. com

Acknowledgements

This edited collection stems from a workshop hosted in Trinity College Dublin in March 2017. This workshop and the subsequent edited collection was supported by funding from the Irish Research Council (IRC) under the New Horizons Research Scheme 2015 for the project 'The New Urban Ruins: Vacancy and the Post-crisis City' (IRC/REPRO/2015/118). We would like to thank the IRC for enabling this scholarly exchange and facilitating the building of this scholarly community. We also thank all those who helped in the running and attended the workshop, especially those who chaired sessions. We would like to thank our supportive colleagues at the Department of Geography, Trinity College Dublin; the Department of Geography and the Maynooth Institute for Social Sciences (MUSSI) in Maynooth University; the School of Geography, Geology and the Environment, University of Leicester; and the Department of Natural Sciences, Manchester Metropolitan University. Thanks to Maedhbh Nic Lochlainn, Tommy Gavin and Kathleen Stokes for proofreading. Finally, we thank our families for allowing us the time to finalise this collection amid the difficulties of lockdowns in 2020 and early 2021.

Introduction

Cian O'Callaghan and Cesare Di Feliciantonio

Empty cities

During the early months of 2020, cities appeared to stop working. The global spread of the COVID-19 pandemic resulted in a wave of nationwide lockdowns as governments mandated restrictions on the movement of populations and the shuttering of all but essential services. Sublime images of familiar cities emptied and at a standstill reached socially distanced audiences via social media. Excepting the ghostly vigil of essential workers – bus drivers, food retail workers and Deliveroo cyclists, as well as medical staff – the pandemic had put our cities on pause.

The empty city became a key representation trope of the pandemic. This is unsurprising given the increasing centrality of urbanisation to contemporary social and economic life. Moreover, as Connolly et al (2020) argue, 'extended urbanisation' is itself a key factor in the spread and mitigation of infectious diseases, with interconnected supply chains and deeply unequal urban cores acting as conduits for the spread of COVID-19. However, the pandemic city was one of interconnection, and mobility collapsed. In this way, it bore some relation to the city in ruins: the sense of linear time suspended; the denuded folly of progress visible in streets aggregating windswept litter; and the return of flora and fauna to landscapes usually dominated by humans. If the images were sublime, the experience on the ground was one of the uncanny (Freud, 2003), with familiar urban environments abruptly rendered strange.

The pandemic also signalled urban cavities of different form by exposing the fragility of cities under neoliberalism: underfunded healthcare systems; inadequate and overcrowded housing; and a social apparatus completely dependent on the private sector. A range of cities quickly adopted unprecedented political responses aimed at banning evictions, forgiving delayed rent and mortgage payments, and ensuring access to temporary accommodation through the sourcing of vacant properties. As the pandemic exposed the impact of years of

1

austerity, privatisation and rentier capitalism on cities (Sassen, 2014; Madden and Marcuse, 2016), it also challenged us to rethink our understandings of urban density (McFarlane, 2020) and, by extension, vacancy. While the city during lockdown has the appearance of being empty, it is paradoxically full, with inhabitants confined mostly to private residences. As McFarlane (2020) notes, the problem for cities tackling COVID-19 'is not with high population density per se, but with the imbalance between good quality urban provisions – including housing, services and infrastructure – and the population density of an area'. Like density, vacancy provides a challenge to urban scholars to move beyond normative thinking.

The city in ruins, characterised by starkly visible emptiness and decay, and the gleaming neoliberal city that, nevertheless, is peppered with invisible cavities may seem diametrically opposed. Our aim in this collection, put simply, is to show that this is not the case. Like McFarlane's comments on density, understanding urban vacancy requires us to look beyond its appearance and into the more opaque task of parsing how 'empty' spaces factor into the ordinary – and unequal – apparatus of the city.

Although the topics of this book – ruins and vacant space – have been subject to voluminous literatures, they have often failed to adequately speak to one another. The scholarship on ruination has focused on highly visible, visually spectacular and culturally resonant sites (DeSilvey and Edensor, 2013). This literature has challenged the view that vacant spaces are empty by documenting the material and discursive engagements occurring in and through them. Nevertheless, by foregrounding 'the ruin', these approaches privilege the most visible and often culturally significant forms of vacancy, and thus cover over the more mundane ways in which vacancy functions as part of the capitalist city. On the other hand, the literature on property studies and urban political economy tends to treat vacancy (in different ways) as an unavoidable and transient, but largely passive, feature of the built environment (Gore and Nicholson, 1991). The former understands vacancy as a residual outcome of property market cycles, which may also be mobilised as a 'powerful planning tool, a sort of "reboot button" ... to bring about economic growth' (Freire Trigo, 2020: 262), while the latter views vacancy as a core component in processes of devaluation that pave the way for new forms of reinvestment and redevelopment (Smith, 1987). However, in both sets of literature, vacant spaces themselves are viewed as largely inert until they are again targeted for substantive processes of land transformation. In this sense, vacant spaces often only come into the frame through the analysis of processes that herald their *dis*appearance.

Thus, a range of common approaches to understanding vacancy do not adequately capture the abundant and diverse forms it takes in cities or its multiple roles in processes of urban transformation. As this book seeks to show, vacant spaces in cities are active, lively and heavily contested. We therefore centre our analysis on the diverse spatialities, temporalities and cultural imaginaries of vacant spaces themselves. In this task, we draw from, and bring together, a range of conceptual and disciplinary approaches.

Ruins, rubble and the vacant spaces in between

Recent decades have witnessed an extraordinary resurgence of interest in spaces of ruination and abandonment in urban scholarship and popular discourse (DeSilvey and Edensor, 2013). Established critical work on modern ruins in geography, planning and cognate disciplines has viewed vacant and abandoned spaces as disruptive of narratives of progress and decline, particularly in relation to deindustrialisation (Edensor, 2005; Mah, 2012). According to DeSilvey and Edensor (2013: 465), 'The ruined form is one of the most enduring and complex representational devices in western tradition, and contemporary perspectives are inevitably inflected with traces of earlier engagements.' Renewed interest in the representational qualities of ruins has also coincided with a wealth of interventions that seek to understand and shape the materiality of vacant spaces. Writing from an architectural perspective, Jill Desimini (2019) has used design ideas to intervene in vacant spaces and disrupt capitalist development processes by proposing imaginative futures for abandoned property. These forms of design-led thinking have also become prevalent across a range of temporary use initiatives (Bishop and Williams, 2012) that proliferated after the 2008 global financial crisis (GFC). Similarly, a new sub-strand of work on urban political economy has foregrounded vacancy as an active component in relation to housing, real estate speculation and contestations over property (O'Callaghan et al, 2018; Fererri and Vasudevan, 2019; Noterman, 2020). This work extrapolates the insights nascent in the literature on property studies and urban political economy, which suggests vacancy is significant in a host of urban processes, ranging from urban regeneration (Freire Trigo, 2020) to resistance movements (Noterman, 2020) and alternative claims on land (Safransky, 2017).

These diverse literatures have begun to cross-pollinate in an exploratory but wayward fashion. Their hitherto fragmentation, however, suggests the under-theorisation of the concept of vacancy in urban studies, while, at the same time, highlighting the potential of more dynamic conceptualisations to unlock new ways of thinking about urban processes. This collection puts these approaches into a more substantive and systematic dialogue by drawing together the rich conceptual and methodological approaches of work on ruins and the insights of recent work focusing on what does, and potentially could, happen in vacant spaces in order to reveal the role that diverse forms of vacancy play in the governance of cities. In this section, we briefly sketch out the parameters, intersections and lacuna of recent research on ruins and vacant spaces.

Ruins research provides a rich set of conceptual and methodological tools to understand vacant spaces as material and discursive sites that are perpetually in – and of – use. However, their object of analysis – the ruin – has at once been limited in scope (as a form of vacancy) and eluded precise definition. As Dillon (2011: 11) notes, ruins 'embody a set of temporal and historical paradoxes. The ruined building is a remnant of, and portal into, the past; its decay a concrete reminder of the passage of time.' Ruins are, therefore, as much a representational form and 'an invitation to thought' (Dillon, 2011: 11) as they are material sites. Traditional tropes of ruins as remnants of distant pasts have been complicated throughout the 20th century, as ruins of antiquity gave way to 'modern ruins' resulting from deindustrialisation and geopolitical change (Edensor, 2005; Mah, 2012). As processes of capitalist creative destruction sped up, societies were increasingly confronted with ruins of the recent past. In contrast to the ruins of antiquity, these modern ruins were in living memory. Already anticipated by Walter Benjamin (1999) in his dissection of the Parisian arcades, the modern ruin was the unacknowledged remainder that haunted the vision of progress propping up capitalist modernity and urbanisation. Therefore, they constituted a problem of *present* capitalist urbanisation rather than of *past* society. These processes of accelerated creative destruction reached an apotheosis in the aftermath of the 2008 GFC, when property crashes in various countries left vast landscapes of unfinished and vacant developments. For Kitchin et al (2014), these constituted a novel form of 'new ruins', both 'new and derelict' and characterised by a 'speculative future' that never became a reality, rather than by an abandoned past. In combination with spectacular future ruins like Chinese 'ghost cities' (Woodworth and Wallace, 2017), the proliferation of new forms of ruination has troubled existing scholarship. Rather than the slow decline of civilisations, these examples presented ruins that seemed to appear, as if in real time, out of collapse in the circulatory system of global finance and the speculative futures it conjured. In having to rethink the basis and import of these 'new ruins', recent ruins research has had to conceptualise the processes through which sites are *made* into ruins.

If the ruin is an allegory of regional or global political and economic forces, vacant space constitutes a much wider and more nebulous aspect of the urban. There is no internationally accepted definition of what constitutes vacant land (Pearsall et al, 2014), and those that exist tend to be highly context specific. Vacant space can be seen as the ordinary and cruddy ancillary to the ruin's melancholic grandeur, created by the same processes but either associated with more negative terminology (for example, 'blight') or largely invisible within the urban landscape. This is because 'ruins' are characterised by a particular representational mode of narrating progress and decline. As Gordillo (2014) argues, 'the ruin' is a Western construct that attaches grand narratives of progress and decline (whether colonialism or waves of capitalist expansion and destruction) onto derelict spaces. In contrast, vacant spaces often fall outside of any clear representational frame. Gordillo can again help us here. In contrast to the singular narrative of 'ruins', he offers the concept of 'rubble' to account for the multiplicity and, indeed, negativity created in the void of 'vacant space'. For Gordillo, rubble captures the refusal of vacant spaces to give themselves over absolutely to representational form. Whereas the ruin signals a teleology linking together a defined historical use, (con)temporary reuse and possible future redevelopment, rubble collapses this into a multiplicity of historical meanings, conflictual (con)temporary uses and contestations over future forms of redevelopment. In this sense, rubble suggests the vibrancy of contestations over the making of ruins, while asking us to cast our net wider to see the conflict hidden in 'vacant spaces', as well as their capacity as sites of possibility to create, through bricolage, the conditions under which alternative presents and futures can come into being.

This view of ruins and vacant spaces as vibrant, contested and processual has emerged alongside a body of work conceptualising abandonment as an active and ongoing process. This work has paid particular attention to the people living in and through places of extensive vacancy and processes of ruination (Povinelli, 2011; Tsing, 2015; Safransky, 2018; Dawney, 2020). Recent anthropological and geographical scholarship, for example, has explored the ways in which 'abandoned' sites (Povinelli, 2011) are also important spaces in the formation of 'nascent commons' (Tsing, 2015) amid competing claims over future redevelopment (Vasudevan, 2015; Safransky, 2017). Critical urban scholarship has also sought to focus on the ways in which life and survival continue for residents of places normatively viewed as abandoned (Safransky, 2018; Dawney, 2020).

Likewise, the dynamic character of vacant spaces has become the focus of scholarly attention in debates on urban regeneration and, more recently, temporary use (Ferreri, 2015; Ferreri and Vasudevan, 2019). The vast literature on gentrification has long explored the role that vacant land and derelict spaces play in capitalist urban development processes, whereby running down and naming areas of cities *as blighted* can pave the way for further rounds of urban development (Smith, 1987). The associations between vacancy and gentrification have been further highlighted through the recent popularity of temporary use in post-crisis cities.[1] Following the 2008 GFC, urban vacant spaces became increasingly visible and politicised (O'Callaghan et al, 2018). The prevalence of unfinished developments stemming from localised property bubbles (Kitchin et al, 2014), coupled with the dispossessions first associated with mortgage foreclosures (García-Lamarca and Kaika, 2016) and then as a result of increasingly financialised rental housing (Fields, 2018; Janoschka et al, 2020), focused attention on urban vacancy. If the 2008 GFC put a spotlight on urban vacancy, it simultaneously drew attention to and mainstreamed an emergent set of interventions in the management of vacant spaces by policy and market actors. Most prevalently, a range of temporary use projects became a vehicle for reinvigorating properties left fallow from the downturn, as well as sites of longer-term vacancy (Bishop and Williams, 2012). Although celebrated in policy and design circles for their transformative potential, a range of critical voices have suggested how these projects were co-opted in the service of neoliberal policy agendas to support 'creative city' initiatives and kick-start gentrification (Mould, 2014; Ferreri, 2015). Moreover, the selective framing and mobilisation of such supposedly bottom-up projects is indicative of the growing governance of vacant spaces in post-crisis cities, whereby various actors seek to intervene to shape what kinds of uses (temporary or longer-term) are made possible (O'Callaghan et al, 2018). A similar set of practices are evident in property guardianship, which can be seen to protect vacant properties against squatting by exploiting the precarious housing conditions of urban residents (Fererri et al, 2017). In this way, urban vacancy can be seen as a key part of instituting precarity (Madanipour, 2018) and making the precarious city (Ferreri and Vasudevan, 2019), while interrogating various interventions in vacant spaces can reframe our understandings of entrepreneurial urban governance (O'Callaghan et al, 2018).

To further a scholarly agenda to bring these literatures together, this book takes as its point of departure two overlapping claims. The first claim is that although the topics of ruins and vacant spaces have been widely discussed in the urban studies literature, their role in the production of both urban landscapes and the economic, social and cultural geographies of cities is not adequately understood. We, therefore, take a critical view of the categories of both 'ruins' and 'vacant space'. If the literature on modern ruins has long offered a rich set of conceptual and methodological tools for engaging with vacant sites (for example, Edensor, 2005; Mah, 2012; DeSilvey, 2017), its focus on exceptional forms of vacancy (sites of often already-existing material and cultural significance) does not simply map onto less visible, more mundane, forms of urban vacancy. In contrast, until recently, the literature on property studies and urban political economy has treated vacancy as largely inert. Furthermore, the diverse and overlapping terminology used in planning and policy frameworks – including 'stalled development', 'underutilised land' and 'brownfield land', or 'vacant' and 'derelict' property – suggest a lack of clarity on what constitutes vacant land and property as a 'measurable object' (Freire Trigo, 2020). All of this is to suggest that vacant space is an important and dynamic characteristic of cities that warrants greater conceptual and empirical attention. We seek to address this problematic in this collection by putting different approaches into dialogue, both across the three sections of the book and through the synthesis of different theories and approaches within individual chapters. Following these principles, our aim is to move away from ruins as traditionally conceived and to stretch to more complex and differentiated processes (O'Callaghan, 2018).

The second claim is that urban vacancy will play an even greater role in urban development, politics and experimentation in the future. By focusing our analysis on vacant spaces, the book builds on work that seeks to problematise the notion that any space is inherently abandoned, unused or unoccupied; rather, spaces officially designated as 'vacant' are the sites of contested activity, use and representation. We develop this theme throughout the collection by framing the governance of vacant spaces as a central concern for cities in historic as well as contemporary contexts, and by suggesting the ways that such attempts are resisted by activists. The range of new literatures taking an interest in vacant spaces as lived and actively governed offer a novel and exciting entry point to rethink urban vacancy.

The book, therefore, aims to expand the conceptual and empirical lexicon of urban vacancy, centring it within the research agenda of urban scholars. It seeks to animate 'vacant spaces' as discursively and materially contested sites, and as relationally important nodes in urbanisation processes. The collection is structured around animating three high-level conceptual and empirical propositions. Each of these advances our thinking on ruination and urban vacancy, while, in total, they contribute towards producing a more holistic, nuanced and critical understanding of these urban processes.

On the relationship between ruins and vacant spaces

Our first proposition is that the relationship between ruins and urban vacancy is under-theorised. Critically considering how ruins are used as sites negotiating urban pasts and essaying urban futures can show us how vacant spaces are claimed and performatively staged as mechanisms of reuse and repair.

Conceptually drawing out the distinction between 'ruins' and 'vacant space', chapters in Part I – 'Rethinking ruination in the post-crisis context' – animate these processes in two major respects. First, contributions view ruins and vacant spaces as inflected by specific histories, as well as being lived spaces. This is a multilayered process. On the one hand, this involves historical conditions of urban and economic development, planning policy, and property speculation. Specific forms of vacancy are produced out of particular boom–bust cycles and more residual forms of abandonment (Mah, 2012). On the other hand, collective cultural imaginaries differentially frame vacant spaces: some gain the cultural significance of ruins by being tied to particular place-based narratives that negotiate between 'troubled' pasts and future possibilities (Till, 2012; Pohl, 2019); others are cast simply as blight or altogether disappear into the urban fabric (O'Mahony and Rigney, 2016). In both instances, however, this involves active contestation over the use and meaning of these spaces.

Lucas Pohl, in his chapter 'Rem(a)inders of loss: a Lacanian approach to new urban ruins', explores how new urban ruins are *transformed into ruins* in the first place. Drawing on Lacanian psychoanalytic theory, Pohl argues that new urban ruins are not just remainders, but reminders of loss, while also engendering a strange type of 'enjoyment' that can be associated with the 'death drive'. Reflecting on Michigan Central Station in Detroit, Pohl's chapter interrogates why, in the context of the demolition of tens of thousands of buildings in Detroit (see also the chapter by Koscielniak), concerted efforts were made to save this particular empty building. He argues that ruins operate as objects of crisis, pivoting around what is lost or changed from a pre-crisis world in a post-crisis reality.

Reflecting on the legacies of anti-Semitism and National Socialism in Berlin, Karen E. Till's chapter, 'Dignifying the ruins: a former Jewish girl's school in Berlin', shows how spaces can be made into ruins by extreme forms of violence and spatial injustice. Focusing on a former Jewish girls' school in Central Berlin, her chapter critically reflects on the temporary art exhibition 'Hannah Arendt *Denkraum*' ('Hannah Arendt Thinking Space') hosted in the building as part of a series of 'interim uses'. Using the exhibition as a focal point, Till documents how these interventions reanimated the building 'as a historical place of Jewish life and culture in Berlin'.

Second, contributions seek to trouble the stability of ruin narratives by emphasising how the meaning and use of vacant spaces shifts over time. Sandra Jasper's chapter, 'Traversing wastelands: reflections on an abandoned railway yard', adds another dimension to the discussion on Berlin by emphasising how urban vacant spaces function as ecological and more-than-human habitats. Excavating the city's complex geopolitical, economic and natural history, Jasper shows how wastelands have been an essential, lively and contested component of urban life and development in Berlin. Taking a long historical view, and weaving together an approach to political ecology, political economy and landscape geography, her chapter reanimates how wastelands have functioned as 'rubble' and how such alternative uses are increasingly threatened by property development.

In her chapter, 'Building the new urban ruin: the ghost city of Ordos Kangbashi, Inner Mongolia', Christina Lee positions China's ghost cities in the context of the literature on 'new ruins'. She uses a psychogeographic and autoethnographic approach to think beyond the view of these developments as inevitable failures. Starting with the dominant view or Ordos as a monumental 'ghost city' stemming from rapid urbanisation, Lee considers the strangeness of these new gleaming ruins of the future. However, she disrupts this narrative by focusing more attentively on the signs of habitation and future possibility that are visible just beneath the surface of the monumental emptiness.

On urban vacancy as an ordinary component of urbanisation

The emerging urban economy in Ordos anticipates our second proposition: that vacancy is an ordinary and constitutive component of urbanisation. Building on the literature on blight and decline

(Hackworth, 2019), as well as predatory property practices, a growing body of work has sought to interrogate how competing claims on vacancy are actively governed, primarily in the interests of propertied elites (Roy, 2017; Safransky, 2017; Akers and Seymour, 2018), but also contested by other groups (O'Callaghan et al, 2018; Ferreri and Vasudevan, 2019; Noterman, 2020). Chapters in Part II, 'The political economy of urban vacant space', approach urban vacancy as a core feature of cities, constituting the interface between urban land markets and cultural understandings of use/exchange value. In doing so, the contributions extend and trouble existing theorisations of gentrification, regeneration and a range of other urban processes.

Vacancy, as Nathan McClintock's chapter, '*Nullius* no more? Valorising vacancy through urban agriculture in the settler-colonial "green city"', shows, is never simply a blank canvas. His chapter looks at the relationships between urban agriculture, vacant space and uneven patterns of urban development. Like vacancy, he argues, urban agriculture is associated with the troughs of urban economic development, 'serving as placeholders for future development'. Building on the gentrification literature that emphasises 'pioneer' or 'frontier' narratives of 'reclaiming' inner cities, McClintock links the ambivalent development processes bound up in urban agriculture to wider processes of settler colonialism and racial capitalism via a discussion of Montreal, Vancouver and Portland.

The chapters by Nina Gribat and by Sara Caramaschi and Alessandro Coppola demonstrate that urban vacancy presents a challenge and an opportunity in context-specific ways that respond to local development agendas and are shaped by the confluence of actors. Nina Gribat's chapter, 'Conflicting rationalities and messy actualities of dealing with vacant housing in Halle/Saale, East Germany', examines differentiated policies responding to vacant housing stock in two areas of the city following reunification. She positions her intervention at the intersection between literatures of shrinking cities, urban regeneration and 'new ruins'. Through a detailed empirical examination of conflicting policy and market interventions in two neighbourhoods – a city-centre district of mostly vacant former private houses and a peripheral district of mostly vacant former German Democratic Republic public housing – Gribat shows how different types of vacancy are 'problematised' and resolved in highly divergent ways.

Sara Caramaschi and Alessandro Coppola's chapter, 'Post-disaster ruins: the old, the new and the temporary', echoes Pohl's assertion that ruins operate as objects of crisis. Focusing on the ruination produced by the earthquake in L'Aquilla, Italy, their contribution interrogates the long-term trajectories of the built environment. Reflecting on the reality on the ground ten years after the earthquake, they show how initial emergency responses have melded into wider post-crisis redevelopment goals. Their chapter accordingly documents two main processes: the disjuncture between reconstruction and a shifting demographic reality; and how emergency housing solutions have transitioned into longer-term policies, coupled with the progressive evacuation and disinvestment of parts of the urban realm.

While these chapters show how dereliction is factored into urban development strategies, the chapter by Michael R.J. Koscielniak, 'The post-crisis properties of demolishing Detroit, Michigan', investigates vacancy and dereliction as an economic sector in itself. Focusing on the city of Detroit, Koscielniak examines the demolition industry as a constitutive component of producing vacancy. Drawing on both political economy and ecology, he demonstrates how a vast land regime of decline has grown out of the city's overlapping fiscal and urban crises. Focusing on demolition and the associated economy of 'backfilling' (that is, dirt to cover over newly vacant lots), Koscielniak assembles a view of a form of shadow urbanisation that renders land vacant and profitable even without development.

Chapters in Part II also emphasise the multiple temporalities of vacancy. The chapters by McClintock and Gribat demonstrate the different ways interim uses factor into urban development and property speculation agendas (as placeholders or signposts for desirable types of future redevelopment), while Caramaschi and Coppola show how the temporary can become a more permanent fix to provide (precarious) housing solutions. Lauren Wagner's chapter, 'Guarding presence: absent owners and the labour of managing vacancy', focuses on another problematic: that of the everyday labour of taking care of second homes. Using the case of Tangier in Morocco, a city characterised by high levels of vacant second residences or investments bought by domestic and diasporic Moroccans, Wagner's chapter shows how forms of guardianship can fill the temporary vacancies left by mobile owners. Drawing on the experience of property guardians to tease out the complexities of everyday housing vacancy, Wagner shows how vacancy can be partial or temporary when connected to circulatory mobility.

On ruins and urban vacant spaces as political antagonism

Our third proposition is that ruins and vacant spaces are an important point of political antagonism. In the post-crisis period, high-profile occupations of vacant buildings have become a strategy used by housing activists across a range of cities (Di Feliciantonio, 2017; Roy, 2017). These strategies demonstrate the extent to which, in a wider sense, urban vacancy has become more visible and politicised in the aftermath of the GFC because of the tension between unaffordability, vacancy and increasing rates of people experiencing homelessness, eviction and arrears. The pervasiveness of underutilised urban space has stimulated wider engagements with reusing vacant spaces in cities on the part of different actors, including public institutions, social movements, private companies and cultural actors (Ferreri, 2015). The popularity of 'temporary uses' at a grass-roots and policy level, for example, or the growth of property guardianship (Ferreri et al, 2017), are testament to the increased visibility of vacant spaces and to a mounting pressure to allow for new models of access in order to create 'alternative' projects or modes of habitation. However, these alternatives are not inherently progressive, that is, they might reproduce precarity or enable the 'reactivation' of private redevelopment (Colomb, 2012; O'Callaghan et al, 2018). Against commodification and the violence of neoliberalism, grass-roots movements around the globe have made use of the conceptual framework of the *commons* to claim their access to, and control over, vacant buildings (Di Feliciantonio and Aru, 2018). While the defence of the commons has traditionally concerned natural resources (for example, water), an increasing number of voices in academia and across social movements have stressed the need to engage with the urban and relational dimension of the commons under informational capitalism. Building on feminist thought (for example, Federici, 2011), they emphasise the importance of 'common' as a verb rather than a noun in order to account for the performative character of the commons as based on the practices that constitute them. The coming together of practices, relations, bodies, desires and the interactions between human and more-than-human actors manifests itself within specific material places – like occupied squares (Kaika and Karaliotas, 2016) and buildings – that challenge hegemonic rationalities and reproduce themselves over time, even after their material eviction.

The four chapters composing Part III, 'Reappropriating urban vacant spaces', analyse the contentious character of vacancy in post-crisis cities shaped by rapid dispossession and increasing precarisation (Beswick et al, 2016). Focusing on Barcelona, one of the Spanish cities most hit by the housing crisis that followed the GFC, Mara Ferreri's chapter, 'Politicising vacancy and commoning housing in municipalist Barcelona', engages with the ambivalent and contested character of the process of politicising vacancy. Analysing the controversies around data availability, and the direct action of reappropriating vacant buildings on the part of neighbourhood-based assemblies that contest official data – even if coming from a 'progressive' and 'friendly' city administration – the chapter emphasises the need for careful scrutiny of how vacancy is imagined, governed and contested.

The contested character of vacancy is also at the core of Matthew Caulkins' chapter, 'Spatio-legal world-making in vacant buildings: property politics and squatting movements in the city of São Paulo', in which he unpacks the three conflicting spatial logics behind a vacant building in the Brazilian metropolis: (1) the market logic of the owner who wants to dispose of the building; (2) the state's ambivalent logic, divided between private property rights and the social function of property included in the Brazilian constitution; and (3) the squatters' logic, reclaiming the social function of property as owned by those inhabiting it. The clash among different rationalities, Caulkins argues, highlights how the meaning of vacancy relies on the rationalities behind the practices *making* them.

While Ferreri's and Caulkins' chapters highlight contrasting rationalities behind the construction of vacancy, the two remaining chapters focus on the 'world-making' character (Vasudevan, 2015) of autonomous initiatives reclaiming urban vacant spaces. In the chapter '(Im)Material infrastructures and the reproduction of alternative social projects in urban vacant spaces', Di Feliciantonio and O'Callaghan produce a comparative analysis of what sustains the reproduction of these initiatives over time, as well as against institutional violence. Their chapter focuses on two European capitals – Rome and Dublin – with very different legacies of autonomous politics. Their analysis highlights the central role of (im)material infrastructures made of people, personal relationships, shared practices and histories, and cultural and social capital, but also including urban vacant spaces themselves because they enable contentious actions and experiments in commoning.

The focus on vacant spaces as offering the possibility to imagine alternative urban futures through commoning continues with Rachel McArdle's chapter, 'Tracing the role of material and immaterial infrastructures in imagining diverse urban futures: Dublin's Bolt Hostel and Apollo House'. Centred around Dublin, a city experiencing a rampant homelessness crisis related to the fast recovery of the real estate market after the collapse that followed the GFC, the chapter claims that occupied buildings contribute to an activist landscape made of new lifeworlds and radical infrastructures. These initiatives, she argues, survive the end of specific actions, opening new possibilities for further projects to emerge. Taken together, the four chapters in

Part III call for urban scholars to engage more with the everyday, lived and experimental 'world-making' dimension of vacant spaces, avoiding the reification of those readings that reduce them to mere tools of financial accumulation.

Conclusion

In summary, *The New Urban Ruins* offers critical insights that help us think beyond existing understandings of ruins and vacant space, and to see the intersections between different approaches. The book builds on and critically synthesises different strands of literature that have sought to problematise and rethink urban vacancy and ruination. By bridging different debates, disciplinary approaches, topics of concern and case studies across the globe, the book sheds new light on the complexity of forces and processes shaping urban vacancy and its reuse considered as *lived spaces*, *economic spaces* and *sites of political antagonism*. As such, by foregrounding urban vacancy, the collection helps us to understand the reconfiguration of the urban process at work under late neoliberalism.[2] This is an urgent task given the confluence of highly unequal and financialised urban cores, the growth of a suite of policies and mechanisms that aim to govern alternative uses of vacant spaces, and the copacetic emergence of grass-roots movements to reappropriate vacant property. The book seeks to provide a framework for thinking through the relationships between ruins and wider processes of vacancy, to reorient vacancy from an inert to an active component in our understandings of urban property development, and to critically interrogate how vacancy forms an infrastructure and a resource in a range of contemporary social movements. The empty spaces and stalled time of the city under lockdown have provided an appropriate juncture to consider these questions; we must look amid cities' interstitial spaces to imagine alternative urban futures. Vacancy, the book argues, will be at the core of questions of equity and justice in post-crisis cities.

Notes

[1] 'Post-crisis' is used here to refer to both cities that have been affected by property crashes and the more general ways in which the ideological legitimacy of 'entrepreneurial urbanism' has been challenged following the GFC (O'Callaghan et al, 2018).

[2] Although the book will take a global focus, we are conscious of the geographical differences with regard to the role that vacancy plays in the city. Our primary aim in the collection will be to draw out how urban vacant spaces in Global North and particular post-crisis cities have become key sites of urban governance – reframing

the sets of actors involved in urban development and the possibilities of, and in, urban space – while learning from the longer-term trajectories of informality in Global South cities.

References

Akers, J. and Seymour, E. (2018) 'Instrumental exploitation: predatory property relations at city's end', *Geoforum*, 91: 127–40.

Benjamin, W. (1999) *The Arcades Project*, Cambridge: Harvard University Press.

Beswick, J., Alexandri, G., Byrne, M., Vives-Miró, S., Fields, D., Hodkinson, S. and Janoschka, M. (2016) 'Speculating on London's housing future: the rise of global corporate landlords in "post-crisis" urban landscapes', *City*, 20(2): 321–41.

Bishop, P. and Williams, L. (2012) *The Temporary City*, London: Routledge.

Colomb, C. (2012) 'Pushing the urban frontier: temporary uses of space, city marketing, and the creative city discourse in 2000s Berlin', *Journal of Urban Affairs*, 34(2): 131–52.

Connolly, C., Keil, R. and Ali, S.H. (2020) 'Extended urbanisation and the spatialities of infectious disease: demographic change, infrastructure and governance', *Urban Studies*, online first, DOI: 0042098020910873.

Dawney, L. (2020) 'Decommissioned places: ruins, endurance and care at the end of the first nuclear age', *Transactions of the Institute of British Geographers*, 45(1): 33–49.

DeSilvey, C. (2017) *Curated Decay: Heritage beyond Saving*, Minneapolis: University of Minnesota Press.

DeSilvey, C. and Edensor, T. (2013) 'Reckoning with ruins', *Progress in Human Geography*, 37(4): 465–85.

Desimini, J. (2019) *From Fallow: 100 Ideas for Abandoned Urban Landscapes*, San Francisco, CA: ORO Editions.

Di Feliciantonio, C. (2017) 'Spaces of the expelled as spaces of the urban common? Analysing the re-emergence of squatting initiatives in Rome', *International Journal of Urban and Regional Research*, 41(5): 708–25.

Di Feliciantonio, C. and Aru, S. (2018) 'Dai Commons al Commoning (urbano): Pratiche e Orizzonti Politici Nel Contesto Mediterraneo. Introduzione al numero speciale', *ACME: An International Journal for Critical Geographies*, 17(2): 258–68.

Dillon, B. (2011) *Ruins*, Cambridge: MIT Press and Whitechapel Gallery.

Edensor, T. (2005) *Industrial Ruins: Space, Aesthetics and Materiality*, Oxford: Berg Publishers.

Federici, S. (2011) 'Feminism and the politics of the commons', *The Commoner: A Web Journal for Other Values*, 24 January.

Ferreri, M. (2015) 'The seductions of temporary urbanism', *Ephemera*, 15(1): 181–91.

Ferreri, M. and Vasudevan, A. (2019) 'Vacancy at the edges of the precarious city', *Geoforum*, 101: 165–73.

Ferreri, M., Dawson, G. and Vasudevan, A. (2017) 'Living precariously: property guardianship and the flexible city', *Transactions of the Institute of British Geographers*, 42(2): 246–59.

Fields, D. (2018) 'Constructing a new asset class: property-led financial accumulation after the crisis', *Economic Geography*, 94(2): 118–40.

Freire Trigo, S. (2020) 'Vacant land in London: a planning tool to create land for growth', *International Planning Studies*, 25(3): 261–76.

Freud, S. (2003) *The Uncanny*, London: Penguin.

García-Lamarca, M. and Kaika, M. (2016) ' "Mortgaged lives": the biopolitics of debt and housing financialisation', *Transactions of the Institute of British Geographers*, 41(3): 313–27.

Gordillo, G.R. (2014) *Rubble: The Afterlife of Destruction*, Durham: Duke University Press.

Gore, T. and Nicholson, D. (1991) 'Models of the land-development process: a critical review', *Environment and Planning A*, 23(5): 705–30.

Hackworth, J. (2019) *Manufacturing Decline: How Racism and the Conservative Movement Crush the American Rust Belt*, New York, NY: Columbia University Press.

Janoschka, M., Alexandri, G., Ramos, H.O. and Vives-Miró, S. (2020) 'Tracing the socio-spatial logics of transnational landlords' real estate investment: Blackstone in Madrid', *European Urban and Regional Studies*, 27(2): 125–41.

Kaika, M. and Karaliotas, L. (2016) 'The spatialization of democratic politics: insights from Indignant Squares', *European Urban and Regional Studies*, 23(4): 556–70.

Kitchin, R., O'Callaghan, C. and Gleeson, J. (2014) 'The new ruins of Ireland? Unfinished estates in the post-Celtic Tiger era', *International Journal of Urban and Regional Research*, 38(3): 1069–80.

Madanipour, A. (2018) 'Temporary use of space: urban processes between flexibility, opportunity and precarity', *Urban Studies*, 55(5): 1093–110.

Madden, D. and Marcuse, P. (2016) *In Defense of Housing: The Politics of Crisis*, New York, NY: Verso Books.

Mah, A. (2012) *Industrial Ruination, Community, and Place: Landscapes and Legacies of Urban Decline*, Toronto: University of Toronto Press.

McFarlane, C. (2020) 'The urban poor have been hit hard by coronavirus. We must ask who cities are designed to serve', *The Conversation*, 3 June. Available at: https://theconversation.com/the-urban-poor-have-been-hit-hard-by-coronavirus-we-must-ask-who-cities-are-designed-to-serve-138707 (accessed 6 July 2020).

Mould, O. (2014) 'Tactical urbanism: the new vernacular of the creative city', *Geography Compass*, 8(8): 529–39.

Noterman, E. (2020) 'Taking back vacant property', *Urban Geography*, online first, DOI: 10.1080/02723638.2020.1743519.

O'Callaghan, C. (2018) 'Planetary urbanization in ruins: provisional theory and Ireland's crisis', *Environment and Planning D: Society and Space*, 36(3): 420–38.

O'Callaghan, C., Di Feliciantonio, C. and Byrne, M. (2018) 'Governing urban vacancy in post-crash Dublin: contested property and alternative social projects', *Urban Geography*, 39(6): 868–91.

O'Mahony, E. and Rigney, S. (2016) ' "What's the story buddleia?": a public geography of dereliction in Dublin City', *Irish Geography*, 48(1): 88–99.

Pearsall, H., Lucas, S. and Lenhardt, J. (2014) 'The contested nature of vacant land in Philadelphia and approaches for resolving competing objectives for redevelopment', *Cities*, 40: 163–74.

Pohl, L. (2019) 'The sublime object of Detroit', *Social & Cultural Geography*, online first, DOI: 10.1080/14649365.2019.1683760.

Povinelli, E.A. (2011) *Economies of Abandonment: Social Belonging and Endurance in Late Liberalism*, Durham: Duke University Press.

Roy, A. (2017) 'Dis/possessive collectivism: property and personhood at city's end', *Geoforum*, 80: A1–11.

Safransky, S. (2017) 'Rethinking land struggle in the postindustrial city', *Antipode*, 49(4): 1079–100.

Safransky, S. (2018) 'Land justice as a historical diagnostic: thinking with Detroit', *Annals of the American Association of Geographers*, 108(2): 499–512.

Sassen, S. (2014) *Expulsions*, Cambridge: Harvard University Press.

Smith, N. (1987) 'Gentrification and the rent gap', *Annals of the Association of American Geographers*, 77(3): 462–65.

Till, K.E. (2012) 'Wounded cities: memory-work and a place-based ethics of care', *Political Geography*, 31(1): 3–14.

Tsing, A.L. (2015) *The Mushroom at the End of the World: On the Possibility of Life in Capitalist Ruins*, Princeton, NJ: Princeton University Press.

Vasudevan, A. (2015) 'The autonomous city: towards a critical geography of occupation', *Progress in Human Geography*, 39(3): 316–37.

Woodworth, M.D. and Wallace, J.L. (2017) 'Seeing ghosts: parsing China's "ghost city" controversy', *Urban Geography*, 38(8): 1270–81.

PART I

Rethinking ruination in the post-crisis context

Rem(a)inders of loss: a Lacanian approach to new urban ruins

Lucas Pohl

What is new about new urban ruins?

In recent years, human geography and other related fields have developed an increasing interest in ruins of the recent past. Expressions such as 'ruins of modernity' (Dawdy, 2010; Hell and Schönle, 2010), 'industrial ruins' (Edensor, 2005; Mah, 2012) or 'new ruins' (Kitchin et al, 2014; Martin, 2014) bear witness to rising attention to the relevance of studying material leftovers of our time. Throughout these debates, several attempts have been made to define what is 'new' about ruins of today. Kitchin et al (2014) consider the ruins that appeared after the global financial crisis in 2008 as a new form of ruination because, here, ruins were not a result of disuse, but a product of speculation about a promised future. The 'ghost estates' in Ireland, for instance, have never been used and are therefore considered testimonies of novel financialised forms of urbanisation. Another differentiation between 'old' and 'new' ruins can be found in Dylan Trigg's (2009: 142–50) *The Aesthetics of Decay*. Comparing 'classical' and post-industrial ruins, Trigg pursues the argument that the classical ruin, in contrast to the ruin of the present, is no longer considered as in an active process of decay, which allows us to perceive it as an absolute object in order, which might even be viewed as a beautiful object. In the ruin of the present, however, the process of decay is still ongoing, offering an understanding of ruins as structures in which decay is still hovering. In the new ruin, disorder and ongoing destruction predominate aesthetic perception.

Relying on the basic assumption that ruins of today – more so than the classical ruins of Rome and elsewhere – operate as objects of loss, this chapter contributes to the debate on new urban ruins. What is 'new' about new urban ruins is, in my view, not only their active process of decay, but also, and more importantly, their active transformation into ruins in the first place. The novelist Rose Macaulay was the first who addressed new ruins in this way. In her book *Pleasure of Ruins*, she writes:

What was last week a drab little house has become a steep flight of stairs winding up in the open between gaily-coloured walls, tiled lavatories, interiors bright and intimate like a Dutch picture or a stage set; the stairway climbs up and up, undaunted, to the roofless summit where it meets the sky. The house has put on melodrama; people stop to stare; here is a domestic scene wide open for all to enjoy. (Macaulay, 1953: 454)

While ruins are, by definition, waste products, leftovers of other objects, new ruins can hardly be perceived without imagining their 'lost' origin. They carry memories, fantasies and dreams of what once 'was' and no longer is. In this chapter, I develop a psychoanalytic framework to further engage with new urban ruins in this perspective. The aim of the chapter is twofold. First, it aims at understanding how new ruins emerge not only as remainders, but also as reminders, of loss. Second, it aims at retracing the reasons why the perception of new ruins goes along with a strange sort of 'enjoyment' that we can understand only by considering the psychoanalytic concept of the 'death drive'.

Post-crisis cities: a Lacanian approach

Psychoanalytic theory, especially the work of Jacques Lacan, has been roaming the fields of philosophy, cultural theory and human geography for decades (for a recent overview of psychoanalytic geographies, see Pohl, 2020a). In this section, I introduce it into the field of urban ruins research. However, since it is still questioned from time to time whether psychoanalysis can be consulted outside its clinical background, I start my exploration with the following quote from Alain Badiou, who points to the relevance of Lacan for understanding the world of today:

The contemporary world is haunted by uncertainty, disorientation, and the spectre of permanent crisis. And Lacan is a great thinker of disorder. More generally, it is even possible to define psychoanalysis as an orderly, methodical thought of subjective disorder.... If one extrapolates starting from Lacanian thought, you could say that the crisis of the contemporary world is a crisis of the symbolic. From there, Lacanian categories can be mobilised to understand, once more, an entire series of phenomena. (Badiou, quoted in Badiou and Roudinesco, 2014: 60–1)

To further engage with the potential of reading Lacan as a thinker of crisis, it is key to insist that every crisis is defined through a 'pre-' and 'post-crisis' condition, whereby the situation *after* the crisis is considered worse than the situation *prior* to it. While terms like 'revolution' are oriented towards a better future – Marx, for instance, speaks of revolutions as the 'locomotives of history' – crises are oriented towards a better past. There is a nostalgic dimension lingering in the narrative of a crisis, a moment of loss as well as a longing for compensating this loss. In contrast to the idea of the revolution symbolising a better future (that is, through signifiers like 'communism'), crisis stems from an attempt to evoke the pre-crisis state (which, of course, does not mean that one cannot pass over from one to the other).

The most prominent crisis in the psychoanalytic framework is 'castration', which Lacan refers to not to denote the loss of the penis, but to understand how the subject emerges as a subject of desire. Castration, or, better, 'symbolic castration', is Lacan's way of engaging with the subject's attempts to fill out the lack that has been left after its world has been forever shattered through the symbolic order. What characterises the post-crisis situation, for Lacan, is the inability of overcoming castration by either forgetting about the loss located in the pre-castrated state or bringing back this state by translating it into the coordinates of the castrated reality.

The big question, of course, concerns the reason for this impossibility to restore the pre-crisis status quo. The obvious argument would be that the crisis has created such a brutal transformation that the pre-crisis state cannot be restored. This is, however, not Lacan's point; rather, he assumes that the crisis does not really change anything in the 'here and now'. What really changes throughout a crisis does not affect the world *after* the crisis so much as it affects the world *prior* to it. The reason why it is impossible to go back to the moment before a crisis is that this moment, strictly speaking, never existed. There is a retroactive fantasy taking place in the post-crisis reality that sheds new light on the world before the crisis. From the standpoint after the crisis, 'we exist in the aftermath of a fall, and from the perspective of the fall, we can see the possibilities for complete satisfaction in the world we have lost' (McGowan, 2013: 42).

Transferring Lacan's notion of the crisis into the field of urban analysis and theory allows us to read the post-crisis city through the emergence and persistence of its pre-crisis state. What matters in the city after it went through the rupture of a crisis is the way it creates a new (and better) narration of its past. The post-crisis city is essentially a nostalgic city. It is a place from which we cannot perceive the present without facing the (retroactive) loss of a past. As such, the post-crisis city is organised around an attempt, one could say, a desire, to overcome the present by re-establishing the previous status quo.

Rem(a)inders

The whole issue of crisis stems from the lingering of the pre-crisis situation; it does not simply disappear after the crisis, but obtains a peculiar place within the post-crisis reality. There is a remainder or leftover – Lacan speaks of 'waste' ('*reste*' in French) – that relates between the subject and its loss. With reference to castration, Mladen Dolar (2015: 135) states that, 'paradoxically, one can maintain that for Lacan the problem of castration is not the problem of lacking something, but of having something too much'. This 'too much' lies at the heart of Lacanian psychoanalysis, and the name Lacan uses to refer to this surplus is 'object *a*'. In contrast to other kinds of objects, 'object *a*' does not simply exist independently from the subject, but obtains its quality from the place it occupies in the subject's fantasy. It only exists after the subject went through castration. 'Object *a*' is a post-crisis object, a particular kind of waste – or surplus – that binds the subject to its loss (Pohl, 2020b). Through this object, loss derives a material existence in post-crisis reality: 'loss is not simply a lack, an absence, something missing. It is very much there (as waste always is)' (Zupančič, 2006: 157). Lacan also calls 'object *a*' the 'object-cause of desire' because it embodies a possible marker guiding the subject to the world before castration. There seems to be a trace of the pre-crisis world clinging to this object, a spectre, which provides the subject with a glimpse of what has been lost in the past. However, since we already know about the retroactive emergence of the pre-crisis world, 'object *a*' ultimately turns out to be a lure, a semblance. 'Object *a*' cannot keep its promise because the world it refers to did not exist. Lacan is therefore concerned with the question of how an object can take the place of 'object *a*':

> How does this transformation of the object come about, one which from an object that can be located, pinpointed, and exchanged, forms this kind of … incommunicable and yet dominant object that is our correlative in the fantasy? Where exactly is the moment of this metamorphosis, this transformation, this revelation, to be placed? (Lacan, 2014: 88)

The basic premise of my theoretical approach is to grasp the ruin in relation to Lacan's 'object *a*'. The transformation of a building into a ruin mirrors the transformation of an object that can be located, pinpointed and exchanged into an incommunicable and yet dominant object in the fantasy. In the emergence of a ruin, as a post-crisis object, I locate the retroactive generation of a world of wholeness and completeness, a world that is structurally lost but still powerful in the way it organises the desire of the post-crisis subject. To substantiate this claim, Dolar reflects in a similar way on the relation between loss and ruin:

> What kind of thing is a ruin? The ruin is an object, which is the rest of an object. It is by definition a partial object, part of an object, a damaged object … it's less than an object. It is an object minus, a minus inscribed and included in the object. Of course, the automatic supposition is that the object has once been whole and it has undergone an impermeant and insurant loss, a depletion, for it to be turned into a ruin. But perhaps what makes its objecthood is precisely the minus, which inhabits it, and the natural supposition has always something of a retroactive fantasy, even when completely founded and supported by all the data, the documented reconstruction of its original state. (Dolar, 2017)

A great part of my psychoanalytic approach of urban ruination goes back to in-depth research on Michigan Central Station in Detroit, which I consider to be a new urban ruin *avant la lettre* (Pohl, 2019). Against the background of the massive interest with which journalists, artists, scholars and popular culture more generally has used Detroit as a blueprint for contemporary urban decline, Michigan Central Station became 'America's most famous ruin' (Vergara, 2016: 29) and the 'world's most photographed abandoned building' (Wells, 2018: 15). However, what interested me more than the national and international popularity of Michigan Central Station was the local perception of this ruin. Opened in 1913 as the tallest train station in the world, Michigan Central Station was built at a time when Detroit was one of the most prosperous and wealthy US cities of the 20th century. In the wake of the crisis of Fordism and political riots motivated by racist police behaviour in the mid-1960s, the city gradually shrank by more than half its population. Some 75 years after its opening, the last train left Detroit's train station. Today, Michigan Central Station functions as a nostalgic reminder of Detroit's glory days (and, more recently, after Ford Motor Company purchased the ruin, also as a symbol for Detroit's comeback [see later]). No other ruin stirs people more with what George Galster (2012) coined Detroit's 'hypernostalgia', namely, the fact that Detroit is often portrayed as a place of loss, a city that was once the 'City of the American Dream' before it ended up becoming one of the most dangerous and poorest cities in the country. More than any other ruin in Detroit, Michigan Central Station stimulates a 'desire … to re-experience the bustling metropolis as it is remembered or has been described' (Steinmetz, 2008: 218). Michigan Central Station occupies a special place in the fantasy of all those who see in Detroit 'more' than its immediate reality. For them, Michigan Central Station functions as an 'object *a*', the stronghold of the world before castration.

Enjoyment of ruins

In April 2009, the City Council of Detroit passed a resolution to demolish Michigan Central Station. Shortly after the announcement, 'The Michigan Central Station Preservation Society' was formed, a civil society-led initiative supported by local and international activists, leading to demonstrations, online petitions and attempts to sue the city of Detroit to stop the demolition effort – successfully. A few months later, the demolition plans were cancelled. In June 2018, Detroit's Mayor, Mike Duggan, gave a talk in front of Michigan Central Station to celebrate the recent plans by Ford Motor Company to reinvent the building. Justifying the decision of the City Council in 2009, Duggan stated that at that time, "there was no hope to bring this building and the city back" (participant observation, 19 June 2018). It is remarkable that despite the apparent hopelessness regarding a possible comeback of the ruin and the city, hundreds of people were actively engaged in saving the train station. While tens of thousands of buildings in Detroit have been demolished over recent years (Hackworth, 2016), this ruin could not disappear without resistance.

To understand why people in Detroit were clinging on to the abandoned train station, it helps to take a brief look at the relation between ruins and enjoyment. There is a long debate surrounding the pleasurable experience of ruined landscapes. Originating from Macaulay's *Pleasure of Ruins*, 'ruin lust' became an emblematic signifier to describe the 'strange human reaction' driven 'by morbid pleasure in decay, by righteous pleasure in retribution … by mystical pleasure in the destruction of all things mortal … by masochistic joy in a common destruction … and by a dozen other entwined threads of pleasurable and melancholy emotion' (Macaulay, 1953: xvf). While scholars frequently adopt Macauley's term 'ruin lust', the 'strangeness' with which she introduced the term is often neglected. The pleasure of ruins is instead either used to describe the artistic or scholarly interest in ruins (DeSilvey and Edensor, 2013; Dillon, 2014), or critically referred to as a way of overemphasising the aesthetic value of urban decay (Apel, 2015; Galviz et al, 2017). In recent years, a discursive change in talking about ruins has occurred. In the age of photography, 'ruin porn' became the new master signifier to denote the common fascination with ruins. While the terms are changing, the ways urban scholars refer to notions like 'ruin pleasure' or 'ruin porn' are hardly distinguishable. In the same vein as ruin lust, ruin porn is primarily used to capture the popularity of urban decay, as well as its limited reliance on the ruin's aesthetic quality (Millington, 2013; Safransky, 2014; Arnold, 2015; Fraser, 2018). Ruin porn turns out to be the ruin lust of the 21st century, which also explains why Brian Dillon (2012) writes: 'The story that Macaulay tells in *Pleasure of Ruins* is … still alive today in photographs of post-industrial Detroit.'

In her introduction to the recently published volume *Ruin Porn and the Obsession with Decay*, Siobhan Lyons (2018: 1–2) argues that images of ruins 'retain something of a Freudian death drive', since they resemble the 'fascination with our own death and a tangible image of the precise form it will take'. While Lyons shifts the focus on ruin porn back to what Macaulay originally referred to as ruin lust, namely, the strange pleasure deriving from an apparently unpleasant condition, she misses the point when she considers the death drive as a human striving for death. Psychoanalysis insists that the death drive is not an 'instinct to return to the state of equilibrium of the inanimate sphere' (Lacan, 1992: 212). Nevertheless, mobilising the concept of the death drive for understanding the pleasure of ruins appears fruitful. Let us consider the Freudian approach to the death drive, and his reflections on why someone would repeat an unpleasurable experience: 'this is Freud's explanation: what we find at the origin of repetition is a repression of a traumatic event – repetition appears at the place of remembering; one repeats something one cannot remember.... The trauma which is being repeated is outside the horizon of experience' (Zupančič, 2017: 107).

The reason for going through an unpleasurable experience again and again, which Freud also called the 'compulsion to repeat', lies in the fixation on a traumatic event that cannot be properly remembered because, strictly speaking, it never existed. Such an event is what Michigan Central Station evokes as soon as it is considered to be an 'object *a*', an event that can only be re-experienced by repeatedly missing it. Whatever fascinates us about ruins is, in the sense of death drive, not a morbid pleasure to imagine our death in the future, but rather a pleasure to re-experience the irrecoverable loss at the bottom of the post-crisis reality in which the ruin is located.

Throughout the last decade, Michigan Central Station became an important attraction for people to visit, with up to one hundred people arriving at the ruin on a daily basis. As part of my research, I spent up to eight hours per day in front of the ruin, speaking to people who came to see it. I observed a tendency of many visitors to neglect facing the immediate state of the ruin and instead talk about 'what' the ruin stands for (Pohl, 2019). Especially those visitors who considered themselves as 'real' Detroiters[1] often preferred to watch the ruin from a distance or to drive around it in cars instead of thinking about going inside of it. I argue that this particular view allows people to derive a certain pleasure that is oriented not towards a decreasing, but rather towards a maintenance or even an increase, of tension. In Lacanian terms, one could speak of this pleasure in the sense of *jouissance*, a strange enjoyment that 'gives us simultaneous pleasure and displeasure: it gives us displeasure because of its inadequacy to the Thing-Idea, but precisely through this inadequacy it gives us pleasure by indicating the true, incomparable greatness of the Thing' (Žižek, 1989: 229). Of course, the abandoned train station is not a proper representative for the 'idea' of Detroit's glorious past. However, precisely in this forlorn state, as the 'mocking symbol of its lost greatness' (LeDuff, 2013: 81), the train station indicates the (fantasy of) tremendous legacy that lies behind it.

I argue that the reason why someone would visit Michigan Central Station again and again is the same reason why someone would fight for saving it in 2009 – to keep enjoying the loss it stands for. People are clinging to the ruin because it allows a compulsion to repeat the traumatic vanishing of Detroit's glorious past, a loss that no one really experienced, as it was retroactively created after the crisis, but that nonetheless animates the painful enjoyment of the post-crisis subject. 'In Detroit nothing arrives or leaves from the former station; only the imagination travels', Camilo José Vergara (1999: 57) writes in an early portrait of Detroit's ruins. What was at stake with the demolition of Michigan Central Station was not the possible reinvention of the building, but the end of this fantastic journey.

There is no comeback!

In recent years, there were several political attempts to put an end to the crisis in Detroit. More than ever in Detroit, desire is directed towards an actual revival of loss, a way of bringing the past back to life. After Detroit became a refuge for so-called 'do-it-yourself urbanism' in the 1990s and 2000s, today, million-dollar investments spread over the city and lead to widespread claims of Detroit's 'comeback'. Michigan Central Station plays a key role with regards to establishing this comeback narrative. While investors like Dan Gilbert have already spent billions on Detroit since 2010, renovating and reinventing historical skyscrapers and office buildings in the inner city, the ultimate comeback of Detroit could not be imagined without bringing back the train station. I already mentioned the celebration of Ford Motor Company's plans to reinvent Michigan Central Station. More than 1,000 people gathered in front of the ruin that day in June 2018, listening to the plans of Ford to turn the ruin into their new headquarters. After the Mayor gave his speech, the organisers prepared a big screen to show the trailer for 'Detroit Comeback City', a documentary produced by rapper and Detroit-native Big Sean for the History Channel. Next to a few pictures of the historic Detroit and a few shots of the abandoned Packard Plant and downtown area, the trailer focused entirely on Michigan Central Station. Starting from the moment when this magnificent building had started to fall apart, the film framed the comeback of the train station as a sort of precondition for the rebirth of Detroit.[2]

There is a significant change taking place in the way Detroit's past is narrated throughout the comeback of Michigan Central Station. The loss that remained after the city went through crisis now turns into something manageable and accessible, something one can master: 'The narrative tale of a rebirth of a city, and by extension the American auto industry, in the face of epic decline makes the story of Detroit the ultimate comeback tale – a phoenix rising from the ashes of destruction' (Kinney, 2016: xxvi). This tale is intrinsically bound to the way capitalism handles crises. In capitalism, there is no such thing as irrecoverable loss. There always seems to be a way of translating loss back into the coordinates of the post-crisis reality, and the key to overcoming every crisis lies in the form of a commodity:

> Lacan identifies the lost object (which he calls the object a) as what orients the subject's desire even though the subject has never had it. But in capitalism the lost object acquires

a substantial status it doesn't actually have. It appears as something substantial that the subject has lost through a traumatic event insofar as it appears accessible in the form of the commodity. (McGowan, 2016: 26)

By turning it into their new headquarters, Ford promises to bring Michigan Central Station back in the form of a commodity. The logic behind the reinvention is basically, 'let the money solve the issue'. However, from a Lacanian standpoint, this whole idea appears to be highly problematic. Since the loss of the city is structurally related to a retroactive fantasy, there can, strictly speaking, be no 'comeback'. As Todd McGowan (2013: 40) points out: 'By insisting that loss is constitutive for the subject, psychoanalytic thought works to combat nostalgia and its poisoning of contemporary politics.' Similarly, one could say that a psychoanalytic reading of Michigan Central Station allows us to combat the contemporary local politics in Detroit by stating that whatever the future might hold for this ruin (and the city), it will never live up to the nostalgic fantasies embedded in it. To that extent, it is true that 'Michigan Central Station had never looked better and will never look better than when it was at its most neglected' (Vergara, 2016: 281).

Traversing the ruin's fantasy

I would like to conclude this chapter with a quote from an interview with Scott Hocking, an artist I interviewed during my research in Detroit. Asked about the local perception of Michigan Central Station, Hocking mentioned a way out of the painful enjoyment that is not restricted to the fantasy of the ruin's commodified comeback:

> 'If you got married at the Colosseum when it was still functioning and then you saw it as a ruin, you might also feel sad. It is hard for those people to not see the ruin as a symbol of our failure and a symbol of sadness and decay ... I feel like the only way for people who have that memory, or who feel that way, is to change their perception from a ruin to a monument. There must be some sort of separation over time. It has got to be long enough that you do not have any memory of what it used to be.' (Interview, 1 May 2017)

What Hocking calls for is a perception of Michigan Central Station that allows us to face the ruin not as part of a glorious past, but rather as its immediate present. As long as the reality surrounding the ruin is haunted by the past, it can only be considered as a symbol of loss. Only when the memories disappear and the spectres of crisis fade away is one truly able to perceive Michigan Central Station in the same way as one perceives ancient ruins like the Colosseum. However, from a psychoanalytic standpoint, one can question whether the transition from ruin to monument is really only possible through time. Rather than simply accepting that new urban ruins, in contrast to ancient ruins, cannot be viewed without the loss from which they emerge, a psychoanalytic approach allows a radical questioning of the relationship between the ruin and its loss. To perceive the ruin as part of the present, there is no need to forget about the past, as Hocking suggests. What it takes is, to put it in Lacanese, a 'traversing of the ruin's fantasy', an attempt to retrace the retroactive insertion of loss into the ruin and to face the void, the 'nothing', that the ruin conceals. After going through the fantasy, one is able to go beyond the desperate attempts to restore the loss and instead enjoy the ruin's structural incompleteness.

A psychoanalytic engagement with new urban ruins, therefore, originates from the relationship between fantasy and materiality. Ruins like Michigan Central Station derive their radiance not so much from their 'objective' qualities as from the 'subjective' standpoints from which we look at them. However, this does not mean that ruins are reducible to subjective experience. There is, indeed, something material about them, so that ruins turn out to be 'objectively subjectivised'. Ruins are prime examples of what Japhy Wilson and Manuel Bayón (2017) call 'fantastical materialisations', eliciting a need for a psychoanalytic geography of urban decay (see also Pohl, 2019). Such a geography not only takes as buzzwords psychoanalytically informed expressions like pleasure, perversion, fetish, desire, anxiety or death drive, which regularly appear in scholarly engagements with ruination, but rather aims to understand how these categories shift our understanding of the matter. While Lyons (2018: 9) is right to state that there still 'is an overwhelming tendency to trivialize ruins', I argue that psychoanalysis offers a silver bullet against this trivialisation because it takes seriously the fantasy that a ruin embodies.

Notes

[1] In the context of Detroit, one should certainly mention that most of the people who visited the train station on purpose, for instance, not walking by on their way to work, were white Detroiters who told me that they had once lived in the city but moved to the suburbs after it 'got rough'.

[2] See: www.youtube.com/watch?v=UtGTQSqLflU

References

Apel, D. (2015) *Beautiful Terrible Ruins: Detroit and the Anxiety of Decline*, New Brunswick, NJ: Rutgers University Press.

Arnold, S. (2015) 'Urban decay photography and film: fetishism and the apocalyptic imagination', *Journal of Urban History*, 41(2): 326–39.

Badiou, A. and Roudinesco, É. (2014) *Jacques Lacan Past and Present: A Dialogue*, New York, NY: Columbia University Press.

Dawdy, S.L. (2010) 'Clockpunk anthropology and the ruins of modernity', *Current Anthropology*, 51(6): 761–93.

DeSilvey, C. and Edensor, T. (2013) 'Reckoning with ruins', *Progress in Human Geography*, 37(4): 465–85.

Dillon, B. (2012) 'Ruin lust: our love affair with decaying buildings', *The Guardian*, 17 February. Available at: www.theguardian.com/artanddesign/2012/feb/17/ruins-love-affair-decayed-buildings (accessed 11 October 2019).

Dillon, B. (2014) *Ruin Lust*, London: Tate Publishing.

Dolar, M. (2015) 'Anamorphosis', *S: Journal of the Circle for Lacanian Ideology Critique*, 8: 125–40.

Dolar, M. (2017) 'Power and the architectural unconscious', lecture presented at the symposium 'On Power in Architecture', Ljubljana.

Edensor, T. (2005) *Industrial Ruins: Space, Aesthetics and Materiality*, Oxford and New York, NY: Berg.

Fraser, E. (2018) 'Unbecoming place: urban imaginaries in transition in Detroit', *Cultural Geographies*, 25(3): 441–58.

Galster, G.C. (2012) *Driving Detroit: The Quest for Respect in Motown*, Philadelphia, PA: University of Pennsylvania Press.

Galviz, C.L., Bartolini, N., Pendleton, M. and Stock, A. (2017) 'Reconfiguring ruins: beyond ruinenlust', *GeoHumanities*, 3(2): 531–53.

Hackworth, J. (2016) 'Demolition as urban policy in the American Rust Belt', *Environment and Planning A*, 48(11): 2201–22.

Hell, J. and Schönle, A. (2010) *Ruins of Modernity*, Durham: Duke University Press.

Kinney, R.J. (2016) *Beautiful Wasteland: The Rise of Detroit as America's Postindustrial Frontier*, Minneapolis, MN: University of Minnesota Press.

Kitchin, R., O'Callaghan, C. and Gleeson, J. (2014) 'The new ruins of Ireland? Unfinished estates in the post-Celtic Tiger era', *International Journal of Urban and Regional Research*, 38(3): 1069–80.

Lacan, J. (1992) *The Ethics of Psychoanalysis. The Seminar of Jacques Lacan. Book VII*, New York, NY: W.W. Norton & Company Inc.

Lacan, J. (2014) *Anxiety. The Seminar of Jacques Lacan. Book X*, Cambridge: Polity.

LeDuff, C. (2013) *Detroit: An American Autopsy*, New York, NY: Penguin Books.

Lyons, S. (2018) 'Introduction: ruin porn, capitalism, and the Anthropocene', in S. Lyons (ed) *Ruin Porn and the Obsession with Decay*, Basingstoke: Palgrave Macmillan, pp 1–10.

Macaulay, R. (1953) *Pleasure of Ruins*, London: Weidenfeld & Nicolson.

Mah, A. (2012) *Industrial Ruination, Community, and Place: Landscapes and Legacies of Urban Decline*, Toronto: University of Toronto Press.

Martin, D. (2014) 'Introduction: towards a political understanding of new ruins', *International Journal of Urban and Regional Research*, 38(3): 1037–46.

McGowan, T. (2013) *Enjoying What We Don't Have: The Political Project of Psychoanalysis*, Lincoln, NE: University of Nebraska Press.

McGowan, T. (2016) *Capitalism and Desire: The Psychic Cost of Free Markets*, New York, NY: Columbia University Press.

Millington, N. (2013) 'Post-industrial imaginaries: nature, representation and ruin in Detroit, Michigan', *International Journal of Urban and Regional Research*, 37(1): 279–96.

Pohl, L. (2019) 'The sublime object of Detroit', *Social & Cultural Geography*, online first, DOI: 10.1080/14649365.2019.1683760.

Pohl, L. (2020a) 'Psychoanalysis', in A. Kobayashi (ed) *International Encyclopedia of Human Geography* (2nd edn), London: Elsevier, pp 61–4.

Pohl, L. (2020b) 'Object-disoriented geographies: the Ghost Tower of Bangkok and the topology of anxiety', *Cultural Geographies*, 27(1): 71–84.

Safransky, S. (2014) 'Greening the urban frontier: race, property, and resettlement in Detroit', *Geoforum*, 56: 237–48.

Steinmetz, G. (2008) 'Harrowed landscapes: white ruingazers in Namibia and Detroit and the cultivation of memory', *Visual Studies*, 23(3): 211–37.

Trigg, D. (2009) *The Aesthetics of Decay: Nothingness, Nostalgia, and the Absence of Reason*, New York, NY: Peter Lang.

Vergara, C.J. (1999) *American Ruins*, New York, NY: The Monacelli Press.

Vergara, C.J. (2016) *Detroit Is No Dry Bones: The Eternal City of the Industrial Age*, Ann Arbor, MI: University of Michigan Press.

Wells, K. (2018) 'Detroit was always made of wheels: confronting ruin porn in its hometown', in S. Lyons (ed) *Ruin Porn and the Obsession with Decay*, Basingstoke: Palgrave Macmillan, pp 13–29.

Wilson, J. and Bayón, M. (2017) 'Fantastical materializations: interoceanic infrastructures in the Ecuadorian Amazon', *Environment and Planning D: Society and Space,* 35(5): 836–54.

Žižek, S. (1989) *The Sublime Object of Ideology*, London and New York, NY: Verso.

Zupančič, A. (2006) 'When surplus enjoyment meets surplus value', in J. Clemens and R. Grigg (eds) *Jacques Lacan and the Other Side of Psychoanalysis: Reflections on Seminar XVII*, Durham and London: Duke University Press, pp 155–78.

Zupančič, A. (2017) *What is Sex?*, Cambridge: MIT Press.

2

Dignifying the ruins: a former Jewish girls' school in Berlin

Karen E. Till

Introduction

De Silvey and Edensor (2013: 467) define ruins as 'structures and places that have been classified (by someone, at some time) as residual or unproductive, but equally most of these sites remain open to appropriation and recuperation'. Urban ruins, therefore, are more than physical by-products of capitalist 'creative destruction' (Harvey, 1985); they may offer the touchstone for alternative imaginings of the city. As O'Callaghan et al (2018) argue, urban 'remainders' have the potential to create spaces of discursive and material struggle over questions of social and spatial justice, such as when alternative communities create urban commons during times of economic austerity. However, what happens when inhabitants are violently removed from a 'productive' place, which is made into a ruin by racist policies? Years later, what does it mean to 'inherit' ruins of spatial injustice – for groups and individuals that were traumatised, for bystanders, and for perpetrators?

This chapter contributes to discussions of the 'dynamic and unsettled' nature of ruins (DeSilvey and Edensor, 2013: 466) by considering their complex and shifting geopolitical temporal-spatial relations in cities marked by extreme forms of violence and spatial injustice, including forced removals and genocide. I focus on a rather mundane 'ruin', a former Jewish girls' school in Central Berlin that was created by the virulent anti-Semitism of National Socialism. Located on Auguststrasse in the central residential district, Berlin-Mitte, the heart of Jewish Berlin, the school was closed in 1942 by the Nazis and later converted to a wartime hospital. It survived the bombings of the Second World War, and was reused by the former German Democratic Republic (GDR) as the 'Bertolt Brecht' grammar school until 1966. In post-reunification Berlin, the building stood empty until 2006, when it was briefly reanimated for a few months by artistic exhibitions while its ownership was being determined. One exhibition was the *Hannah Arendt Denkraum* ('Hannah Arendt Thinking Space') (hereafter, the

Denkraum), which marked the 100th anniversary of the political philosopher Hannah Arendt's birthday. Open from 14 October to 19 November 2006, this 'experimental art project' invited artists and visitors to explore Arendt's writings on free thought and democracy in a then empty building with a not-yet clear future land-use and property status (Funken, no date).

As I describe later, the temporary exhibition created a critical presence for residents and visitors to reflect upon that called attention to the importance of Jewish life and the inheritance of Jewish political thought in their city. Audiences could explore the building, by then already empty for 50 years, wander through the 13 artistic installations and central reading room, and consider Arendt's significance, both past and present. Through the exhibition, this building – which was violently made into a ruin – was again reanimated as a historical place of Jewish life and culture in Berlin. This form of repair, which contributes to what Atuahene (2014) describes as 'dignity restoration', enhances spatial justice in ways that are often ignored by urban managers, especially when pressures of economic development are a priority. Moreover, few academics explain how acknowledging difficult pasts and absences can interrupt the reproduction of legacies of spatial injustice. This chapter provides a first step in filling this gap by considering this particular form of 'chronic urban trauma' (Pain, 2019). Before describing the exhibition, I first comment on the significance of ruins in wounded cities, after which I briefly describe the political, economic and cultural context of Berlin at the time of the exhibition. I then consider how the exhibition reclaimed a historical place from a ruin of spatial injustice by calling attention to the loss of Jewish life and political thought in the city.

Ruins in wounded cities

Cities like Berlin have been 'wounded' by extreme acts of state-perpetrated violence, such as forced removals tied to racist and anti-Semitic regimes (Till, 2012). The physical destruction, displacement of people and trauma from genocide, racism, discrimination and oppression do not end with regime change. According to Atuahene (2014), such acts demolish more than physical buildings and material possessions; vibrant communities, social capital and inheritance are also destroyed, and the dignity of individuals and their social groups is denied. Atuahene (2014: 3) refers to this process as '*dignity takings*': 'when a state directly or indirectly destroys or confiscates property rights from owners or occupiers whom it deems to be sub persons without paying just compensation or without a legitimate public purpose'. Fullilove (2004) argues further that the physical fabric of the neighbourhood one grows up in provides the cues and opportunities for the intergenerational transmission of stories. If one is violently uprooted from a familiar emotional ecosystem that provided stability, the 'root shock' of displacement affects multiple generations through mental and physical health consequences, as well as forms of economic and social injustice.

Berlin's history of violent forced removals, dignity takings and root shock remains part of the city's heritage in the built environment. With each transition to a new German state, changes were made to the material and symbolic fabric of the capital city, communicating new national ideologies. Under National Socialism, the (re-)creation of Berlin as an idealised Aryan Germania was dramatic (Richie, 1998). The transformation of Berlin included: imprisoning and murdering communists, socialists and political dissenters; deporting or murdering Jewish families, as well as confiscating their belongings; razing neighbourhoods to the ground; changing street names; creating new transportation and communication systems; building forced-labour, concentration and death camps; renovating existing buildings for new purposes; and constructing new buildings and boulevards. Urban ruins were created from otherwise healthy places, spaces and communities to realise the new political economies, which included genocidal goals, of the National Socialist regime. Ruin making continued during the war, and following 1945, when Berlin was occupied and divided, the city's built environment communicated Cold War geopolitical agendas. Even after German reunification in 1990, many of the city's buildings, neighbourhoods, streets and transportation and communication structures remain marked by these difficult pasts.

Following the war, a complex set of compensation, rehabilitation and restitution processes were established by the Federal Republic of Germany (FRG) to compensate for past harms. Demands for 'indemnification for the material damages to Jewish individuals and to the Jewish people caused by Germany through the Holocaust' were negotiated through the Conference on Jewish Material Claims Against Germany (hereafter, Claims Conference), established by the World Jewish Congress in 1951 (Claims Conference, no date). While Jews had limited property rights before the rise of National Socialism in Berlin (Nachama et al, 2001), this was the first time an international reparations system was established by government bodies (the FRG and new state of Israel) and corporate bodies (international Jewish organisations). Land claims could be submitted by individuals and collectives for properties stolen under the Nazi regime during the Second World War, as well as under the GDR after reunification. In the GDR, buildings, infrastructure and land were reappropriated as the 'people's property' (*Volkseigentum*), and justified as a form of war repayment. In 1990, GDR 'public' property was privatised, leading to new rounds of land claims for owners whose land and property were taken by the Nazi regime or the GDR. As I describe in the next section, some of the 'ruins', buildings and properties that fell into this category were squatted and/or reused, informally or through 'temporary use agreements' until claims were settled (Forkert, 2016 [2013]).

Even this limited sketch indicates how the legacies of National Socialism continue to haunt present-day social-spatial relations, including the supposedly neutral category of 'property'. Germany remains exemplary in the process of reparations, having paid over US$60 billion to individuals and groups (Claims Conference, no date), and also establishing numerous centralised and decentralised memorials, which, in Berlin, have resulted in significant public debates about remembering the violence and effects of National Socialism and the Holocaust, notwithstanding ongoing calls for critical memory-work (Till, 2005). However, restitution and commemoration cannot address the forms of social repair and 'dignity restoration' (Atuahene, 2014) needed to redress historical and ongoing forms of spatial injustice. Dignity restoration takes more time, is more complicated and is more expensive than a process of property reparations, which also 'sanitizes existing property rights and removes the stench of past theft' (Atuahene, 2014: 6). However, when citizens are harmed, so too are the places and cities in which they live(d) (Till, 2012). The negative legacies of the loss remain part of the fabric of the everyday lived city, including through the rhythms and relational spaces that animate particular places, which, at any given moment in time, are tied to psychosocial geographies that unfold through inhabitants' movements in daily routines and mazeways. Therefore, ruins resulting from previous moments of state-perpetrated violence are fragile, yet especially important, presences in wounded cities. As reminders of past violence in a city, they embody losses that interrupt hegemonic understandings of the city as having dealt with its past.

Recognising past wrongs and seeking to repair what has been damaged is part of imagining healthier places to live. In wounded cities, caring for ruins contributes to the work of restorative justice by seeking to 'repair' what has been damaged, by reclaiming the city and by asserting the right to return, even if that is only possible symbolically (Bennett and Stephens, 2019). Restorative justice as a form of memory-work includes a place-based ethics of care for the city's inhabitants, former residents and those that remain missing (Till, 2011b). For feminist political theorists Berenice Fischer and Joan Tronto, care is a 'species activity that includes everything that we do to maintain, continue, and repair our "world" so that we can live in it as well as possible' (Tronto, 1993: 103). Extending Tronto's discussion to include caring for place, I argue that when inhabitants in wounded cities engage in attending to ruins of spatial injustice, they acknowledge past forms of violence, and in the process of caring for places, they begin to receive care and care for others (Till, 2008, 2010, 2012). For example, the ornate gold-leafed dome of the New Synagogue on Oranienburger Strasse in Berlin-Mitte (not too far away from the former girls' school), built in 1866 and expanding to include a museum of Jewish Culture that opened in 1933 just before the Nazi rise to power, had only begun to be restored in 1991, following repair of the interior space begun in 1988. The reappearance of this landmark gestures to the important presence of those who were once forcibly removed. Even small acts restore dignity and allow those once excluded to risk considering the city once more a home. Place names, stories, historic preservation, forms of heritage and living cultural landscapes can communicate a past/future non-racist city where people or their children might feel as though they can belong.

However, when ruins and remainders that have the potential to restore a group's rightful presence in the city are labelled as 'empty', 'blighted', 'marginal', 'unproductive' or 'redundant', the urban manager (developer, planner, government official, engineer or architect) transforms places that speak of difficult pasts into empty sites. Such practices are often justified through the discourses of development and the public good that assume linear chronologies of 'progress' that locate 'the past' as separate from the present and future. In this way, the past is spatially contained through functionality, for instance, by designating specific types of place, such as memorials, for public memory, or by erasing historical complexity through planning land-use and zoning maps. Devaluing places of past injustice as empty sites is a second form of violence in wounded cities. By ignoring the depth and value of inhabitants' attachments to place, and denying possibilities of restorative justice through a place-based ethics of care, a form of place injustice may exacerbate legacies of earlier forms of structural and institutional violence.

As urban scholars, it is our responsibility to document the ways healthy places were made into ruins through violent acts, as well as to note acts of repair and care for ruins of spatial injustice. Urban spaces are never neutral backdrops. As Soja (2009) reminds us, the 'normal' redistributive functions of the city in a capitalist economy are uneven and a 'primary source of inequality', 'aggravated further by [legacies of] racism, patriarchy, heterosexual bias, and many other forms of spatial and locational discrimination'. The work of confronting and reanimating difficult pasts calls attention to these 'aggravated' violent legacies. In other words, ruins of spatial injustice are not simply 'in the past', but very much part of the present-day city.

In the following sections, I discuss Berlin and the critical function of its 'interim spaces' when the *Denkraum* exhibition opened. I then discuss how these artistic installations and the later renovation contributed to dignity restoration by acknowledging the loss of Jewish life in the city, and creating space for a new, if commodified, Jewish presence in Berlin.

Interim space in Berlin

In 2006, Berlin was facing bankruptcy. More than 15 years after reunification, the city was still trying to develop a service and information economy, without the federal subsidies it had formerly enjoyed. It sought to promote artistic and alternative renovations of previous large factory buildings in former East Berlin, redesigned as trendy information technology (IT) and loft offices (Ward, 2004). This was happening at the same time the city and region were experiencing high levels of unemployment. The spectacle of renovation and growth of the 'New Berlin' used to market the city and attract international investment was not so successful (Colomb and Kalandides, 2010). Moreover, the government bodies responsible for privatising East German socialist enterprises and lands continued to be the largest real estate holders in the 'new' states (of the former East Germany created after reunification). This meant that property claims for parts of the city were still being negotiated at a time when the nearby 'new' states of former East Germany were facing high unemployment, in part, due to the closures of many former collective agricultural and industrial institutions. Many structures, buildings and networks deemed 'redundant' were awaiting new uses, just as were many newly built offices.

What was functioning well in the city during this uncertain economic time was its 'cultural economy', including design, music, clubs, arts and creative industries, which supported a related 'symbolic economy' (Colomb, 2012; Forkert, 2016 [2013]). On the one hand, independent artists, entrepreneurs, initiatives and alternative groups squatted and/or (re)used 'redundant' material spaces. City authorities would later call these artists 'space pioneers' (Berlin Senatsverwaltung für Stadtentwicklung, 2007). Especially concentrated in former East Berlin along the former Berlin Wall and in the outskirts of the city, where property rights and claims were still in question, people created informal markets, parks, allotments, mobile caravan neighbourhoods, experimental workshops, urban beaches, outdoor theatres, exhibitions, creative projects and alternative social spaces, all of which contributed to the energy and romantic attraction of living in the 'new' Berlin (Colomb, 2012).

On the other hand, as real estate markets stalled, developers used Berlin's creative and artistic activity as a form of free advertising. The edginess of the creative and artistic (re)use of urban space generated symbolic capital rather than rental income. Forkert (2016 [2013]: 99) discusses the sophisticated use of the often unpaid labour of artists and creatives to promote the reputation of a neighbourhood and, indeed, the 'promise of seemingly living without money … [was] essential to Berlin's appeal' (referring to Jens Bisky). If developers let 'space pioneers' use their properties for low to no rents for unspecified periods of time, they received cheap or free marketing in return (Colomb, 2012). Similarly, international art galleries set up satellite offices to promote their 'image', even if they made no profits from selling the art. Unlike other cities, much of this so-called 'temporary use' was managed by the city.

Yet, few scholars have paid attention to the fact that such (re)use is not 'new' (Till and McArdle, 2016). Squatting, alternative communities and so-called 'temporary uses', therefore, are not one-off events in Berlin, but a regular and quite permanent feature of the city at different moments in time that may contribute to political activism and memory-work (Vasudevan, 2011). For this reason, I use the term 'interim space' (Till, 2011a) rather than 'temporary use' to refer to how individuals and groups in the past and present appropriated media images, buildings, streets, remnant matter and parcels of land for their own uses to make their city liveable. Some interim spaces directly questioned the privatisation of property, and others called attention to how government authorities ignored the legacies of a once-divided city, itself a consequence of National Socialism. The non-normative, critical spatial and historical imaginaries of the city created through interim spaces invited other residents and guests to encounter the city as an enacted and dynamic environment of rights and responsibilities.

In the next section, I describe the *Denkraum*, an exhibition one can interpret according to the creative 'temporary use' prevalent in the city at the time. Curators were searching for an appropriate venue for a critical exhibition about Arendt's legacy, and the historic building became a possibility when it was used earlier in 2006 as part of the city's fourth Art Biennial. Hosted by the relatively new Kunst-Werk Institute for Contemporary Art (KW), located on Auguststrasse down the road from the former girls' school, one could say that the success of the festival set a precedent for another 'temporary use' by the *Denkraum* exhibition. However, such an interpretation does not recognise the importance of Berlin's historical culture of interim spaces, which includes critical reflections on German society and politics. Such an understanding was clearly articulated by the *Denkraum* exhibition curator, Peter Funken (no date), who noted, 'without artistic forms of realization we will not get very far in dealing with and solving the complicated problems that grow out of … freedom of thought; the right to express our own point of view; the chance to build a democracy for the future'. It is significant that the *Denkraum* exhibition took place in a building made residual by the history of National Socialism, with a pending claim made by the Claims Conference on behalf of the Jewish Community of Berlin (JCB).

(Re)Animating ruins in Berlin: the *Denkraum*

According to Funken (no date), while 'totalitarianism, culminating with the extermination of the European Jews and many others', was not the explicit 'focal point of the exhibition', Germany's past and present inspired exhibitions on 'the topics of freedom and self-determination'. One artist's work directly commented upon the absence of the former Jewish girls' school in the city. Ram Katzir's 'Milk Teeth' was a sculpture of one child's chair sitting upturned on a small desk, carved out of white marble (see Figure 2.1). The remainders of marble dust from the carvings were shaped into a pile in one corner of a former classroom. This small but solid sculpture contrasted with the modernist functional design of the room and the building's subsequent decay. The visitor experienced this installation in a school originally built to accommodate the growth of the Jewish community in Berlin. At the time the school opened in 1930, about 160,000 Jews lived in the city, and its location 'in the heart of a posh Jewish quarter' (Rayasam, 2012), close to the New Synagogue, indicated its significance for the community. Using the '*Neue Sachlichkeit*' ('New Objectivity') style, the prominent Jewish architect Alexander Beer (1873–1944, murdered in Theresienstadt concentration camp) designed 'one of the most modern' buildings in the city, a five-storey structure with 14 classrooms, a sports hall and rooftop garden for the girls (EJMB, no date). In 1933, shortly after

Figure 2.1: Detail of Ram Katzir's 'Milk Teeth', 2006

Source: Photo by the author

Hitler's rise to power, a new law was passed to prevent 'overcrowding in German schools'. As most Jewish families in Berlin considered themselves German and sent their children to public schools, the number of pupils rose that year from 400 to 1,000. After Kristallnacht in 1938, student numbers diminished rapidly, and by 1942, all Jewish schools were closed, 'with the majority of its pupils and teachers later deported to be murdered in death camps' (EJMB, no date). After having read this history as part of the exhibition material, and then experiencing Katzir's sculpture, the visitor was powerfully reminded of how the city still continues to experience the loss of Jewish life. The white pile of dust in the corner alluded to the tragic loss of young girls' lives sent to their death by an anti-Semitic regime and society, and the title of the work, alluding to children's baby teeth, suggested their innocence, as well as the fact that the girls would never become adults in the city.

'Milk Teeth' was linked to another sculpture by Katzir marking the absence of Jewish life elsewhere in the city. In the foyer of Berlin–Brandenburg Academy of Science, where Arendt was arrested by the Gestapo in 1933, a suitcase carved from pink-brown stone from Israel was located. At the time of her arrest, Arendt was researching anti-Semitic propaganda for the Zionist Federation of Germany in Berlin and briefly imprisoned. This stone suitcase and a glass case filled with remainders of stones and stone dust from the carved case were placed in the lobby in close proximity. The geotemporal tension between 'Petrification/Versteinerung', as an installation in a living German institution of scholarly prestige, and the dust of 'Milk Teeth' in the former girls' school, critically commented upon the effects of Jewish genocide on the status and future of the nation's institutions of education and knowledge production.

The haunting presence of Hannah Arendt marked all exhibition spaces. At its core was a central reading room, where curators posed the following question on the walls: 'In what kind of a world do we want to live in the future, and what needs to be done in order for us to construct a society that allows us to live in self-determined freedom?' This well-visited room offered guests the opportunity to peruse significant publications and texts (in German and English) written by Arendt. Around the reading room were viewing and listening rooms, which included video interviews with the philosopher and highlighted 'the reading movement that Hannah Arendt's writing have established over the years' (Hefti and Heuer, no date). Some artists were inspired to create new spaces of learning and critical self-reflection in reunified Germany. Judith Siegmund, for example, organised a participatory reading course, entitled 'Vocation – Job Graft. Labour Work Action', in Weissenfels, a town in Saxony-Anhalt in former East Germany, which had high levels of unemployment at the time. Individuals who enrolled in the course read Arendt's (1958) *The Human Condition* and responded to it through their own experiences, fears and insights. For the exhibition, the artist created a place of virtual education and reading in a former classroom, with videos, quotations and other materials they generated on display.

A number of artists focused on Arendt's political thinking in the then political climate five years following 11 September 2001 (9/11) and the launch of the 'Global War on Terror' initiated by former US President George W. Bush. At the time of the exhibition, the German army's involvement with coalition troops in Afghanistan was controversial not because of the number of civilian deaths, but because German deployments abroad were the highest since the Second World War and marked the first time since 1945 that German ground troops had faced an organised enemy and been killed in action. Sebastian Hefti, Susanne Hofer and Kartri Oettli's video installation, 'Auditorium Elements and *Origins of Totalitarianism*', displayed a 45-hour public reading by public figures of the well-known 1951 text as a form of commemoration. One walked into a room of wooden bookshelves housing television monitors, each screening a different person reading a different part of the text. The multivocal simultaneous reading of Arendt's work created a sense of political urgency.

American artist Martha Roseler's work, 'Reading Hannah Arendt (Politically)', selected a range of Arendt's texts that spoke to her of the current political situation in the US, including the retrenchment of civil liberties, breaking of international law, censorship of media and scholarly work, and creation of a popular culture of fear. Passages of Arendt's work were printed in English and German on clear large plastic panels and hung in an overlapping, yet free-flowing, way from the ceiling, allowing visitor to see through to other texts, other readers and the walls and windows of the classroom/Thinking Space (see Figure 2.2). The powerful texts of Arendt, juxtaposed and read in relation to one another, questioned the 'transparency' of US political rhetoric, while suggesting, like other scholars, that the current US democracy must be compared to other democracies that became totalitarian. In addition to Rosler's work, Iranian artist Parastou Forouhar explored Arendt's ideas about freedom in a contemporary state. Her installation, 'Sag mir wo die Menschen sind/Where Have All the People Gone?', and flash animation, 'Just a Minute', depicted torture scenes using the aesthetic language of the circus to comment on her experiences living under a totalitarian dictatorship.

This exhibition created an emotional presence and tactile canvas through which to encounter the absence of Jewish life in the city and

Figure 2.2: Detail of Martha Rosler's 'Reading Hannah Arendt (Politically)', 2006

Source: Photo by the author

Arendt's thinking about democracy and totalitarianism during the so-called 'War on Terror'. For curator Peter Funken (no date):

> Ideally, the Denkraum, housed in the building of a former Jewish girls' school, resembles a think tank and a memorial simultaneously, while being neither, serving instead to connect people as diverse as scientists and business persons … [to] those whose primary orientation to the world is through action, to politics, philosophy and art.

Funken's description of the exhibition project emphasises the importance of this interim historic space in the city. No longer a ruin, audiences experienced a historic building in which to consider the meanings of democracy and freedom in Germany, while becoming aware of the absence of Jewish life in the city.

Conclusions

Through caring for place, the lived geographies and symbolic-material fabric of the city at any moment in time may be (re)animated to include the stories of former residents and groups now largely absent in the city due to past forced removals and systematic murder. As Andreas Huyssen (2003: 6) has argued, the work of memory has become even more critical 'to regain a strong temporal and spatial grounding of life and the imagination' in a cultural present marked by 'a fundamental crisis in imagining alternative futures' due to 'a media and consumer society that increasingly voids temporality and collapses space'. In Berlin, the *Denkraum* exhibition specifically called attention to the critical absence of Jewish life and knowledge production in the city. Practices of reparative justice through legal restitution prevented the historical building from being treated as an empty site for redevelopment following reunification. However, through creative practices and later renovation, forms of dignity restoration, or restorative justice, took place.

In 2009, the run-down building was finally returned to the JCB following a long-standing application submitted by the Claims Conference. At this point in time, the economic liability and costs of renovation are now the responsibility of the JCB. Although they originally wanted to restore the school, with upkeep and insurance costing €40,000 a year, the JCB voted to support a modified proposal by a local gallery owner and developer, Michael Fuchs, to renovate the building in a way that would 'honour the past' and 'bring life back' to the building (cited in Rayasam, 2012). In 2012, 70 years after the Nazis closed down the school, the building reopened as Ehemalige Jüdische Mädschenschule Berlin (The Former Jewish Girls School). The importance of Jewish life in the city and nation is remembered through the centre's place name, the preservation of many original architectural and design features, historical placards with text and photos about the history of the building, and a memorial plaque. In the former classrooms, there are now high-end art galleries and exhibition spaces, including the 'Salon Berlin' gallery of the Museum Frida Burda, and a 'Kosher Classroom' Jewish restaurant offering Shabbat meals. In addition, a 'Rooftop Playground' exhibition space exists on the top floor, a high-end restaurant, the Pauly Saal and Bar, in the former gym, and a small 'Moog' New York-style deli on the ground floor. Described by Jewish Heritage Europe (2012) as a 'chic cultural centre', the building offers visitors a sense of the density of meanings, bodies, ideas and rhythms that once inhabited this modern building, while providing a trendy presence in the present day.

Caring for place (and each other) is an intergenerational right and responsibility for more just urban futures. Even in a limited way, the centre has contributed to dignity restoration. As part of the opening ceremonies, Beate Hammet, the 82-year-old daughter of the building's architect who, as a child, escaped in 1939 and now lives in Sydney, was invited by the city and the JCB to return to dedicate a memorial plaque to her father's memory (Rayasam, 2012). The JCB had contacted her years earlier with a map of the buildings her father had built in the city, and she wrote letters to the Berlin Mayor, lobbying him to restore the former girls' school. She noted that: 'The last time I saw this building it was covered in graffiti and cigarette butts were everywhere. It was revolting'; she was 'delighted' to return for the dedication ceremony, saying how 'emotional' the trip had been (cited in Rayasam, 2012). The building now reflects the multiple functions it has had since it first opened as a school in 1930, which, for Greg Schneider, Vice President of the Claims Conference, is quite unusual: 'You have a prewar thriving Jewish community, you have the Nazis, you have the Communists, and now you have a renewal' (cited in Doyle, 2012). While the new centre can be criticised for consumerist forms of philo-Semitism and extending the gentrification of the area, the name of the building (online, on the street and in publications), the memorial plaque on the exterior and the historical preservation work gesture to the historical legacies of loss; exhibition spaces, the museum and, to a lesser degree, some of the restaurants suggest new possibilities that include Jewish life in the present and future city.

In August 1952, Arendt wrote in her *Denktagebuch*, 'freedom can only be real in plurality, in the space that exists between people, granted they live and act as a community' (quoted in Pfütze, no date). For this reason, 'each retreat from the world results in an almost demonstrable world loss; what is lost is the specific, and in most cases irreplaceable, *interspace* that would have evolved between exactly the retreated and those around him or her' (quoted in Pfütze, no date, emphasis added). Arendt's notion of community and interspace captures the cross-generational and societal conversations made possible through the *Denkraum* exhibition and the building's restoration, which dignified the ruins to become a living place again in the city. As I finished writing this chapter, Arendt's words also resonated with the acts of numerous protestors taking to the streets around the world who are removing statues of and monuments to perpetrators of past violences. These activists are calling attention to expressions of systemic structural forms of racial injustice and their ongoing legacies in particular places in the city. They are demanding radical changes in the hegemonic frames of reference used to understand and live in the city and, indeed, the world. Systemic injustice is cumulative and interwoven into the fabric of the city across generations. State-perpetrated and socially supported forms of violence are never temporally or spatially isolated.

When walking in the city, despair should not be the 'normal' experience for people who have inherited the legacies of racist violence across generations (Hamilton, 2020). As privileged academics and citizens of our world, we have a responsibility to listen to, document and learn from civil rights and justice movements in our cities, including projects of memory-work with ruins. No matter how small, the process of transforming ruins of spatial injustice into historically relevant living places begins the work of restorative justice that is needed to make our cities healthy for all people to live in.

References

Arendt, H. (1958 [2013]) *The Human Condition*, Chicago, IL: University of Chicago Press.

Atuahene, B. (2014) *We Want What's Ours: Learning from South Africa's Land Restitution Process*, Oxford: Oxford University Press.

Bennett, B. and Stephens, M. (2019) *Reclaiming the Name 'District Six'*, report submitted to the Western Cape Provincial Place Names Commission (June), Cape Town: District Six Museum. Available by email request at: researcher@districtsix.co.za

Berlin Senatsverwaltung für Stadtentwicklung (2007) *Urban Pioneers: Berlin: Stadtentwicklung durch Zwischennutzung*, Berlin: Jovis.

Claims Conference (Conference on Jewish Material Claims Against Germany) (no date) 'History'. Available at: www.claimscon.org/about/history/ (accessed 22 June 2020).

Colomb, C. (2012) *Staging the New Berlin: Place Marketing and the Politics of Urban Reinvention in Berlin Post-1989*, London: Routledge.

Colomb, C. and Kalandides, A. (2010) 'The new Be Berlin campaign: old wine in new bottles or innovative form of participatory place branding? Reflections on the evolution of Berlin place marketing and branding', in G.J. Ashworth and M. Kavaratzis (eds) *Towards Effective Place Brand Management: Branding European Cities and Regions*, Cheltenham: Edward Elgar, pp 173–90.

DeSilvey, C. and Edensor, T. (2013) 'Reckoning with ruins', *Progress in Human Geography*, 37(4): 465–85.

Doyle, R. (2012) 'New chapter for Berlin school', *New York Times*, 12 March. Available at: www.nytimes.com/2012/03/11/travel/historic-school-building-now-a-cultural-center-in-berlin.html (accessed 22 June 2020).

EJMB (Ehemalige Jüdische Mädschenschule Berlin) (no date) 'Home page'. Available at: www.maedchenschule.org (accessed 22 June 2020).

Forkert, K. (2016 [2013]) *Artistic Lives: A Study of Creativity in Two European Cities*, London: Routledge.

Fullilove, M.T. (2004) *Root Shock: How Tearing Up City Neighborhoods Hurts America, and What We Can Do About It*, New York, NY: One World/Ballatine Press.

Funken, P. (no date) 'Hannah Arendt's Denkraum (Thinking Space): the experience of an experimental exhibition'. Available at: www.wolfgang-heuer.com/denkraum/eng/space.htm (accessed 28 June 2020).

Hamilton, A. (2020) 'The geography of despair (or all those rubber bullets)', blog post on 'Medium | Race', 4 June. Available at: https://medium.com/@blackgeographer/the-geography-of-despair-or-all-these-rubber-bullets-6f6d711159f5

Harvey, D. (1985) *The Urbanization of Capital*, Oxford: Blackwell.

Hefti, S. and Heur, W. (no date) 'On the century of Hannah Arendt's birth a Denkraum (Thinking Space) is born'. Available at: www.wolfgang-heuer.com/denkraum/eng/centenary.htm (accessed 28 June 2020).

Huyssen, A. (2003) *Present Pasts: Urban Palimpsests and the Politics of Memory*, Redwood City, CA: Stanford University Press.

Jewish Heritage Europe (2012) 'Germany – former Jewish girls school in Berlin is now a chic culture center'. Available at: https://jewish-heritage-europe.eu/2012/03/11/germany-former-jewish-girls-school-in-berlin-is-now-a-chic-culture-center/ (accessed 21 June 2020).

Nachama, A., Schoeps, J. and Simon, H. (eds) (2001) *Juden in Berlin*, Leipzig: Henschel.

O'Callaghan, C., Di Feliciantonio, C. and Byrne, M. (2018) 'Governing urban vacancy in post-crash Dublin: contested property and alternative social projects', *Urban Geography*, 39(6): 868–91.

Pain, R. (2019) 'Chronic urban trauma: the slow violence of housing dispossession', *Urban Studies*, 56(2): 385–400.

Pfütze, H. (no date) 'Freedom of movement'. Available at: www.wolfgang-heuer.com/denkraum/eng/freedom.htm (accessed 28 June 2020).

Rayasam, R. (2012) 'Old Jewish girls' school reborn as Berlin hotspot', *Speigel International*, 20 April. Available at: www.spiegel.de/international/zeitgeist/old-jewish-girls-school-converted-into-berlin-gallery-and-restaurant-a-828763.html (accessed 21 June 2020).

Richie, A. (1998) *Faust's Metropolis: A History of Berlin*, New York, NY: Carroll and Graf.

Soja, E. (2009) 'The city and spatial justice', *Justice Spatiale*, 1. Available at: https://www.jssj.org/article/la-ville-et-la-justice-spatiale/

Till, K.E. (2005) *The New Berlin: Memory, Politics, Place*, Minneapolis, MN: University of Minnesota Press.

Till, K.E. (2008) 'Artistic and activist memory-work: approaching place-based practice', *Memory Studies*, 1: 95–109.

Till, K.E. (2010) 'Resilient politics and a place-based ethics of care: rethinking the city through the District Six in Cape Town, South Africa', in B. Goldstein and W. Butler (eds) *Planning for the Unthinkable: Building Resilience to Catastrophic Events*, Cambridge: MIT Press, pp 293–308.

Till, K.E. (2011a) 'Interim use at a former death strip? Art, politics and urbanism at Skulpturenpark Berlin Zentrum', in M. Silberman (ed) *The German Wall: Fallout in Europe*, New York, NY: Palgrave Macmillan, pp 99–122.

Till, K.E. (2011b) 'Resilient politics and memory-work in wounded cities: rethinking the city through the District Six in Cape Town, South Africa', in B. Goldstein (ed) *Collaborative Resilience: Moving from Crisis to Opportunity*, Cambridge: MIT Press, pp 283–307.

Till, K.E. (2012) 'Wounded cities: memory-work and a place-based ethics of care', *Political Geography*, 31(1): 3–14.

Till, K.E. and McArdle, R. (2016) 'The improvisional city: valuing urbanity beyond the chimera of permanence', *Irish Geography*, 48(1): 37–68.

Tronto, J.C. (1993) *Moral Boundaries: A Political Argument for an Ethic of Care*, New York, NY: Routledge.

Vasudevan, A. (2011) 'Dramaturgies of dissent: the spatial politics of squatting in Berlin, 1968–', *Social and Cultural Geography*, 12(3): 283–303.

Ward, J. (2004) 'Berlin, the virtual global city', *Journal of Visual Culture*, 3(2): 239–56.

3

Traversing wastelands: reflections on an abandoned railway yard

Sandra Jasper

Introduction

A long patch of vacant land appears through the windows of the train moving from the airport to the centre of Berlin. This linear zone of grasslands stretches alongside the tracks passing through the south-eastern district of Schöneweide. A former roundhouse drifts by, followed by a derelict brewery covered in shrubs and a banner appealing to 'leave no one behind'. Traversing Berlin's track wilderness has long stirred the imagination of artists and filmmakers. In the 1981 film *Berliner Stadtbahnbilder*, the German writer and director Alfred Behrens secretly captured his train journeys across the divided city. The film portrays a marooned transport network of geopolitically induced disrepair: deserted platforms and defunct tracks overgrown by birch trees; a railway landscape suspended in time; or, as Behrens describes it, 'a post-industrial wilderness at the heart of the city'.[1]

Over the past two decades, patches of this urban wilderness have been absorbed into prize-winning public parks. An example includes the Natur-Park Südgelände in Schöneberg that opened in May 2000 – an abandoned railway yard that was designated a nature reserve and conservation area, with grassland biotopes and wild-growing woodlands (Kowarik and Langer, 2005). Another example, which has been widely celebrated in the field of landscape design, is Park am Gleisdreieck in Kreuzberg, completed in 2013. The park design evokes a new type of 'wasteland aesthetic' (Gandy, 2013: 1306) by integrating *Gleiswildnis* ('track wilderness'), as signs label the remnants of wild forest, with various leisure and sports facilities.

Other abandoned railway zones, notably, those in more peripheral locations in the former East Berlin, have remained hidden and, until recently, attracted little public curiosity. However, with increasing pressure on land development, the track wilderness north and south-east of the city centre in boroughs like Pankow and Treptow-Köpenick is gradually being razed for speculative interests. The corporate seizure of *Stadtbrachen* (the German word for urban fallow or wasteland) now extends to the smallest vestiges alongside the tracks. The financialisation of the city that is reshaping Berlin's housing sector (Fields and Uffer, 2016) visibly seeps into the realm of urban nature. Thus, the rapid loss of liminal zones and their distinctive flora and fauna needs to be placed in the wider context of contemporary urban change in Berlin.

Berlin has been a focal point for ongoing research on urban ruins, vacancy and wastelands. Berlin's voids have played a key role in excavating the intersections of memory, place and culture in the economic and political restructuring of post-1989 Berlin, including preoccupations with 'post-traumatic' space and the rapid erasure of the city's socialist past (for example, Huyssen, 1997; see also Till's chapter, this volume). The notion of 'vacant space' has been challenged by geographers studying the reanimation of abandoned spaces by activists and artists, whose critical spatial practices have led to new conceptions of urban space like the autonomous 'makeshift urbanism' of mending and care that emerged in West Berlin's squatting scene in the 1970s (Vasudevan, 2015) and the 'interim spaces' produced through new art practices responding to wastelands in the early post-Wende years (Till, 2011). Both Till and Vasudevan highlight how the 'interim use of space' that characterised spontaneous appropriations of wastelands in the 1990s has been taken up as a policy strategy in official planning discourse and city marketing since the late 2000s. Policy strategies like 'urban pioneering' capitalised on improvised responses to unplanned zones to lay the groundwork for attracting developers, at a time when the city-state of Berlin almost faced bankruptcy.

Spontaneous appropriations of urban wastelands are not restricted to human activities; rather, wasteland spaces are also reanimated by non-human life (Jasper, 2020a). Urban ecologists in Berlin have highlighted that wastelands provide the substrate for novel kinds of biotopes to emerge (Kowarik, 1991). In the 1960s, the wastelands created through wartime destruction, geopolitical division and economic decline became open-air laboratories for botanists in West Berlin, who discovered novel assemblages of plants in bombed plots, rubble fields and truncated infrastructural environments (Scholz, 1960; Sukopp et al, 1979). As experimental fields, Berlin's wastelands have generated new scientific and cultural interpretations of nature, raised environmental awareness of the value of spontaneous ecologies flourishing in abandoned spaces, and shifted conservation strategies to consider the protection of these unusual urban biotopes (Gandy, 2013; Lachmund, 2013).

While the fall of the Berlin Wall and the city's ongoing economic crisis created new abandoned zones like the former death strip, many wastelands were lost in the wake of the 'New Berlin' and its building boom. In parallel to radical urban restructuring, nature conservation policies in reunified Berlin have been gradually diluted, making it increasingly difficult for activists and scientists to draw on ecological data for the valorisation and protection of wasteland spaces against their development.

Berlin's current phase of accelerated property development, which has been critically examined in the wider context of the rental housing market (for example, Holm, 2013), is also driving the dramatic loss of inner urban wastelands. Berlin's distinctive infrastructure of cultural and scientific experimentation – vacant buildings, derelict industrial facilities, disconnected railways and other abandoned plots of land that fostered various non-capitalist projects, from clubs, art studios, squats and activist spaces, to unusual urban biotopes – is now rapidly disappearing, even in more peripheral areas of the city.

Taking an abandoned railway yard on the urban periphery as an example, this chapter examines the multiple histories, contemporary responses to and prospective futures of wasteland spaces in Berlin. German and English terminologies commonly used for ostensibly vacant land such as '*Brache*' or 'wasteland' imply that these spaces are devoid of human and non-human life. The chapter argues that rather than being voided, ruined or fallow terrain, *Brachen* are, in fact, rich repositories of urban life from which alternative socio-ecological futures can be gleaned.

Urban wilderness on the periphery

Since its abandonment in 1998, the former Schöneweide railway yard has developed into a 40-hectare ecological experiment. The two-kilometre stretch of railway land runs parallel to the active tracks that mark the boundary between the districts of Schöneweide, Adlershof and Johannisthal in the south-eastern borough of Treptow-Köpenick. On entering the site by foot, the grass rustles with every step. It is a warm and sunny morning in June and the wasteland is brimming with life. The petals of wild flowers stand out brilliantly against the light sandy soil, gravel and rusty railway relics – a colourful assemblage of blue, red and white, with *Anchusa officinalis* ('alkanet'), *Papaver rhoeas* ('poppy') and *Reseda lutea* ('wild mignonette') (see Figure 3.1). Insects whizz around and the hypnotic song of skylarks draws the ear towards the sky. This island of urban nature sounds is periodically drowned out

Figure 3.1: Assemblages of plants flourishing in the abandoned Schöneweide railway yard, Berlin, May 2020

Notes: *Reseda lutea* is an old cultivated plant that originates in the Mediterranean and now flourishes on roadsides across Eastern Germany. *Anchusa officinalis*, a South-Eastern European plant, is originally associated with steppes, and is now a common feature of spontaneous railway ecologies. A newly paved cycling path transects the site.

Source: Photo by the author

by trains rushing by. Aside from a few people cycling past on a new path running parallel to the tracks, the site seems unnoticed.

Among the many rare species that have appropriated this wasteland is the *Lacerta agilis* ('sand lizard'). Its German name, *Zauneidechse* ('fence lizard'), stems from the lizard's preference for richly textured habitats alongside roads, railways and fences. In Berlin, the interstices of railway tracks are a key refuge for the sand lizard and make up 75 per cent of its urban habitat (Becker and Buchholz, 2016). The sites' grasslands harbour insects such as the *Oedipoda caerulescens* ('blue-winged grasshopper') and the *Papilio machaon* ('swallowtail'). Fragments of oak forest with *Quercus robur* ('pedunculate oak') provide pockets of shade. In a central part of the site, a small pioneer woodland is developing with aspen, robinia and birch trees. In the past two decades, non-human life has transformed this site that is deeply marked by its infrastructural past (see Figure 3.2). The signal boxes, tracks, gravel and wooden ties that have fallen out of use are now part of 'a new

Figure 3.2: The abandoned tracks of the Schöneweide railway yard, Berlin, provide habitats for the sand lizard and various ground-breeding birds, May 2020

Source: Photo by the author

kind of socio-ecological synthesis' that blurs the boundaries between nature and the city (Gandy, 2011: 150).

Rather than being despoiled or vacant, wastelands can be read as vital ecological and cultural zones. Environmental groups in Berlin consider the Schöneweide railway yard of exceptional ecological value. The many rare and endangered forms on non-human life – several of which are 'target species' of conservation concern – make the site an integral segment to reconnect fragmented urban space into a citywide green corridor or network (BLN, 2015: 7). Railway corridors – active and abandoned – can help facilitate the dispersal of seeds and the movement of animals across urban space. In a recent survey of the Schöneweide railway yard, urban ecologists have examined the effects of intensifying urban fragmentation on seed dispersal to speculate about the plants that will be able to adapt in an increasingly sealed and fragmented city (Westermann et al, 2011).

The abandoned railway yard is also a place of social and cultural significance. Some industrial structures like a water tower and roundhouse have been retained as part of a local railway museum, other traces of the past have been lost in the aftermath of war, geopolitics, industrial decline and the memory politics of post-unification Berlin.

Today, Schöneweide is little known to people outside of Berlin, except from passing through on their journey to the airport. However, in the late 19th century, when industrialisation reached the outskirts of Berlin, the riparian settlement Schöne Weyde, meaning 'beautiful meadow', rapidly developed into one of the city's largest industrial complexes that remained throughout the German Democratic Republic (GDR). The abandoned railway yard originates from an expansive junction of over 40 tracks that connected the famous AEG electrical company and other factories in Schöneweide to one of the oldest railway lines in Germany, the Berlin-Görlitz train line that was opened in 1866. The area became a soaring *Ausflug* ('excursion') destination when the railway brought thousands of Berliners to Schöneweide. On weekend trips, workers enjoyed the riverfront in beer gardens and restaurants with elaborate pavilions, bowling alleys and ballrooms (Schultheiss Brauerei, 1910). By the early 1900s, much of the riverfront and its leisure spaces had been destroyed due to the rapid expansion of the AEG industrial complex of factories and housing, several designed by the German modernist architect Peter Behrens, a proponent of making corporations provide critical services for workers, including housing and spaces for recreation (Hake, 2008: 28). In 1929, the S-Bahn was connected to the Schöneweide railway network. Workers now travelled further out to the south-eastern lakes to enjoy nature. With the overcrowding of the city in the late 1920s, public access to nature became increasingly important. The lakes and pine forests on the periphery of Berlin became essential leisure spaces for the workforce and were vehemently defended against privatisation by Weimar-era progressive city planners like Martin Wagner (Gandy, 2014: 55–79).

However, the lakes not only served as leisure spaces. At the height of the economic recession and housing crisis, with rent strikes and occupations, hundreds of homeless and unemployed who had been evicted from their Berlin flats built a camp at the south-eastern lake Müggelsee. Public spaces of nature became indispensable, serving the dire need for shelter. For his 1932 film *Kuhle Wampe oder Wem gehört die Welt?*, director Slátan Dudow recreated the tent city of lake Müggelsee on an airfield just opposite the Schöneweide railway yard. In 1920, when Berlin emerged as an experimental city across the arts, architecture and moving-image culture, the Jofa-Atelier film studios opened next to the railway yard on the Johannisthal airport. Two former hangars were converted into halls for filming and the railway tracks that had serviced the airport were now repurposed by camera operators (Giesen, 2019: 74). For a brief period, the Jofa studios – Berlin's 'forgotten dream factory' (May, 2020) – turned the south-eastern periphery into a focal point for Weimar-era leftist and expressionist cinema. *Kuhle Wampe* was the last major leftist film production before the Nazis' rise to power (Sprink, 2001). The studios were later used for Nazi propaganda films and, after the war, for GDR television. In the 1990s, a German media group bought the film complex and later demolished it, razing nearly all material traces of moving-image culture.

After 1939, the railway serviced the export of arms when the AEG factories started to produce weapons. The area continued to be a left stronghold for the communist resistance against fascism. Until 1945, thousands of forced labourers from across Europe worked in the factories. They were housed in a labour camp on railway-owned land just north of Schöneweide station (Wörmann, 2010). After the division of Berlin, the railway yard that was now located in East Berlin continued to service the public, but it lost its significance as a major trade and transport hub. In 1990, many factories were dismantled or privatised and later went bankrupt, leaving industrial facilities and their infrastructures abandoned. Schöneweide became a declining industrial zone, with rapidly increasing unemployment and a rising neo-Nazi scene.

Compensation landscapes

Wastelands in the former East Berlin like the Schöneweide railway yard have remained blank spots on ecological maps for a long time. The geopolitical division of Berlin mirrors the production of ecological knowledge on both sides of the Berlin Wall. While West Berlin became one of the most intensely surveyed cities, especially botanically (Lachmund, 2013), much less is known about marginal spaces of spontaneous nature beyond the walled-in enclave. In the post-war period, travel restrictions, which made journeys beyond the confinements of the walled-in city difficult, led botanists in West Berlin to study previously undiscovered spaces on their doorstep; bomb sites, abandoned industrial zones and the large network of truncated railway spaces became scientific field laboratories in which the botanist Herbert Sukopp and his colleagues discovered unknown species, many of which were new arrivals to the city (Lachmund, 2003).

In the 1970s and 1980s, various artists reanimated the truncated 'phantom limbs' of abandoned railway stations with sound installations and forensic excavations of everyday objects in an archaeology of the present (Jasper, 2011). At the same time, urban ecologists produced detailed surveys of the wilderness flourishing in the interstices of railway tracks (Kowarik, 1991: 50) The botanist Ullrich Asmus, for example, surveyed the vegetation of defunct inner-city railway yards, counting over 400 different ferns and flowering plants, almost half of them so-called 'non-native' species. Asmus (1980: 2; see also Jasper, 2018) considers wastelands as multifarious public spaces of leisure and play, urban gardening, environmental protection, scientific discovery, and education and learning, as well as spaces that enhance the quality of the urban experience, including the sensory realm, by easing the effects of urban heat and noise.

The revaluation of urban wastelands by scientists, artists and environmental activists led to a convergence of interests around their protection when municipal plans envisioned large-scale transport projects that would have turned these spaces of nature into surfaces of asphalt. In 1981, landscape planners and members of the newly formed left-wing environmental party Alternative Liste: Für Demokratie und Umweltschutz ('Alternative List: For Democracy and Environmental Protection') developed a counter-proposal in which railway wastelands were reimagined as future green corridors stretching across the island city. The *Grüne Mitte* ('green centre'), as the plan was called, proposed the protection of wasteland biotopes as public spaces, alongside the retention of squats and housing collectives, cultural spaces, and flea markets, and the expansion of cycling paths and public transport (Alternative Liste, 1984).

Much less is known about the history of wastelands in the former East Berlin. Bottom-up responses to urban nature include the work of volunteers and citizen science groups who carried out ecological surveys of urban avifauna, amphibians and reptiles in the 1980s (Degen and Otto, 1988). Botanical knowledge of the city was patchy compared with the comprehensive biotope maps of West Berlin (Pobloth, 2009). More in-depth botanical studies of unusual zones in the former East Berlin and in nearby Potsdam were first carried out in the early 2000s (Maurer et al, 2000). Equally, the role of wasteland spaces in the history of illegal occupation in the former East Berlin has yet to be fully explored (Vasudevan, 2015).

In post-unification Berlin, the planning paradigm shifted towards redeveloping the centre as a new capital, with government buildings, corporate offices and consumption spaces. The dramatic transformation of the post-Berlin Wall inner city marks a shift from an ambitious phase of environmental politics that integrated social and ecological concerns towards a more pragmatic approach of mitigation that prevailed throughout the 1990s (Lachmund, 2013: 195–220). After long and laborious activist struggles, some wasteland spaces of ecological value like the former Johannisthal airport and the Südgelände railway yard were turned into public parks in the early 2000s. These parks have been celebrated for defending spaces of spontaneous nature against development, but they embody an ambivalent trajectory. Natur-Park Südgelände, for example, is the outcome of compensation schemes mitigating the destruction of nature in the inner city (Gandy, 2013; Lachmund, 2013). Rather than focusing on protecting particular wastelands from encroachment, the policy shift towards compensation created a landscape of 'phantom biotopes', as the sociologist Jens Lachmund (2013: 196) refers to the real or latent sites that are considered as potentially equivalent to the biotopes destroyed for construction projects. The aim to protect species and biotopes was watered down further in subsequent years through the introduction of quantification, metrics and flexibilisation: the possibility to disconnect compensation measures temporally and spatially from the wasteland ecologies that are destroyed.

Speculative ecologies

In their contemporary reinvention as parks, former railway wastelands challenge us to reconsider questions of social and ecological justice, even more urgently now in the wake of various strategies of accumulation by greening (see McClintock, this volume). Berlin has been at the forefront of turning abandoned railway yards into public parks prior to 'the high line effect', the circulation of the New York High Line model of railway-to-park revitalisation that is now circulating in various cities (see Rosa and Lindner, 2017; Gulsrud and Steiner, 2020). Like in New York, Barcelona, Los Angeles and other cities, processes of environmental gentrification that exhibit the paradoxical effects of securing public spaces of nature for local neighbourhoods (for example, Anguelovski et al, 2019) can now also be observed in Berlin. Although not initially intended as assets for financial investments, the linear verges of railway parks now proliferate with new-build luxury housing developments in a 'third wave' of gentrification in Berlin (Holm, 2010). In Park am Gleisdreieck, remaining pockets of spontaneous nature that flourish on the edges of the park are now encroached upon by booming construction, or have already been razed and replaced by ruderal-looking flowerbeds and front lawns. In neighbourhoods like Schillerkiez in Neukölln, the transformation of the noise-polluted Tempelhof airport into a public park has sparked the so-called 'Tempelhof effect': the steep rise

Figure 3.3: A newly paved road with street trees and bike racks cutting through the Schöneweide railway wasteland, May 2020

Source: Photo by the author

in rents that drastically affects poorer and migrant residents (Huning and Schuster, 2015).

The south–east of Berlin has become another frontier of gentrification. High-profile artists and investors have bought factories and land along the riverfront in the abandoned industrial core of the former East Berlin. The industrial heritage of Schöneweide is being rediscovered in new arts-based revitalisation schemes led by the municipal government and local authorities. In Oberschöneweide, the northern part of the district, the rents for studio spaces have become unaffordable for many local artists and musicians, who had already moved further out from Central Berlin. Along the southern riverfront in Niederschöneweide, Germany's largest real estate company, the notorious Vonovia, is planning to build 800 new housing units for their long-term investment portfolio in a shift from 'pure speculation to long-term investment' or 'financialisation 2.0' (Wijburg et al, 2018: 1098).

Some clubs and art studios are now following upstream to Schöneweide. Steep rises in rent, the short-term termination of leases and noise complaints make it difficult for non-profit cultural spaces to prevail in Central Berlin. The city's *Clubsterben* – as the disappearance of nightlife spaces is called in German, alluding to the term *Artensterben* ('species extinction') – reveals how the speculative interest in abandoned zones affects cultural spaces and spaces of nature alike in a wider encroachment on public life. Not unlike developments in cities like New York or London, many clubs that have been forced to close were hosting LGBTQ events. The Griessmühle is a recent, prominent example of the loss of 'queer infrastructure' in Berlin (Trott, 2020: 92). Its lease of a former industrial building in the district of Neukölln was terminated on short notice in February 2020 after long negotiations with the real estate developers and numerous solidarity protests. Under the new name of Revier Südost, Griessmühle has now found a *Zwischennutzung* ('interim use') in an abandoned brewery in Schöneweide that once served workers of the industrialising metropolis as an *Ausflug* destination. The makeshift urbanism of the 1970s and 1980s has entered a new phase of transiency, with mobile parties and 'fluid infrastructure' that can quickly be disassembled and reassembled elsewhere, as clubs and other cultural organisations not primarily aiming at profit cannot easily afford to invest labour and care in uncertain material spaces and futures.[2]

Upon returning to the abandoned railway yard in Schöneweide, cranes are looming over the site. Since 2016, this unique wasteland biotope has been disappearing bit by bit. The land is being sold for commercial use and marketed as part of a new 'tech corridor' connecting the south-east of Berlin with the airport. A newly paved street transects the site. Young street trees have been planted in symmetrical rows that appear strangely out of place in the midst of the track wilderness. The southern edge of the wasteland is now a car park. Another section has been fenced off and bulldozed; plants are piled up together with layers of earth, refuse, an old sofa and other remnants of human habitation. Behind signs by a real estate investor that advertise future office buildings lies a deep construction pit.

In 2009, in the early planning phase of this new commercial zone – a project that was initiated by the landowner, the private German railway company Deutsche Bahn AG, together with the municipality and local authority – landscape consultants conducted an in-depth ecological survey of the Schöneweide railway yard that considered half of the 40-hectare site as rare or endangered biotopes (Berlin House of Representatives, 2016: 28–9). Of the 38 species of birds that were found on the site, several are listed as critically endangered and protected under nature conservation law, including *Anthus campestris* ('tawny pipit'), *Oenanthe oenanthe* ('wheatear'), *Lullula arborea* ('wood lark'), *Carduelis cannabia* ('common linnet') and *Sylvia communis* ('common whitethroat'). Other legally protected species include the sand lizard and various assemblages of plants, such as fragments of oak forest and semi-dry grasslands. In 2016, the land-use plan was approved on the basis of a compensation scheme to mitigate the destruction of these rare wasteland ecologies, which was vehemently opposed by various environmental groups for its flawed offsetting metrics and lack of scientific grounding (BLN, 2015).

The compensation scheme includes the creation of a small linear park with a bicycle path. Most of the legally protected species and biotopes will be offset in existing parks elsewhere: the sand lizards will be moved to a landscape park in Lichtenberg; and habitats for birds will be created 30 kilometres outside of Berlin in Brandenburg (Berlin House of Representatives, 2016: 10), severing the synthesis of nature and city that has evolved over more than two decades. All other forms of non-human life on the site will be destroyed.

The focus of nature conservation on endangered species and biotopes frames nature according to its likelihood of extinction, as the anthropologist Timothy Choy (2011) describes such 'politics of endangerment'. Similarly, the geographer Gerhard Hard (2001: 258) questions the sole focus on endangerment as reflecting a '*Biotoppolitik*' ('biotope politics') that divides nature into a 'first-class nature' that is valued with protection and a 'second-class nature' that can be destroyed.

New planning strategies like the *Ökokonto* ('eco account') currently pioneered in Berlin, Hamburg and other cities reveal the increasing financialisation of urban nature. In Berlin, the eco account is introduced to speed up development by preponing mitigation measures. The costs for such measures are initially covered by the municipality and later reimbursed by developers once land-use plans are approved. The geographers Elia Apostolopoulou and Bill Adams (2017) have highlighted the multiple problems of using offsetting in conservation. Biodiversity offsetting reframes nature through a market lens and isolates nature in abstract and quantifiable units through metrics like the *Biotopwert* ('biotope value') that was first introduced by urban ecologists in Berlin in 1970 as an effort to gain influence in planning policy (Lachmund, 2013: 110). From a scientific perspective, the uniqueness of wastelands as biotopes that have emerged in a complex and place-specific synthesis of nature and city cannot be numerically abstracted or easily recreated elsewhere (Sukopp and Markstein, 1983). Offsetting does not account for the cultural and social histories of a place, the relations between people and nature, and the long-term costs of sealing open space, including the social costs of losing wastelands as surrogate forms of public space. In this sense, such compensation measures are not a robust enough tool to counter a speculative financial view that seeks to treat wastelands as abstract and ahistorical space to be developed as real estate.

Within the finitude of urban space, wastelands become antagonistic spaces, especially at moments when cities are densifying. The new *Ökokonto* can be considered a tool of post-politics designed to bypass participation and contestation. Its explicit aim is to 'speed up the development of new urban quarters' and 'compensate for the inevitable encroachment on urban nature' (SenUVK, 2019). Implying that the destruction of nature is 'inevitable' depoliticises the inherently conflictual process of development. As Apostolopoulou and Adams (2017: 28) argue: 'Offsetting forecloses discussion of the nature of the social and economic forces behind the environmental impacts of development.' Offsetting further distances conservation from activists' struggles for a socially and environmentally just city, as well as from wider political debates on the 'right to nature' and the 'rights of nature' in cities.

In June 2020, the Berlin Senate published its *Charta für das Berliner Stadtgrün* ('*Charter for Berlin's urban green*'), a voluntary political commitment together with a green action plan for the next decade. The charter highlights the importance of railway wastelands for urban biodiversity, but the commitment to protect these spaces remains vague.

Abandoned railway yards and other urban–industrial wasteland spaces will only be permanently integrated in the existing network of green spaces if 'no other uses are envisioned' (SenUVK, 2020: 17). Recent botanical and ornithological studies of railway wastelands in the former East Berlin emphasise that the rare grassland biotopes flourishing in these sites provide the only remaining habitats for ten bird species of European conservation concern across Berlin, and should become the core focus for future conservation strategies (Maurer et al, 2000; Meffert et al, 2012). At the same time, Deutsche Bahn AG is selling more and more of its railway properties in Berlin for profit, even smaller pieces of land on the fringes of downscaled infrastructure. The current Mayor of Berlin has recently stated that he aims to acquire all possible railway-owned land, though not to protect wasteland ecologies, but to tackle the housing crisis (Bünger, 2019). Not unlike previous moments in the city's history of environmental activism, the future of urban wastelands cannot be discussed in separation from the future of housing, and both are fundamentally tied into wider processes of land speculation.

Conclusions

The future of wastelands remains caught between efforts to secure these spaces for public life and forceful attempts to extract value from ostensibly vacant land. Recent examples like the Tempelhofer Feld – an abandoned airfield with unique spontaneous biotopes that was successfully protected as a public park through a bottom-up, citywide public referendum (Jasper, 2020b) – show that in order to preserve wastelands, strong alliances across civil society are needed, together with radical political tools for creating a more socially and ecologically just city. Another previously abandoned zone is the Mauerweg, a section of the former 'death strip' cutting across Berlin that has become part of a pan-European initiative to transform the former Iron Curtain into a green corridor (Kowarik, 2019). However, unlike these prominent examples, the Schöneweide railway yard is not going to be integrated in the city's 'green belt' or official memorial landscape, and is bound to soon be forgotten.

This chapter has recovered some of the historical uses and present activities that shed light on other ways of valuing wastelands as lived and inhabited spaces to counter the narrow sense of temporality reflected in the utilitarian idea of wastelands as spaces in between the 'no longer' and 'not yet'. The speculative value of wastelands is not merely economic; rather, wastelands are repositories holding traces of human pasts and actions. Wastelands are future oriented in the myriad possibilities of prospective appropriation and use that they promise. For architectural historian Vittoria Di Palma (2014: 244), the wasteland is 'our terrain of contestation ... a space of resistance, of challenge, and ultimately, of possibility and change'. The city of Berlin now encompasses a considerable archive of wasteland activism that goes back at least to the 1970s. Many activist groups in Berlin have laboured militantly to preserve wastelands in their essential role as ecological and cultural spaces, often against corporate and municipal interests. Wastelands constitute the material grounds for building an alternative city. They foster a counter-aesthetic of urban life that cannot be fully exhausted by capitalist projects.

Wastelands can still be found on the periphery of Berlin, alongside canals, railways, industrial installations and other infrastructural spaces. As field laboratories for ecological research, they propel scientists to speculate about future ecologies in future cities. In and through wastelands, more-than-human urban futures are at stake. To speculate about a future for wasteland ecologies poses difficult questions about the presence of non-human life in cities: where do we tolerate or even perhaps accommodate non-human life? Which forms of nature do we value and protect? The current species-centred politics that drives conservation (Gandy, 2019) is increasingly decoupled from protecting actual wasteland sites. By losing more and more wasteland spaces, Berlin is gradually dissolving the synthesis of spontaneous nature and the city that has characterised its urban landscape for decades.

Acknowledgements

This research was supported by the European Research Council Advanced Grant entitled 'Rethinking Urban Nature'.

Notes

[1] The quote is taken from the DVD booklet to *Berliner Stadtbahnbilder* (1981), DVD, directed by Alfred Behrens, Basis Film Verleih, Berlin.

[2] I would like to thank the students of the 'Wastelands' class for sharing their insights from the interview with the organiser of the Griessmühle club, conducted in June 2020.

References

Alternative Liste (1984) *Zum Thema: Stadtentwicklung. Die 'Grüne Mitte'. Das Konzept der Alternativen Liste zum Zentralen Bereich*, Berlin: Hilberts & Pösger.

Anguelovski, I., Connolly, J.J.T., Garcia-Lamarca, M., Cole, H. and Pearsall, H. (2019) 'New scholarly pathways on green gentrification: what does the urban "green turn" mean and where is it going?', *Progress in Human Geography*, 43(6): 1064–86.

Apostolopoulou, E. and Adams, W.M. (2017) 'Biodiversity offsetting and conservation: reframing nature to save it', *Oryx*, 51(1): 23–31.

Asmus, U. (1980) *Vegetationskundliches Gutachten über den Potsdamer und Anhalter Güterbahnhof in Berlin*, Berlin: Senator für Bau- und Wohnungswesen.

Becker, M. and Buchholz, S. (2016) 'The sand lizard moves downtown: habitat analogues for an endangered species in a metropolitan area', *Urban Ecosystems*, 19(1): 361–72.

Berlin House of Representatives (2016) 'Entwurf des Bebauungsplans 9-60 für eine Teilfläche des ehemaligen Rangierbahnhofes Schöneweide', 17 February.

BLN (Berliner Landesarbeitsgemeinschaft Naturschutz e.V.) (2015) 'Stellungnahme B-Plan 9-60 (Rangierbahnhof Schöneweide, Adlershof)', 21 October, pp 1–8.

Bünger, R. (2019) 'Ausgediente Flächen im Stadtgebiet: Berlin möchte alle Bahnbrachen für den Wohnungsbau kaufen', *Der Tagesspiegel*, 13 July. Available at: www.tagesspiegel.de/wirtschaft/immobilien/ausgediente-flaechen-im-stadtgebiet-berlin-moechte-alle-bahnbrachen-fuer-den-wohnungsbau-kaufen/24589684.html (accessed 15 July 2020).

Choy, T. (2011) *Ecologies of Comparison: An Ethnography of Endangerment in Hong Kong*, Durham: Duke University Press.

Degen, G. and Winfried Otto, W. (1988) *Atlas der Brutvögel von Berlin. Aus dem Arbeitskreis Avifaunistik der Fachgruppe Ornithologie Berlin*, Berlin, Potsdam: Gesellschaft für Natur und Umwelt im Kulturbund der DDR.

Di Palma, V. (2014) *Wasteland: A History*, New Haven, CT: Yale University Press.

Fields, D. and Uffer, S. (2016) 'The financialisation of rental housing: a comparative analysis of New York City and Berlin', *Urban Studies*, 53(7): 1486–502.

Gandy, M. (2011) 'Interstitial landscapes: reflections on a Berlin corner', in M. Gandy (ed) *Urban Constellations*, Berlin: Jovis, pp 149–52.

Gandy, M. (2013) 'Marginalia: aesthetics, ecology, and urban wastelands', *Annals of the American Association of Geographers*, 103(6): 1301–16.

Gandy, M. (2014) *The Fabric of Space: Water, Modernity, and the Urban Imagination*, Cambridge: MIT Press.

Gandy, M. (2019) 'The fly that tried to save the world: saproxylic geographies and other-than-human ecologies', *Transactions of the Institute of British Geographers*, 44(2): 392–406.

Giesen, R. (2019) *The Nosferatu Story: The Seminal Horror Film, Its Predecessors and Its Enduring Legacy*, Jefferson, NC: McFarland.

Gulsrud, N. and Steiner, H. (2020) 'When urban greening becomes an accumulation strategy: exploring the ecological, social and economic calculus of the High Line', *Journal of Landscape Architecture*, 14(3): 82–7.

Hake, S. (2008) *Topographies of Class: Modern Architecture and Mass Society in Weimar Berlin*, Ann Arbor, MI: The University of Michigan Press.

Hard, G. (2001) 'Natur in der Stadt?', *Berichte zur Landeskunde* 75(2/3): 257–70.

Holm, A. (2010) 'Townhouses, urban village, car loft: Berliner Luxuswohnanlagen als "dritte Welle" der Gentrification', *Geographische Zeitschrift*, 98(2): 100–15.

Holm, A. (2013) 'Berlin's gentrification mainstream', in M. Bernt, B. Grell and A. Holm (eds) *The Berlin Reader: A Compendium on Urban Change and Activism*, Bielefeld: Transcript, pp 171–87.

Huning, S. and Schuster, N. (2015) '"Social mixing" or "gentrification"? Contradictory perspectives on urban change in the Berlin district of Neukölln', *International Journal of Urban and Regional Research*, 39(4): 738–55.

Huyssen, A. (1997) 'The voids of Berlin', *Critical Inquiry*, 24(1): 57–81.

Jasper, S. (2011) 'Phantom limbs: encountering the hidden spaces of West Berlin', in M. Gandy (ed) *Urban Constellations*, Berlin: Jovis, pp 153–7.

Jasper, S. (2018) 'Sonic refugia: nature, noise-abatement, and landscape design in West Berlin', *The Journal of Architecture*, 23(6): 936–60.

Jasper, S. (2020a) 'Abandoned infrastructures and nonhuman life', *Society & Space*. Available at: www.societyandspace.org/articles/abandoned-infrastructures-and-nonhuman-life (accessed 25 December 2020).

Jasper, S. (2020b) 'Acoustic botany: listening to nature in a former airfield', in M. Gandy and S. Jasper (eds) *The Botanical City*, Berlin: Jovis, pp 221–8.

Kowarik, I. (1991) 'Unkraut oder Urwald? Natur der vierten Art auf dem Gleisdreieck', in Bundesgartenschau 1995 GmbH (ed) *Dokumentation Gleisdreieck morgen. Sechs Ideen für einen Park*, Berlin, pp 45–55.

Kowarik, I. (2019) 'The "Green Belt Berlin": establishing a greenway where the Berlin Wall once stood by integrating ecological, social and cultural approaches', *Landscape and Urban Planning*, 184: 12–22.

Kowarik, I. and Langer, A. (2005) 'Natur-Park Südgelände: linking conservation and recreation in an abandoned railyard in Berlin', in I. Kowarik and S. Körner (eds) *Wild Urban Woodlands: New Perspectives for Urban Forestry*, Berlin: Springer-Verlag, pp 287–99.

Lachmund, J. (2003) 'Exploring the city of rubble: botanical fieldwork in bombed cities in Germany after World War II', *Osiris*, 18(1): 234–54.

Lachmund, J. (2013) *Greening Berlin: The Co-production of Science, Politics, and Urban Nature*, Cambridge: MIT Press.

Maurer, U., Peschel, T. and Schmitz, S. (2000) 'The flora of selected urban land-use types in Berlin and Potsdam with regard to nature conservation in cities', *Landscape and Urban Planning*, 46: 209–15.

May, W. (2020) *Berlins vergessene Traumfabrik: Johannisthaler Filmgeschichte(n)*, Berlin: Kulturring Berlin.

Meffert, P.J. and Dziock, F. (2012) 'What determines occurrence of threatened bird species on urban wastelands?', *Biological Conservation*, 153: 87–96.

Pobloth, S. (2009) 'Die Entwicklung der Landschaftsplanung in Berlin im Zeitraum 1979 bis 2004 unter besonderer Berücksichtigung der Stadtökologie', PhD dissertation, Technische Universität Berlin, Germany.

Rosa, B. and Lindner, C. (2017) 'From elevated railway to urban park', in B. Rosa and C. Lindner (eds) *Deconstructing the High Line*, New Brunswick, NJ: Rutgers University Press, pp 1–20.

Scholz, H. (1960) 'Die Veränderungen in der Ruderalflora Berlins. Ein Beitrag zur jüngsten Florengeschichte', *Willdenowia*, 2(3): 379–97.

Schultheiss Brauerei (1910) *Die Schultheiss Brauerei in Vergangenheit und Gegenwart*, Berlin: Meisenbach, Riffarth.

SenUVK (Senatsverwaltung für Umwelt, Verkehr und Klimaschutz) (2019) 'Das Berliner Ökokonto'. Available at: www.berlin.de/sen/uvk/natur-und-gruen/landschaftsplanung/landschaftsprogramm/gesamtstaedtische-ausgleichskonzeption/ (accessed 15 July 2020).

SenUVK (2020) *Charta für das Berliner Stadtgrün*, Berlin: SenUVK, pp 1–24.

Sprink, C.D. (2001) ' "Wir waren alles einfache Leute," die Geschichte der Arbeiterzeltstadt Kuhle Wampe', *Müggelheimer Bote*, 7(6): 6.

Sukopp, H. and Markstein, B. (1983) 'Möglichkeiten und Grenzen des Ausgleiches von Eingriffen in den Naturhaushalt, dargestellt am Beispiel der Pflanzenwelt urban-industrieller Standorte', *Laufener Spezialbeiträge und Laufener Seminarbeiträge (LSB)*, 9: 30–8.

Sukopp, H., Blume, H. and Kunick, W. (1979) 'The soil, flora and vegetation of Berlin's wastelands', in I. Laurie (ed) *Nature in Cities: The Natural Environment in the Design and Development of Urban Green Space*, Chichester: Wiley, pp 115–34.

Till, K.E. (2011) 'Interim use at a former death strip? Art, politics, and urbanism at Skulpturenpark Berlin_Zentrum', in M. Silberman (ed) *The German Wall*, New York, NY: Palgrave Macmillan, pp 99–122.

Trott, B. (2020) 'Queer Berlin and the Covid-19 crisis: a politics of contact and ethics of care', *Interface: A Journal for and about Social Movements*, 12(1): 88–108.

Vasudevan, A. (2015) *Metropolitan Preoccupations: The Spatial Politics of Squatting in Berlin*, Chichester: Wiley-Blackwell.

Westermann, J.R., von der Lippe, M. and Kowarik, I. (2011) 'Seed traits, landscape and environmental parameters as predictors of species occurrence in fragmented urban railway habitats', *Basic and Applied Ecology*, 12: 29–37.

Wijburg, G., Aalbers, M.B. and Heeg, S. (2018) 'The financialisation of rental housing 2.0: releasing housing into the privatised mainstream of capital accumulation', *Antipode*, 50(4): 1098–119.

Wörmann, H.W. (2010) *Widerstand in Köpenick und Treptow*, Berlin: Gedenkstätte Deutscher Widerstand.

4

Building the new urban ruin: the ghost city of Ordos Kangbashi, Inner Mongolia

Christina Lee

Introduction

In March 2020, when Australia began shutting its borders and non-essential services were restricted due to COVID-19, I took to running outdoors when I could no longer go to the gym. Hitting the pavement at dusk, this ritual would mark the end of my workday. I would follow the same route that would take me past the local McDonald's, where, without fail, there would be a steady stream of cars at the drive-through. I thought this peculiar given the pervasive fear of community transmission, the government mandate for people to stay at home unless absolutely necessary and tightened household spending in light of escalating unemployment rates and a possible recession. In the face of a pandemic that had left no part of society, and no country, untouched, the queue tellingly indicated daily exhaustion, as well as a desperate holding on to some semblance of normality in a world that had completely changed in a matter of weeks. The activity at the fast-food restaurant was a comic juxtaposition to the No. 212 bus that would, as if on cue on my evening runs, trundle by at that point, carrying no more than a handful of passengers. On some nights, there was only the bus driver.

Extraordinary images of cities appeared in news stories and online videos in the weeks following the start of the pandemic, which showed the impact of lockdowns and partial closures: the cleared skies over Delhi due to decreased air pollution; boars from the mountains roaming deserted roads in Barcelona; and the stillness of Siena's dormant streets, interrupted by the fullness of voices singing in unison from apartments above. In a CNN story in early April 2020, reporter Richard Quest walked through Times Square in New York City during an unusual rush hour. There were few pedestrians in the vicinity and minimal traffic flow. In the city that never sleeps, the giant digital screens still provided sensory overload but product placement was now side-by-side with warnings and advice concerning the virus. The post-apocalyptic mood of the story gave way in the end to Quest's uplifting comment: 'Who knows how long this will last. It's good to see it's all still here. Waiting for us to return' (Quest, 2020).

The language of eerie emptiness – of cities falling silent and transforming into ghostly spaces – has become a shared experience globally. While the pandemic has forced people to adapt their ways of living, it is nevertheless a biding of time in the knowledge that the cities will eventually start moving again. There is an endpoint to all of this, whether it is three months, six months or a year from now, and when we emerge from our homes – to go back to schools and workplaces, to share meals with family and friends at a favourite restaurant, or to sit in a cinema for the latest blockbuster – the streets and places of congregation and commerce will once more teem with activity. As Quest poignantly stated, the cities are waiting for us to return.

However, what if there were no people ready to return? What if the shelves in the grocery stores were brimming with items but there were no customers? What if the escalators and the lights remained switched off indefinitely? What if the homes from which the people were supposed to emerge from had never been lived in? This chapter focuses on Ordos Kangbashi in Inner Mongolia to explore the arresting strangeness of this town that has no foreseeable endpoint to its state of seeming emptiness. Eschewing its fetishisation as a terminal new urban ruin, I wish to unpack how its vacant spaces are important sites of spatial and temporal alterity that allow us to move beyond a discourse of crisis. In doing so, I argue that Ordos Kangbashi offers a way of rethinking, or rather thinking beyond, such developments as inevitable failures.

Pretty vacant: Ordos Kangbashi as China's pre-eminent ghost city

China's ghost cities and towns function in international media representations as cautionary tales of heady future planning.[1] Images of barren streets, neglected business districts, uninhabited housing estates and lifeless public zones in places such as Chenggong District, Shenzen City, Caofeidian and Kangbashi New Town are stark and sombre because of their severe underutilisation. They are but a handful of those new establishments erected on the outskirts of existing cities that capitalise on undeveloped land, where the overabundance of the built environment is abruptly unsettled by the absence of the human element. The 'ghost city phenomenon' is a by-product of the demands of an overarching national agenda – to secure China's position as a global superpower and ensure its successful entry into the 21st century – and the particularities of regional governance. As Christian Sorace and William Hurst (2016: 305) state, China's exponential trajectory of urbanisation 'is a powerful ideological commitment to urban growth as the "royal road" to modernity and assessment of political performance'. On the one hand, the twin projects of modernisation and urbanisation materialise as administrative exercises involving the reclassification of places to grant instant 'city' status. On the other, the upgrade entails the dramatic reshaping of topographies that sees land reclaimed from the water, mountains levelled and settlements demolished in order to develop the necessary infrastructure to house the hundreds of millions of new city dwellers – formerly rural citizens – who are expected to migrate to urbanised areas over the next several decades. In his book *Ghost Cities of China*, Wade Shepard (2015a: 5, 7) conveys the magnitude of this undertaking:

> Over the next twenty years China will build hundreds of new cities, thousands of new towns and districts, erect over 50,000 new skyscrapers, wipe untold thousands of villages off the map, and relocate hundreds of millions of people.... Within the past thirty years 400 million Chinese, more than the entire population of the United States, have transitioned from rural to urban areas; throughout the first decade of the twenty-first century the country's urban head count was growing by the population of Australia annually. But China's not done yet. By governmental decree, 300 million more people are expected to become urban by 2030, the much portended year when the country is expected to have 1 billion city dwellers. This means that 1.4 million Chinese, roughly the population of Estonia, will need to urbanize each month for the next sixteen years.

Equally as startling as the sheer scale of this mass migration and urbanisation is the breakneck velocity and intensity of spatial change that accompanies it. This has fuelled a burgeoning discourse and concern around unsustainability and the creation of new urban ruins (which shall be discussed in the following section, from p 80).

While modernisation and urbanisation are the banners under which high-speed, large-scale constructions are occurring throughout China, it is important to contextualise this within local strategic operations.

Since 1978, reforms in China have increasingly decentralised the economic and administrative powers 'from the central government to the local state at the provincial, city, county, town and township levels' as a strategy for nation-building, with cities tasked with playing a major role in the country's economic development (Ma, 2005: 77–8). At a regional level, urbanisation has become a priority because it augments that territorial unit's economic and political influence, and is an indicator of its capabilities in advancing the national agenda. The staggering pace of development is further driven by the unique financial pressures exerted upon regions. With the greater agency bestowed upon local governments comes the greater responsibility to generate their own revenue, much of which derives from land sales and levying various land-development taxes and fees (Woodworth, 2012: 81). Building an entire city reaps enormous monetary rewards in a relatively short period of time but has also led to the ghost city phenomenon.

Ordos Kangbashi in the Inner Mongolia Autonomous Zone is arguably China's most infamous ghost city, exemplifying the drivers and conditions that have enabled rapid urban development and precipitated acute underpopulation. Ordos is comprised of three districts or towns: Dongsheng, Azhen and Kangbashi – the latter of which is the most recent construction. The discovery of rich deposits of rare earth minerals and coal in the late 1990s, and the subsequent favourable market conditions for these resources in the following years, quickly transformed the previously poor and largely rural region in the Gobi Desert into one of the nation's most affluent. Ordos' wealth would be tied up in mining:

> It has one-sixth of the country's total coal reserves, its proven natural gas reserves are equivalent to one-third of the country's total, and its proven rare earth and kaolin deposits account for half of total domestic reserves. These rich underground resources have propelled an economic growth rate of nearly thirty per cent, with urban development to match. (Otede, 2018: 77)

The lucrative extractive industry ensured that by the end of 2007, Ordos' per capita gross domestic product 'surpassed that of Beijing and Shanghai, and by 2010 it exceeded that of Hong Kong' (Sorace and Hurst, 2016: 311). In 2001, Ordos was reclassified from the prefecture-level Yeke-juu League to Ordos Municipality, which marked the beginning of an ambitious urbanisation project. It included expansion of urban spaces and improvements to existing infrastructures and housing stock, and would reach its pinnacle with the creation of a new town. Construction of Kangbashi, positioned approximately 25 kilometres from the established 'old city' of Dongsheng, began in 2003/04. By 2009, 'the town's basic infrastructure was completed along with municipal agency buildings, landmark civic institutions, and a significant amount of commercial property' (Woodworth and Wallace, 2017: 1272). The rapid rise of the new district in the desert, on the former site of two ethnic Mongolian villages, was an exceptional feat in terms of the completion time and its grand designs (see Figure 4.1[2]).

Kangbashi was planned to accommodate a population of 1 million citizens by 2023, and was to spread over 355 square kilometres (Shepard, 2015a: 68). Major development projects were financially supported by local government revenue from the mining industry and injections into the economy by private investors. Feverish construction was also stimulated and sustained by the speculative residential real estate market. Household financial strategies in China heavily depend on property ownership due to limited investment opportunities; therefore, a household may retain several properties in the anticipation that they will appreciate in value over time.[3] As rental yield is low and there is no property tax in China, properties purchased for investment

Figure 4.1: New residential complexes, Kangbashi

Source: Photo by the author

purposes often remain empty for years (Woodworth and Wallace, 2017: 1275). Public and private investors were effectively lying in wait to reap the rich profits that had seemed almost assured given the exponential economic growth of Ordos. However, a sharp decrease in demand and market price for coal in 2011, coupled with the fallout of Ordos' speculative real estate and investment market that had been propped up by a problematic banking system and private lending, proved disastrous for Kangbashi's continued development. Bankruptcy and defaults on repayments rose, leading to swathes of construction sites being abandoned, while the promise of future buyers for investment properties dissipated. In response, 'Kangbashi's original concept was scaled down to a city for 500,000 during its early phases of development, and later on to 300,000' (Shepard, 2015b).

More than a functional space, the 'instant city' of Kangbashi was intended to serve as a trophy and testament to the region's prosperity, culture and commitment to better living, with its open spaces, clean air and orderly urban design (Pond, 2010/11: 42). It boasts state-of-the art amenities, including a sports stadium, cultural and arts centre, and artificial lake near the central business district, which are purposely aesthetically striking. For example, the ostentatious Ordos Museum sits on elevated land like a globular alien pod that contrasts with the sharp lines and symmetry of the buildings, plazas, pathways and roads nearby.[4] Ordos Library has been designed to resemble three books inspired by Mongolian history and culture leaning against one another.[5] Navigating through Kangbashi, I was reminded of classical Chinese paintings showcasing sweeping natural landscapes with the diminutive human figure gently placed in the tableau. In place of towering majestic mountains are row upon row of towering skyscrapers, and uninterrupted fields and waterways morph into sprawling public squares, parks and extensive road and motorway networks.

Instead of the harmonious coexistence between landscape and human in the paintings, in Kangbashi there is the sense of an environment that does not simply dwarf its inhabitants, but engulfs them. That Kangbashi is not built to scale for humans became apparent as I tried to walk around the town. I found myself constantly in a light run trying to cross six laneways at the traffic lights before they turned green, and realised that it took much longer than expected to make my way from one landmark to another even when they were adjacent on the map. The monuments throughout Kangbashi subscribe to the mantra that 'size matters'; they rival the dimensions of landmarks in international megacities that have populations of more than 10 million people. The epic bronze statues in Genghis Khan Square (see Figure 4.2), as with

Figure 4.2: Genghis Khan Square, Kangbashi

Source: Photo by the author

so many of the historic tributes in the town, are statement pieces that are visible from afar. Groups of people strolling by look like listless, tiny ants.

The surfeit of space in Kangbashi is compounded by the dearth of people. Although the estimated population of permanent residents was 153,000 as at 2017, the low residential density is palpable in the experience of the town (Xinhua, 2017). When I arrived at Ejin Horo Airport one September evening in 2016, I was struck by the echoes of my footsteps and suitcase wheels as I crossed the partially illuminated, cavernous terminal, passing a few workers and travellers. The taxi ride from the airport to Dongsheng was eerie and odd; a highway with barely any vehicles and frequent stops at traffic lights and pedestrian crossings where there were no pedestrians. After checking in at The Crowne Plaza, which continued the theme of half-lit establishments and few patrons, I recalled a previous guest's review left on a TripAdvisor site that referred to the hotel's 'David Lynch vibe' (TripAdvisor, 2015).

In the ensuing days, I would travel through the sprawling urbanscapes of Kangbashi and Dongsheng. By night, outlines of lightless complexes were like motionless sentinels in the dark. By day, I saw whole commercial buildings and residential zones in various unfinished states. Many had been deserted several years ago (see Figure 4.3). At

Figure 4.3: Abandoned construction site, Dongsheng

Source: Photo by the author

the time of my visit, the occupancy rate in Kangbashi's six Central Business District towers was approximately 30 per cent.[6] Standing at the top of one of those buildings, the impressive outlook from the roof and helipad belied the incompleteness of Level 42 below, with its dirt floor, soil mounds and exposed concrete columns. In a children's education, entertainment and retail centre in Dongsheng, the words 'Future World' were emblazoned on its glass façade. Apart from six vendors and one child in the foyer, there were no other people I could see there. The ceiling lights and escalators were switched off, the activity rooms were locked up, and several of the shops – aside from exterior signage – were bare. Outside Future World was a colourful merry-go-round surrounded by a metal barrier that was already starting to rust and a pile of concrete slabs that had been dug up.

New urban ruins: spaces of alterity and slow time

As has been discussed previously, the speed of urban development in China arises in large part from the political ambitions of local authorities, as well as the fiscal pressures to raise land-based revenue in a compressed period of time. This has contributed to the problematic short lifespans of new constructions, whether a single building or an entire city. Writing on Kangbashi, Melia Robinson (2016) states that, 'Pressure to build fast and cheap left a number of structures dilapidated shortly after their construction.' When I visited Kangbashi's main landmark, the Ordos Museum, it had only been open for seven years and yet was already showing signs of dilapidation, with plaster peeling away from the ceiling and walls. Hasty workmanship aside, it is symptomatic of the strategic operations of regional governments, where the sooner something falls, the sooner it can be demolished, redeveloped and sold again. It is a cyclical construction of built environments – with built-in expiration dates.

China's ghost cities exemplify what has come to be known in scholarly literature as 'new ruins', resulting from the accelerated creative destruction and volatility of capitalist production (and in China's case, accelerated modernisation and urbanisation). Broadly, ruins are 'associated with spaces that were once occupied but, through economic and social transformations, are no longer in use' (Kitchin et al, 2014: 1070). While they may present as architectural eyesores in the landscape – whether a disused power station, an abandoned airport, a gutted house or the rubble of an ancient site – they symbolise past aspirations and purposes that have been rendered obsolete *over time*. As the casualties of progress, ruins are physical reminders of things and places that were once relevant and useful. By contrast, China's ghost cities constitute new urban ruins that were never occupied; their dereliction is caused by their premature abandonment. They are 'a physical manifestation of the "ruined" future' (Kitchin et al, 2014: 1071).[7] If, as Caitlin DeSilvey and Tim Edensor (2013: 468) propose, 'The ruin indexes both the hope and hubris of the futures that never came to pass', China's ghost cities embody the extremity of unrealised potential. The moniker of the 'stillborn city' widely circulating in international media crudely encapsulates the common view of China's ghost cities as dead on arrival.

As Daryl Martin (2014: 1043) avers, 'New ruins require a fuller reading of the landscape … they require that we dig deeper.' This fuller reading and deeper digging is an appeal to situate new ruins in their broader spatial and temporal context. In relation to Kangbashi, it is to widen the scope to capture what is outside the photographic frame – the dominant mode of visual representation of the ghost city – and to excavate artefacts and sites that have been overlooked. Duo Yin, Junxi Qian and Hong Zhu (2017: 11) astutely point out that because much of the discussion on the ghost city phenomenon has focused on China's political and economic dynamics, this has perpetuated a narrowed view 'that erases the lived experiences of the residents' and the heterogeneity of these urban spaces. On Kangbashi, they write:

> While the concentration of unsold properties and underused public infrastructures exist in these cities-in-waiting, it is nonetheless necessary to understand how these landscapes are inhabited by people who have already moved in, through the lens of daily practices rather than a rigid epistemological distinction between the ghostly and the vibrant. (Yin et al, 2017: 3)

While photographic documentation was an integral aspect of my fieldwork in Ordos, my multidisciplinary approach included psychogeography and autoethnography as a way of broadening the scholarly viewfinder. The act of physically navigating through the environment by foot was a strategy to slow down my own movements to take time to observe, reflect and engage with the locals, and to enable an embodied experience of the place that was more attuned to the human presences within it.

Studying the 'still life' in China's ghost cities requires redirecting our gaze towards sites/sights in our blind spots that may appear unremarkable, quotidian or marginal but often bear the traces of lived presence. After entering a residential complex that was in the middle of a construction site, it was apparent that some residents had already moved in. On one of the floors, there were clear signs of 'home' and daily routines: mushrooms left out to dry on the landing; red banners and lanterns hanging outside the front entrance; a child's bicycle with trainer wheels leaning against a cupboard; a pair of shoes resting on a welcome mat; the sound of a television switched on; and the smell of food emanating from inside the flat. In other cases, there were more furtive presences that undermined the initial impression of absence. Upon closer inspection of an unfinished building, there were dusty beer bottles and flattened cardboard boxes that had been used for seating in one of the apartments. In a psychogeographic wander down a darkened passageway in Kangbashi's Cultural and Art Centre, I saw a man asleep in a storage room that had been converted into his private dwelling (see Figure 4.4). The posters on the wall and personal computer set up on a desk reinforced the homeliness of this hidden space. In the windows of a padlocked commercial building in the cultural precinct, rows of beds were discernible (see Figure 4.5). Whether they were signs of occupancies of bored youth or migrant workers, these sites were being utilised and appropriated in ways that they were not intended

Figure 4.4: Man asleep in the Cultural and Art Centre, Kangbashi

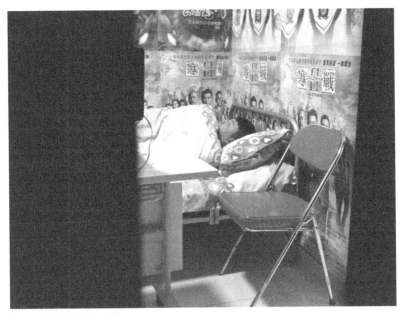

Source: Photo by the author

Figure 4.5: Makeshift dwelling in a commercial building, Kangbashi

Source: Photo by the author

for, and defied the usual strict policing of private and public spaces. Paying attention to these usually unnoticed locales revealed pockets of activity and spaces of alterity that intimated an urban heartbeat.

The lived experience of China's ghost cities runs counter to the culture of speed of the mobile, hyperactive metropolis, with its fast food, fast fashion, fast lifestyles, fast results, fast city building and so forth. Stephanie Hemelryk Donald and Christoph Lindner (2014: 12) argue that a condition of urban life is 'inertia'. Rather than interminable stasis, the suspension, stillness and decay of ghost cities imply movement. In various states of transition and transformation, these 'new towns are ongoing dynamics of change and becoming' (Yin et al, 2017: 2). As spaces of alterity, they gesture to other temporalities and trajectories by which to measure a city's progress, which increasingly recognises vacancy as a component part of urbanisation. Judith Audin (2018: 2) asserts that 'the urbanization of Chinese cities is neither a linear nor a stable process, and spaces that are abandoned or in situations of flux represent a significant stratum of the Chinese urban space'. The torpid rate of growth and pace of life in these cities has necessitated an openness towards slowness itself as a discourse and critical approach for understanding and engaging with contemporary urban life. Instead of signifying lack of progress or productivity, 'slowness today serves a crucial function to challenge deterministic fantasies of mindless progression and develop concepts of meaningful progress instead' (Koepnick, 2014: 14). While the built environment of China's ghost cities manifests economic and political processes in ways that are visually arresting, the (extreme) slow motion within them requires re-evaluation of how people experience and exist in these places.

From a scholarly perspective, 'slow research' can allow for more nuanced, considered readings that benefit from the virtue of patience. A criticism that has been levelled at the international press is that it was reporting on China's ghost cities when they were still construction sites or had only been recently completed, and many were therefore without essential services and facilities, such as schools, shops and medical centres. The assessment of a ghost city, accompanied with haunting pictures as evidence of a place that is not peopled, may be accurate at that *moment*, but it is far too premature to conclude them as having no future. When I first met my translator, Laura Wang – then a 24-year-old native of Ordos who lived in Dongsheng with her family – she reproached Kangbashi for its squandered resources that had made it a national embarrassment. Five months later in February 2017, she informed me that she had secured a job there in one of the public schools (though she remained based in Dongsheng and commuted each day). In October that same year, she spoke with pride about Kangbashi hosting the United Nations Convention to Combat Desertification the month prior, which had prompted additional work to the urban landscape for the high-profile event. Kangbashi was, in Laura's words, beautiful by night. The town was in a state of 'change and becoming', both materially and in the imaginations of Ordos' locals.

Coda

As I completed this chapter in May 2020, COVID-19 restrictions in my state of Western Australia had begun to ease. Most public schools had already returned to face-to-face teaching for several weeks, and social gatherings of up to 20 people were permitted. Cafes, restaurants and pubs resumed dine-in services under strict conditions. Over the course of the month, employees gradually migrated back to the workplace. Noticeably more vehicles were on the roads, with peak-hour traffic resembling the congestion prior to COVID-19. The city was ready for us to return, and we, too, were eager to do so. While the world had experienced a disruption in time and regular activities, life was still moving, however slow, interrupted or invisible it was to the public eye.

Here, I loop back to my stay at The Crowne Plaza in Ordos in my own reflection of the city's stuttered but ever-progressing time. The first morning in the restaurant, I sat alone while eating breakfast. There was scarcely anyone in the dining room and yet the buffet tables were bountiful. The chefs frequently checked the bains-marie as if the food might have magically vanished; the action was poignant and pointless at the same time.[8] I contemplated the waste, not only of the food, but also of the efforts of the chefs and waitstaff, who outnumbered the diners. By the end of the week, however, the restaurant was at capacity.

Throughout the course of my fieldwork in Ordos, it was apparent that timing was critical – timing in the hour of the day, in the day of the week and in the week of the year. I had inadvertently arrived in the city at the start of the week-long National Day holiday, when many people had travelled back to their hometowns to see family, and it was therefore quieter than usual. On a more granular level, in Kangbashi, I needed only wait for a certain time in the day to see crowds congregating in the food halls for the lunch rush hour, and rows of electric bikes lined up outside McDonald's and Subway. Knowing what day of the week in the summertime the free fountain show would be scheduled at the artificial lake allowed me to see the thousands of people who would descend on this public space. Idle the day before, now it was communal, festive and lively. Locals and tourists enjoyed the fountain show and amusement rides as roaming hawkers sold their sticks of candied hawthorn berries, colourful helium balloons, stuffed toys and glow sticks to excited customers, both young and old. My sojourn in Kangbashi demonstrated the value of *giving time*, literally and figuratively, in order to witness the people and life slowly emerging in this ghost city. Who knows how long this will take. In any event, the city is here and mostly ready for the people. To borrow from the adage, good things come to those who wait ... long enough.

Notes

[1] While many of the ghost cities in China are classified as towns, I will use the collective phrase of 'ghost city' as it is more frequently recognised in the media and scholarly literature.

[2] All images in this chapter are copyrighted by Christina Lee, 2016.

[3] This was confirmed by my translator in Ordos, Laura Wang, whose family – like many others – owned multiple investment properties.

[4] MAD Architects was commissioned by the local government to design Ordos Museum. On the MAD website, it states that the museum was to:

> navigate the many contradictions that emerge when local culture meets with visions of the future city. Inspired by Buckminster Fuller's 'Manhattan Dome', MAD conceived of a futuristic shell to protect the cultural history of the region and refute the rational new city outside. Encapsulated by a sinuous façade, the museum sits upon sloping hills – a gesture to the recent desert past and now a favourite gathering place for local children and families. (MAD Architects, 2011)

[5] The three books represented in the library's design are *Mongolian Mystery*, *Mongolian History of Gold* and *Mongolian History of Origin* (de Muynck, 2010: 110).

[6] This occupancy rate was provided by a government employee I spoke to in one of the towers.

[7] Here, I have drawn from Rob Kitchin, Cian O'Callaghan and Justin Gleeson's study of 'ghost estates' in Ireland as exemplars of new ruins. During the prosperous Celtic Tiger era from the mid-1990s to the mid-2000s, Ireland experienced an unprecedented property boom that was spurred on by speculative capitalism, loosened fiscal policies and market-led regulations. The excessive overbuilding led to unfinished estates becoming rife throughout the country. Ireland's ghost estates, similar to China's ghost cities, are markers of spectacular property crashes that followed a period of heightened optimism and untrammelled urban development and capital investment.

[8] I have borrowed Liz Millward's (2017: 105) phrase of abandoned places, in the absence of people, routines and rules, being 'pointless and poignant'.

References

Audin, J. (2018) 'Beneath the surface of Chinese cities: abandoned places and contemporary ruins' (trans O. Waine), *Metropolitics*, 28 September. Available at: www.metropolitiques.eu/Beneath-the-Surface-of-Chinese-Cities-Abandoned-Places-and-Contemporary-Ruins.html (accessed 25 May 2020).

De Muynck, B. (2010) 'Architecture on the move: urban and architectural design in Inner Mongolia', in A. Moran and M. Keane (eds) *Cultural Adaptation*, Abingdon: Routledge, pp 103–13.

DeSilvey, C. and Edensor, T. (2013) 'Reckoning with ruins', *Progress in Human Geography*, 37(4): 465–85.

Donald, S.H. and Lindner, C. (2014) 'Inertia, suspension and mobility in the global city', in S.H. Donald and C. Lindner (eds) *Inert Cities: Globalization, Mobility and Suspension in Visual Culture*, London: I.B. Taurus, pp 1–14.

Kitchin, R., O'Callaghan, C. and Gleeson, J. (2014) 'The new ruins of Ireland? Unfinished estates in the post-Celtic Tiger era', *International Journal of Urban and Regional Research*, 38(3): 1069–80.

Koepnick, L. (2014) *On Slowness: Toward an Aesthetic of the Contemporary*, New York, NY: Columbia University Press.

Ma, L. (2005) 'Urban administrative restructuring, changing scale relations and local economic development in China', *Political Geography*, 24(4): 477–97.

MAD Architects (2011) 'MAD Ordos Museum complete', *Mad*, 26 September. Available at: www.i-mad.com/press/mad-ordos-museum-complete/ (accessed 5 January 2020).

Martin, D. (2014) 'Introduction: towards a political understanding of new ruins', *International Journal of Urban and Regional Research*, 38(3): 1037–46.

Millward, L. (2017) '"Un aéroport-fantôme": the ghost of Mirabel International Airport', in C. Lee (ed) *Spectral Spaces and Hauntings: The Affects of Absence*, New York, NY: Routledge, pp 103–16.

Otede, U. (2018) 'Kangbashi: the richest "ghost town" in China?', in J. Golley and L. Jaivin (eds) *China Story Yearbook 2017: Prosperity*, Canberra: Australia National University Press, pp 77–9.

Pond, E. (2010/11) 'Urbanism on the steppe: the insta-city in Inner Mongolia', *World Policy Journal*, 27(4): 41–7.

Quest, R. (2020) 'CNN anchor: scenes from Times Square are like a "disaster film"', *CNN*, 2 April. Available at: https://edition.cnn.com/videos/us/2020/04/02/us-new-york-coronavirus-covid-19-pandemic-times-square-subway-quest-pkg-intl-ldn-vpx.cnn (accessed 26 April 2020).

Robinson, M. (2016) 'Surreal photos of China's failed "city of the future"', *Tech Insider*, 30 January. Available at: www.businessinsider. com/chinese-ghost-town-2016-1?IR=T#located-in-the-remote-province-of-inner-mongolia-ordos-sits-on-one-sixth-of-chinas-coal-reserves—making-it-an-attractive-center-for-development-1 (accessed 29 November 2016).

Shepard, W. (2015a) *Ghost Cities of China*, London: Zed Books.

Shepard, W. (2015b) 'An update on China's largest ghost city – what Ordos Kangbashi is like today', *Forbes*, 19 April. Available at: www. forbes.com/sites/wadeshepard/2016/04/19/an-update-on-chinas-largest-ghost-city-what-ordos-kangbashi-is-like-today/ (accessed 11 November 2016).

Sorace, C. and Hurst, W. (2016) 'China's phantom urbanisation and the pathology of ghost cities', *Journal of Contemporary Asia*, 46(2): 304–22.

TripAdvisor (2015) 'Review by Beauemmett: Crowne Plaza Ordos', *TripAdvisor Australia*, 18 April. Available at: www.tripadvisor. com.au/ShowUserReviews-g1016967-d565832-r304648039-Crowne_Plaza_Ordos-Ordos_Inner_Mongolia.html (accessed 28 December 2019).

Woodworth, M. (2012) 'Frontier boomtown urbanism in Ordos, Inner Mongolia Autonomous Region', *Cross-Currents: East Asian History and Culture Review*, 1(1): 74–101.

Woodworth, M. and Wallace, J. (2017) 'Seeing ghosts: parsing China's "ghost city" controversy', *Urban Geography*, 38(8): 1270–81.

Xinhua (2017) 'Across China: from ghost town to boomtown – the new look of Kangbashi', *Xinhuanet*, 28 June. Available at: www. xinhuanet.com/english/2017-06/29/c_136402110.htm (accessed 9 January 2020).

Yin, D., Qian, J. and Zhu, H. (2017) 'Living in the "ghost city": media discourses and the negotiation of home in Ordos, Inner Mongolia, China', *Sustainability*, 9(11): 1–14.

PART II

The political economy of urban vacant space

Nullius no more? Valorising vacancy through urban agriculture in the settler-colonial 'green city'

Nathan McClintock

Introduction

Among the brick warehouses and new-build condos of Montreal's hip Mile-Ex neighbourhood, a group of musicians leads a parade a few dozen strong. The intergenerational crowd comes to a stop and circles together in a gravel-covered vacant lot, chattering happily and bouncing in time to the bass drum and snare, while the band's clarinets, accordion, cello and tuba crank out a lively tune. A mother flanked by her two young children scrapes away some of the gravel and begins digging holes in the clay beneath. Another woman places a basil plant in one of the holes and pats some soil back around its base. Someone else empties a basketful of 'seed bombs' on the ground and calls out for people to come and grab some. A young girl picks up one of the small balls of clay packed with herb and wildflower seeds, walks a few feet, cranks her arm back, and hurls it as if it were a Molotov cocktail, the first of many thrown in this battle, in the words of the event's organisers, to *approprier la ville* ('reclaim the city').

In Montreal, as in cities across North America, it is often not long before some group or other replaces the gravel, asphalt or weeds of a vacant lot with something more verdant: beds of rich soil and compost giving life to leafy vegetables, vines, fruits and flowers. Indeed, the relationship between vacancy and urban agriculture is arguably as old as urban food production itself; city dwellers have always opportunistically gardened or grazed animals on the grass and weeds growing in the 'wastelands', those interstitial spaces between and within residential and commercial lots, markets, streets and sidewalks (Vitiello and Brinkley, 2014). They do so for a variety of reasons, from a desire to improve access to fresh and healthy produce, to community building, to recreation and mental health, employing 'motivational frames' that may be entrepreneurial or anti-capitalist, political or apolitical, and individual or collective (McClintock and Simpson, 2018). Like the Montrealers described earlier, many cultivate vacant lots as a means to 'reclaim the commons' or to assert their 'right to the city' (Staeheli et al, 2002; Purcell and Tyman, 2015; Eidelman and Safransky, 2020), in the process, transgressing formal or juridical forms of property, and blurring the boundary between public and private (Blomley, 2004).

Urban agriculture's presence – and its absence – goes hand in hand with the market logics and uneven spatio-temporal patterns of urban development. Like vacancy itself, urban gardens have historically taken root in the troughs of the Kuznets waves of economic expansion and contraction, serving as placeholders for future development (McClintock, 2014). However, in so-called 'green cities' that pride themselves on their leadership and innovations in sustainability, urban agriculture's emergence on vacant land serves another purpose: like other forms of green infrastructure, urban agriculture functions as a form of symbolic 'sustainability capital' that green growth machines can mobilise to attract new investment and more affluent residents (McClintock, 2018). Its role in processes of gentrification has therefore become a growing concern of activists and scholars alike (Quastel, 2009; Sbicca, 2019). Path-breaking geographic work on gentrification emphasises the discursive power of 'pioneer' and 'frontier' imaginaries in the 'reclaiming' of inner-core urban neighbourhoods (Smith, 1996). Building on these insights, a growing area of scholarship makes clear that the language of frontiers and settlement works within wider processes of racial capitalism, and thus functions as more than a metaphor (Blomley, 2004; Safransky, 2014; Peyton and Dyce, 2017; Dorries et al, 2019).

In this chapter, I contribute to these discussions by drawing on research conducted in Montreal (Quebec, Canada), Vancouver (British Columbia, Canada) and Portland (Oregon, USA), three cities in two settler nations located on unceded Indigenous land.[1] I demonstrate how the discursive production of vacancy – as well as the radical assertions of a 'right to the city' underlying efforts to transform such spaces – reproduce settler-colonial logics and racialised dispossession. Following a discussion of how practitioners and 'green growth machines' (Gould and Lewis, 2016) in the three cities employ urban agriculture as a means of valorising vacant properties, I turn to a growing body of literature on settler colonialism and racial capitalism to demonstrate that the discursive and material production of vacancy depends on the effacement of existing uses and relations. Moreover, I argue that even the most progressive of initiatives frequently turn on such pernicious logics.

Valorising vacancy through urban agriculture

Beyond the individual and social benefits it provides, urban agriculture plays a critical role in the seesawing spatio-temporal patterns – including vacancy – that characterise capitalist urbanisation and uneven development. Urban agriculture has long served as a temporary land use, cropping up with the ebb of capital and floundering of land markets, only to be trammelled by bulldozers and covered over with concrete when capital flows back (Drake and Lawson, 2014; McClintock, 2014). Its precarity as a temporary land use lays bare the 'incommensurability' of competing use values (Schmelzkopf, 2002), that is, a parcel's use value as a site of food production and social cohesion, on the one hand, versus its use value as a site of development, and ultimately a site of extraction of exchange value, on the other. This tension has underpinned numerous high-profile cases of urban agricultural 'commons' cleared to make way for development (Staeheli et al, 2002; Irazábal and Punja, 2009). Gardens, in such cases, become sites of contestation over competing visions of the city, as many authors in this volume assert.

In green cities, with their skyrocketing land values and New Urbanist commitments to inner-city densification to enhance walkability and counter suburban sprawl, such tensions are perhaps even more acute. The permanence of vacant parcels in such contexts appears inversely related to their market potential – land simply cannot be 'wasted'. *The Diggable City*, a city of Portland-sponsored inventory of vacant publicly owned parcels of land that could potentially be used for urban agriculture, is illustrative. The report identified more than 200 parcels (Balmer et al, 2005) but later phases of the project winnowed the list down to only a dozen or so 'undevelopable' sites that could realistically be used for urban agriculturalists, only a couple of which were ever turned over to the public.

Yet, while the tension between use and exchange values is an adequate analytical lens in many instances, the growing importance of temporary land uses in the entrepreneurial city (Ferreri, 2015) means that grass-roots gardens are nothing if not *commensurable* with the logics of the market, particularly in cities that have made names for themselves as green and sustainable. More 'developable' areas simply require a more temporary form of urban agriculture. Community-led or guerrilla gardening initiatives on vacant lots and similar forms of 'do-it-yourself [DIY] urbanism' (Iveson, 2013) offer a proverbial 'bang for the buck' in the eyes of urban growth-machine actors: they beautify vacant parcels at little or no cost to the developer and have a spillover effect on the surrounding parcels and neighbourhood (Voicu and Been, 2008).

In Vancouver, for example, developers can receive a tax break if they install a temporary community garden on vacant properties awaiting development. The garden's presence allows the property to be reclassified from 'commercial' to 'non-profit or recreational', leading to significant savings; in 2018 alone, the construction of 28 gardens on vacant lots across the city saved developers CA$2.9 million in taxes (Fumano, 2019). The founder of a Vancouver organisation that constructs these gardens describes the arrangement as a "win–win–win" and "a feel-good project" that benefits the landowner, those who use the garden and the wider public:

> 'A number of the landowners realise the value it brings, both from the community itself, the people using it, and the value that comes out of that. The fact, in general, that something is being used on the site, it's either this vacant lot or a garden. There are very limited things you can put on vacant lots. Our gardens are one of the few things. And the neighbours like it, usually.'[2]

The promotion of urban agriculture as a temporary land use thus reframes both vacancy and its value in new ways.

Many urban agriculturists have come to accept the ephemeral nature of their installations. The founder of one urban agriculture project in a low-income but transitioning area of Portland explains that his group was able to access land thanks to a municipal call for interim uses "to draw attention to this neighbourhood in the hopes of spurring development". He describes the precarious nature of the lease: "We're out here on a temporary use permit. We have to renew every year because, every year, they have to figure out how close they are to this lot being developed. This lot will get built, too, at some point."[3] The founder of a Montreal organisation that facilitates garden builds on vacant parcels also accepts such impermanence: "We aim for something temporary – we like to say 'transitory' because, of course, as an organisation that wants to do tactical urbanism, we don't want to constrain development, whether it is on public or private land."[4] Rather than existing in opposition to capitalist urbanisation, temporary gardens clearly dovetail with development, both in discourse and practice, despite radical claims of reclaiming the city.

Profit-driven growth-machine actors are not the only stakeholders wooed by the 'seductions of low-budget temporary urbanity' (Ferreri,

2015: 181) and DIY urban agriculture's potential role therein. Cash-strapped municipalities are eager to support volunteer-led greening efforts because they buttress weakened state support for beautification, greenspace management and food security programmes (Perkins, 2009; Rosol, 2012; McClintock, 2014), among other things. In Portland, explains a city staffer, "the majority of the maintenance and site management happens in the gardens themselves by the gardeners.... So, we are actually getting tons and tons of service hours, maintenance hours for these properties. So, that's a big benefit."[5] In Montreal, a borough councillor explains that from the city's perspective, there is a practical benefit to "this idea that it's really citizens taking charge because there's a lack of municipal resources. There are so many other issues, potholes, etc. In the grand scheme of things, [for the city, transforming vacant space] is tertiary."[6]

For developers and municipalities alike, gardens function as a symbolic form of 'sustainability capital' (McClintock, 2018) that realtors, developers, city officials and other members of the green growth machine can use to burnish a city's brand and attract investment (Gould and Lewis, 2016; Bunce, 2017). In paradigmatic green cities such as those discussed here, practices such as urban agriculture carry cachet; they serve as a 'performance' of environmental values (Lebowitz and Trudeau, 2017) and signal that a neighbourhood or city is green or sustainable – and open for business. For one Montreal borough councillor, community appropriation of vacant space for urban agriculture actually fosters the entrepreneurialism of the green city by pushing against regulatory barriers. These small acts of reappropriation, in his words, "literally shock, transform, challenge" conventional land-use classifications (industrial, residential and so on) that, in his view, "lead cities to be less productive, less sustainable – in terms of sustainable development – and less entrepreneurial". For this city official, "every square foot won is a small victory".[7]

As the chapters by Di Feliciantonio and O'Callaghan and by McArdle in this volume describe, progressive and radical experiments in commoning are behind many efforts to transform vacant land, and are fundamentally at odds with the entrepreneurial motivations of growth-machine actors. Similar to the Montreal seed bombers we met at the beginning of the chapter, the founder of one Portland farm links the creation of an agro-ecological commons on vacant land with mitigating the deleterious social and environmental impacts of capitalist development:

> We thought it would be a waste to let empty lots around
> town grow weedy when they could be used to produce

cheap, local, and healthy food.... We are able to act independently of large-scale corporations and capitalistic business models which actively destroy intact ecologies in the name of profit. Along these lines, we are able to shift power back into the hands of ourselves and our neighbors through the creation of communal systems for food production and distribution, thereby increasing our health, reducing any negative impacts on our local environment, and gathering together under a common purpose and identity.[8]

While such efforts are laudable, however, the appropriation of urban space 'does not in itself give birth to a new kind of city' (Iveson, 2013: 942). In most cases, there is a scalar mismatch between the politics of transforming vacant space and many of the political-economic processes that make and unmake the food system or the city (Stehlin and Tarr, 2017), resulting in tensions between radical intentions and neoliberal outcomes, with their contradictions unfolding at different scales (McClintock, 2014).

A prime example is urban agriculture's contribution to the widening 'rent gap' – the difference between existing and potential market values – which is central to the process of gentrification (Smith, 1996). Bike lanes, community gardens, farmers' markets, parks, 'whole food' supermarkets and other green infrastructure have become markers of the sustainable, liveable neighbourhood for which affluent consumers are willing to pay a premium. Developers and realtors use proximity to such amenities when marketing properties (Quastel, 2009; Bunce, 2017). In disinvested neighbourhoods where vacancy is widespread and land values are lower, gardens indicate that a transition to the green, liveable neighbourhood is under way. It is this promise of the influx of this more affluent class of resident that widens the rent gap, a reality that concerns many urban agriculturalists. The director of an urban agriculture organisation in Portland acknowledges the role that gardens play in signalling to developers that a neighbourhood is primed for investment: "in some ways, we bolster the gentrification of Portland because we are contributing to that image of Portland as being eco, sustainable, groovy. Urban food production is a part of that image. So, we're facilitating it."[9] However, what imbues these gardens and other DIY transformations of vacant land with symbolic power in the first place, I argue, are entrenched logics, discourses and practices of settler colonialism and racial capitalism, to which I turn now.

Settler urbanism, racial capitalism and vacancy

Sustainability capital's power works by distinguishing certain spaces and populations from others, for example, gardens stewarded by creative, eco-conscious citizens as distinct from the toxic, manicured lawns that symbolise the post-war American dream. At a larger scale, it is precisely the uniqueness of a neighbourhood's or city's reputation as 'green', 'sustainable' or 'liveable' – in contrast to 'bland', 'boring', 'disinvested' or 'dangerous' – that attracts the attention of affluent consumers and investment capital. Gardens help mark streets, neighbourhoods and even cities as 'hip', 'transitioning' or 'up-and-coming', and eventually as 'liveable' (McClintock, 2018).

Such transitions, of course, imply that the space was previously *un*liveable and/or that there was simply nothing there before – *Terra nullius* ripe for the taking. Describing urban space this way – as vacant, abandoned, marginal, empty or underused – turns on the discursive erasure and Othering of whatever existing use value a city lot, block or neighbourhood may already have, and of the population who used or continues to use it. As McKittrick (2006: 130–1) argues, 'to transform the uninhabitable into the inhabitable, and make this transformation profitable', requires discursive differentiation from '"normal," "a normal way of life," or the normally inhabitable'. This transformation, she explains, 'does not fully erase the category of uninhabitable, but rather re-presents it through spatial processes as a sign of social difference' mapped onto the landscape.

A 'romance with pure spaces' (Lipsitz, 2007: 12) – untouched, 'virgin' landscapes awaiting domination – has long undergirded constructions of *Terra nullius*. Settler-colonial origin stories describe '"wasted" or "virgin" landscapes' transformed into 'great hubs of commerce and exchange brought to life by the brilliance and ingenuity of rugged and ambitious arrivistes' (Hugill, 2017: 5); the towns and cities that emerged amid the stumps and slash represented 'the highest and most progressive stage of empire' (Edmonds, 2010: 239). Furthermore, as settlement required both territorial expropriation and erasure of the native population, it was bound up with processes of racial Othering (Nemser, 2015; Bhandar, 2018). Original inhabitants were, on the one hand, rendered as non-human by virtue of their living in a 'natural' but 'uninhabitable', 'unliveable' space, while, on the other, pathologised as unwelcome contaminants of these same empty and pure landscapes. While contradictory, both views served to dehumanise Indigenous people and justify genocide and the theft of their territory. Settlers not only used coercion and force to physically remove Indigenous people from urban spaces and onto rural reserves, but also employed discursive violence, rendering them as primitives anathema to progress and the modernity of urbanisation (Blomley, 2004; Edmonds, 2010; Toews, 2018; Dorries et al, 2019), and eventually as spectral vestiges relegated to the memory of a virgin landscape long since developed (Baloy, 2016; Porter et al, 2020).

Settler colonialism, explains King (2016), also required the discursive, juridical and biological production of Black bodies as a 'fungible' form of property that could be exchanged, substituted and replaced like other commodities. This lens of fungibility draws our attention not only to the dehumanising violence inflicted upon the enslaved, as well as the political-economic centrality of slavery to settler colonialism (Lowe, 2015; Kelley, 2017; Dorries et al, 2019), but also to how the Black enslaved body became 'a figurative and metaphorical value extending into the realm of the discursive and symbolic ... an open sign that can be arranged and rearranged for infinite kinds of use' (King, 2016: 1025). As 'a form of raw material and an expression of spatial expansion' (King, 2016: 1026), Blackness was thus bound up in both the material and discursive transformation of *Terra nullius* into a site of domination and exploitation.

These discursive and symbolic processes are not limited to the past tense, however. Indeed, they continue to serve as 'tool[s] of everyday violence' (Rotz, 2017: 162) that underpin the maintenance of racial-capitalist/settler-colonial power in the present. Contemporary renderings of space as uninhabitable continue to work dialectically, where 'the process of uneven development calcifies the seemingly natural links between blackness, underdevelopment, poverty and place' (McKittrick, 2011: 951). As scholars of racial capitalism have emphasised, accumulation occurs by 'seizing upon colonial divisions identifying particular regions for production and others for neglect, certain populations for exploitation and still others for disposal' (Lowe, 2015: 150). The dual devaluation of urban space and racialised bodies – the rendering of a space as unlivable and its inhabitants as deviating from the normal by virtue of living therein – thus lays the groundwork for occupation or 'reclamation', and is therefore key to the transformation of vacant spaces in the settler city.

Gentrification and displacement in North American cities tend to be highly racialised, and the frontier imaginary is deeply entrenched. Just as Smith (1996) observed of the revanchist gentrification of New York's Lower East Side, Safransky (2014: 238) observes that ongoing redevelopment in Detroit often invokes a frontier imaginary of discovery and pioneering that renders the 'vacant' sites in question as 'empty and underutilized … awaiting inhabitants and transformation, [thus] nullifying existing ways of life'. Dillon (2014: 1214) describes a similar framing in San Francisco, where potential redevelopment sites are classed as 'under-utilized, economically unproductive lands'. Such discourse, she argues, works in tandem with the material and discursive devaluation of the surrounding, predominantly African American, neighbourhood. Racialised and devalued urban space, 'unburdened by Indigenous sovereignties and emptied of Indigenous peoples' (Porter et al, 2020: 230), thus becomes what Coulthard (2014: 176), linking past to present and underscoring that colonisation is ongoing, refers to as '*urbs nullius*'.

Nullius no more?

Vacant, inner-city spaces in settler cities such as Portland, Vancouver and Montreal, where indigeneity has been effaced and Blackness 'calcified' as a marker of a neighbourhood's devaluation, constitute not only the emptiness of *urbs nullius* and the 'uninhabitable', but also the extension of possibility – an abstracted space of latent accumulation. Just as the imposition of the colonial grid onto Indigenous landscapes effaced difference via abstraction (Blomley, 2004; Nemser, 2015; Blatman-Thomas and Porter, 2019), the discursive production of vacancy – the deeming of space as 'wasteland', for example (Goldstein, 2013; Dillon, 2014; Wideman, 2020) – and concomitant erasure of existing use values and socio-ecological relations are a prerequisite to a site's transformation through urban agriculture. The words that a thirty-something white, male urban farmer uses to describe the large parcel of land he farms in a diverse but gentrifying part of Portland are illustrative: "I feel like it's – it was just an empty field here and now it's something that's more of a neighbourhood asset. It's a neighbourhood asset for, like, anybody really, like all different kinds of people."[10]

Beyond viewing such spaces as empty, urban agriculturalists often invoke the language of repair. One of the vacant spaces identified in the Portland's *Diggable City* project was, in the words of a city staffer, "this piece of property that was just sitting there, covered with seven feet of blackberries and God knows underneath that what was there". Considered a "nuisance site" due to low-levels of asbestos and other contaminants in the soil, an activist group secured funding from the state's Department of Environmental Quality to clean up the site:

> 'The work that they've done on this thing! … it's going to be a permaculture site with a food forest. It already has the gazebo in there for their meeting space. And this is in one of the lowest-income neighbourhoods in the city, with a dearth of those sorts of amenities.'[11]

A city planner reflects in a similar manner on the transformation of a vacant lot in Vancouver:

> 'It was a gas station that shut down, it was just a shitty derelict site for years. Just ugly, a really visible corner. A temporary community garden was built there, and it's been there for years now. People use that space now, like, people have their lunch there, there's benches, you see people walking their dogs through there. It's such a community space now.'[12]

In these examples and others, the efforts of urban agriculture activists are often grounded in a worldview that Paperson (2014: 117) calls 'settler environmentalism', whereby calls to transform vacant land turn on a twin discourse of 'land as sacred, wild, and preserve-able' and 'land as desecrated, in pain, in need of rescue'. Such calls for rescue, in turn, justify 're-invasion' and 'resettlement', using a variety of green technologies, including urban gardens. Resettlement may proceed slowly, in fits and starts, or rapidly. When enough newcomers practise urban agriculture in their front yards, community garden plots or vacant lots, their gardens signal to future gentrifiers and investors that the neighbourhood is on the road to being liveable and green. Describing urban agriculture's ability to transform, one Portland farmer invokes a settler imaginary:

> 'It's kind of a [pauses] pioneer. In the same way that maybe artist studios are pioneer uses, so you get these areas which are basically left behind, and so the property value drops to the point where, well, you can do anything with it because nobody's there anymore anyway, it's a shell. And then you get these really creative spaces in there – so, artist studios or urban ag projects or something like that. There starts to be some kind of vibrancy that happens and then the

neighbourhood starts to grow up around that and there gets to be a lot of development.'[13]

The promise of new development and a whiter demographic, in turn, distinguishes a once-vacant site from the surrounding, lower-income, more diverse neighbourhood (Dillon, 2014). As a young white urban farmer in Vancouver explains:

> 'If there are community gardens or a street that looks like people are growing food on it, I think for the people I know, that plays into the "Oh, this is up-and-coming" or "It's okay to live here"-type thing…. I think the presence of food growing in public spaces does contribute to the mindset of less risk to go into this area.'[14]

Similarly, as a Portland farmer explains, urban agriculture "gives the appearance of   it's like something cute or sweet. It makes it cute and neighbourhoody. Desirable. It makes it desirable and feel safe."[15] Discussing the installation of gardens in a disinvested downtown plaza, a former Montreal borough councillor says:

> 'It works really well there; it gave a second life to a site that really lacked – that was sad. There were lots of itinerant people, which is fine, but what we want is a mix. So, now there is a mix and it's good. You can have a homeless person who's chilling, and then next to them, you have a little family eating.'[16]

As critical food scholars have noted, however, agglomerations of white bodies in urban agricultural spaces can alienate those who either previously used or might otherwise be drawn to use these spaces for food production (Ramírez, 2015; McClintock, 2018). In the words of a Black gardener reflecting on Portland's numerous community gardens, "You ain't seeing any people of your kind, and you're kinda like, 'Oh, this ain't for me.'"[17] Another Black farmer in Portland explains that for many African Americans, the proliferation of urban gardens is "a sign of gentrification" under way.[18] Therefore, in the gentrifying green city, urban agricultural spaces – and the sustainability they symbolise – become coded as white. At the same time, a post-political, colour-blind discourse of sustainability (Hammelman, 2019; Harris and Romero, 2019) elides this 'racialisation of space and spatialisation of race' (Lipsitz, 2007).

Even when the transformation of vacant property proceeds under the ostensibly progressive or radical banners of reappropriating the city, claiming a right to the city or reclaiming the urban 'commons', such efforts may be blind to the discursive and material processes of dispossession underwriting vacancy in the first place, unintentionally perpetuating a settler-colonial logic that 'all prior, indeed current as well as future relations between people and land are null and void' (Paperson, 2014: 121). Coulthard (2014: 12, emphasis in original) cautions that claims of reclamation by settlers are fraught precisely because 'the "commons" not only belong to somebody – *the First Peoples of this land* – they also deeply inform and sustain Indigenous modes of thought and behaviour that harbour profound insights into the maintenance of relationships within and between human beings and the natural world built on'. If land is 'a material being that through its being creates the world and the subjects (human and non-human) of that world' (Blatman-Thomas and Porter, 2019: 41), then deeming it 'vacant' and subsequently 'rescuing' it (Paperson, 2014) not only effaces its existing use values, but also unravels the very fabric of Indigenous socio-ecological relations and thus becomes 'a continuation of the practice of settling' (Porter et al, 2020: 224). Capital's fundamental requirement to undo 'metaphysical and material relations of people to land, culture, spirit, and each other' (Kelley, 2017: 269) is thus borne out by the very act of reclamation.

Conclusion

The verdant gardens exploding forth from once-'vacant' parcels of land in North American cities are testament to the love, labour, devotion and determination of a small but growing number of urban agriculturalists. In this chapter, I have attempted to elucidate the role that such transformations play in capitalist accumulation in thriving, green, liveable cities. Vacant lots, for many, serve as a key site of urban commoning, where tilling soil, planting seeds and sharing the harvest serve as a political claim of the 'right to the city', a reclamation of physical space from the market (il)logics of capitalist urbanisation, as well as a site of forging anti-capitalist relations of mutual aid and ecological stewardship. At the same time, the greening of vacant lots, whether by anti-capitalists or entrepreneurs, has come to play an important role for urban growth machines eager to cash in on the symbolic capital of such efforts, resulting in urban agriculture's new entanglements in processes of gentrification, displacement and uneven capitalist development.

In my effort to help rethink urban vacancy, I have also situated these dynamics within the context of racial capitalism and settler colonialism. This lens demonstrates how the discursive and material practices that rendered urban spaces as 'vacant', 'empty' and 'uninhabited' in the first place – that produced *urbs nullius* – are ongoing. Since 'vacant' land in settler cities nevertheless remains embedded in sovereign relations with the original Indigenous inhabitants (and is thus already in use), the construction of vacancy reproduces settler-colonial and racial-capitalist logics working to efface these existing uses and unravel these relations. Vacancy, in this light, takes on new valence as a vital mechanism of (always ongoing) colonisation, and thus also as a lively terrain of (long-standing) contestation. There are always multiple, overlapping claims and conceptions of the commons (Eidelman and Safransky, 2020). Indeed, many of these weedy, interstitial spaces tucked between buildings and pavement are also sites of Black and Brown self-determination and commoning, as well as of Indigenous resurgence and reclamation of territory and the land-based practices and knowledge-imbuing relations between humans, non-humans and the land (Coulthard, 2014; Safransky, 2017; Bledsoe et al, 2019; McClintock et al, 2021).

Efforts to 'reappropriate' the city through urban agriculture under the anti-capitalist banner of the commons are thus rarely cut and dry. My intention here is not to belittle the often admirable motivations and outcomes of the many committed activists in Portland, Vancouver and Montreal, or to gainsay their claims of commoning; indeed, many of them have succeeded in creating new social relations that challenge capitalist logics of food production, labour, land and property. Rather, my observations come from a place of sympathetic critique. Truly 'abolitionist and decolonial renderings of the city' (Ramírez, 2020: 161) require laying bare not only histories of dispossession narrated in the past tense, but also the ways in which efforts to transform urban space today are often inadvertently complicit in ongoing dispossession. Attending to these dynamics cannot be done without recognising and centring the 'underlying continuance of Indigenous sovereignties' that shape urban space (Porter et al, 2020: 232). Further, such renderings demand of us an 'uncomfortable reflexivity' (Pillow, 2003), one that comprises both a critical acknowledgement of our own positionality, as well as that of our forebears (Ramírez, cited in Naylor et al, 2018), and 'an ethic of incommensurability' (Tuck and Yang, 2012: 9) that pushes us to recognise and accept acts of solidarity as 'an unsettled matter that neither reconciles present grievances nor forecloses future conflict' (Tuck and Yang, 2012: 3). I suggest then, in closing, that such an ethic should ground both our rethinking of urban vacancy and our reflections on the role of urban agriculture and other forms of DIY urbanism in transforming vacant space. Vacancy in the settler city clearly remains unsettled.

Notes

[1] I have been conducting research on urban agriculture in all three cities since 2012, and draw here on interviews, open-ended survey responses and participant observation conducted during four separate projects (see McClintock et al, 2016, 2018; McClintock and Simpson, 2018; Bach and McClintock, forthcoming), and acknowledge my positionality as a white settler on the Indigenous territory where I live and work. Greater Montreal lies on the unceded land and waters of the Kanien'kehá:ka (Mohawk) and Anishinaabeg (Algonquin), and Vancouver on the unceded territory of the xʷməθkʷəy̓əm (Musqueam), Skwxwú7mesh (Squamish) and Tsleil-Waututh Nations. Portland lies on the traditional homelands of the Multnomah, Clackamas and Atfalati, who the US government dispossessed and relocated onto reservations following a series of unratified treaties in the 1850s. Their descendants are today members of the Confederated Tribes of the Grande Ronde Community of Oregon and the Confederated Tribes of Siletz Indians.

[2] Interview by the author and Christiana Miewald, Vancouver, BC, June 2016.

[3] Interview by the author, Portland, OR, September 2015.

[4] Interview by Claire Bach, Montreal, QC, August 2015. Translated by the author.

[5] Interview by the author, Christiana Miewald and Eugene McCann, Portland, OR, August 2016.

[6] Interview by Claire Bach, Montreal, QC, April 2016. Translated by the author.

[7] Interview by Claire Bach, Montreal, QC, April 2016. Translated by the author.

[8] Online survey conducted by the author and Michael Simpson, February 2013.

[9] Interview by the author, Portland, OR, September 2016.

[10] Interview by the author, Portland, OR, September 2015.

[11] Interview by the author, Christiana Miewald and Eugene McCann, Portland, OR, August 2016.

[12] Interview by the author and Christiana Miewald, Vancouver, BC, June 2016.

[13] Interview by the author, Portland, OR, September 2015.

[14] Interview by the author and Christiana Miewald, Vancouver, BC, October 2016.

[15] Interview by the author, Portland, OR, August 2015.

[16] Interview by Claire Bach, Montreal, QC, April 2016. Translated by the author.

[17] Interview by the author, Christiana Miewald and Eugene McCann, Portland, OR, August 2016.

[18] Interview by the author, Portland, OR, November 2016.

References

Bach, C.E. and McClintock, N. (forthcoming) 'Reclaiming the city one plot at a time? DIY garden projects, radical democracy, and the politics of spatial appropriation', *Environment and Planning C: Politics and Space*.

Balmer, K., Gill, J., Kaplinger, H., Miller, J., Paterson, M., Rhoads, A., Rosenbloom, P. and Wall, T. (2005) *The Diggable City: Making Urban Agriculture a Planning Priority*, Portland, OR: School of Urban Studies and Planning, Portland State University.

Baloy, N.J.K. (2016) 'Spectacles and spectres: settler colonial spaces in Vancouver', *Settler Colonial Studies*, 6(3): 209–34.

Bhandar, B. (2018) *Colonial Lives of Property: Law, Land, and Racial Regimes of Ownership*, Durham: Duke University Press.

Blatman-Thomas, N. and Porter, L. (2019) 'Placing property: theorizing the urban from settler colonial cities', *International Journal of Urban and Regional Research*, 43(1): 30–45.

Bledsoe, A., McCreary, T. and Wright, W. (2019) 'Theorizing diverse economies in the context of racial capitalism', *Geoforum*, DOI: 10.1016/j.geoforum.2019.07.004

Blomley, N. (2004) *Unsettling the City: Urban Land and the Politics of Property*, New York, NY: Routledge.

Bunce, S. (2017) *Sustainability Policy, Planning and Gentrification in Cities*, New York, NY: Routledge.

Coulthard, G.S. (2014) *Red Skin, White Masks: Rejecting the Colonial Politics of Recognition*, Minneapolis, MN: University of Minnesota Press.

Dillon, L. (2014) 'Race, waste, and space: brownfield redevelopment and environmental justice at the Hunters Point shipyard', *Antipode*, 46(5): 1205–21.

Dorries, H., Hugill, D. and Tomiak, J. (2019) Racial capitalism and the production of settler colonial cities, *Geoforum*, DOI: 10.1016/j.geoforum.2019.07.016.

Drake, L. and Lawson, L.J. (2014) 'Validating verdancy or vacancy? The relationship of community gardens and vacant lands in the U.S.', *Cities*, 40(Part B): 133–42.

Edmonds, P. (2010) *Urbanizing Frontiers: Indigenous Peoples and Settlers in 19th-Century Pacific Rim Cities*, Vancouver: UBC Press.

Eidelman, T.A. and Safransky, S. (2020) 'The urban commons: a keyword essay', *Urban Geography*, DOI: 10.1080/02723638.2020.1742466.

Ferreri, M. (2015) 'The seductions of temporary urbanism', *Ephemera*, 15(1): 181–91.

Fumano, D. (2019) 'Vancouver's community gardens sit on $525 million of land', *Vancouver Sun*, 18 June.

Goldstein, J. (2013) 'Terra economica: waste and the production of enclosed nature', *Antipode*, 45(2): 357–75.

Gould, K.A. and Lewis, T.L. (2016) *Green Gentrification: Urban Sustainability and the Struggle for Environmental Justice*, New York, NY: Routledge.

Hammelman, C. (2019) 'Challenges to supporting social justice through food system governance: examples from two urban agriculture initiatives in Toronto', *Environment and Urbanization*, 31(2): 481–96.

Harris, D.A. and Romero, R. (2019) 'Race, four farms, and a city: color blindness and the Austin, TX, urban farm debate', *Humanity & Society*, 43(3): 227–49.

Hugill, D. (2017) 'What is a settler-colonial city?', *Geography Compass*, 11(5): 1–11.

Irazábal, C. and Punja, A. (2009) 'Cultivating just planning and legal institutions: a critical assessment of the South Central Farm struggle in Los Angeles', *Journal of Urban Affairs*, 31(1): 1–23.

Iveson, K. (2013) 'Cities within the city: do-it-yourself urbanism and the right to the city', *International Journal of Urban and Regional Research*, 37(3): 941–56.

Kelley, R.D.G. (2017) 'The rest of us: rethinking settler and native', *American Quarterly*, 69(2): 267–76.

King, T.L. (2016) 'The labor of (re)reading plantation landscapes fungible(ly)', *Antipode*, 48(4): 1022–39.

Lebowitz, A. and Trudeau, D. (2017) 'Digging in: lawn dissidents, performing sustainability, and landscapes of privilege', *Social & Cultural Geography*, 18(5): 706–31.

Lipsitz, G. (2007) 'The racialization of space and the spatialization of race: theorizing the hidden architecture of landscape', *Landscape Journal*, 26(1): 10–23.

Lowe, L. (2015) *The Intimacies of Four Continents*, Durham: Duke University Press.

McClintock, N. (2014) 'Radical, reformist, and garden-variety neoliberal: coming to terms with urban agriculture's contradictions', *Local Environment*, 19(2): 147–71.

McClintock, N. (2018) 'Cultivating (a) sustainability capital: urban agriculture, eco-gentrification, and the uneven valorization of social reproduction', *Annals of the American Association of Geographers*, 108(2): 579–90.

McClintock, N. and Simpson, M. (2018) 'Stacking functions: identifying motivational frames guiding urban agriculture organizations and businesses in the United States and Canada', *Agriculture and Human Values*, 35(1): 19–39.

McClintock, N., Mahmoudi, D., Simpson, M. and Santos, J.P. (2016) 'Socio-spatial differentiation in the sustainable city: a mixed-methods assessment of residential gardens in metropolitan Portland, Oregon, USA', *Landscape and Urban Planning*, 148: 1–16.

McClintock, N., Miewald, C. and McCann, E. (2018) 'The politics of urban agriculture: sustainability, governance, and contestation', in A.E.G. Jonas, B. Miller, K. Ward and D. Wilson (eds) *The Routledge Handbook on Spaces of Urban Politics*, London: Routledge, pp 361–74.

McClintock, N., Miewald, C. and McCann, E (2021) 'Governing urban agriculture: formalization, resistance, and re-visioning in two "green cities"', *International Journal of Urban and Regional Research*, online first, DOI: 10.1111/1468-2427.12993.

McKittrick, K. (2006) *Demonic Grounds: Black Women and the Cartographies of Struggle*, Minneapolis, MN: University of Minnesota Press.

McKittrick, K. (2011) 'On plantations, prisons, and a black sense of place', *Social & Cultural Geography*, 12(8): 947–63.

Naylor, L., Daigle, M., Zaragocin, S., Ramírez, M.M. and Gilmartin, M. (2018) 'Interventions: bringing the decolonial to political geography', *Political Geography*, 66: 199–209.

Nemser, D. (2015) 'Primitive accumulation, geometric space, and the construction of the "Indian"', *Journal of Latin American Cultural Studies*, 24(3): 335–52.

Paperson, L. (2014) 'A ghetto land pedagogy: an antidote for settler environmentalism', *Environmental Education Research*, 20(1): 115–30.

Perkins, H.A. (2009) 'Out from the (green) shadow? Neoliberal hegemony through the market logic of shared urban environmental governance', *Political Geography*, 28(7): 395–405.

Peyton, J. and Dyce, M. (2017) 'Colony on Main: history and the ruins of imperialism in Vancouver's restaurant frontier', *Cultural Geographies*, 24(4): 589–609.

Pillow, W. (2003) 'Confession, catharsis, or cure? Rethinking the uses of reflexivity as methodological power in qualitative research', *International Journal of Qualitative Studies in Education*, 16(2): 175–96.

Porter, L., Hurst, J. and Grandinetti, T. (2020) 'The politics of greening unceded lands in the settler city', *Australian Geographer*, 51(2): 221–38.

Purcell, M. and Tyman, S.K. (2015) 'Cultivating food as a right to the city', *Local Environment*, 20(10): 1132–47.

Quastel, N. (2009) 'Political ecologies of gentrification', *Urban Geography*, 30(7): 694–725.

Ramírez, M.M. (2015) 'The elusive inclusive: black food geographies and racialized food spaces', *Antipode*, 47(3): 748–69.

Ramírez, M.M. (2020) 'City as borderland: gentrification and the policing of Black and Latinx geographies in Oakland', *Environment and Planning D: Society and Space*, 38(1): 147–66.

Rosol, M. (2012) 'Community volunteering as neoliberal strategy? Green space production in Berlin', *Antipode*, 44(1): 239–57.

Rotz, S. (2017) '"They took our beads, it was a fair trade, get over it": settler colonial logics, racial hierarchies and material dominance in Canadian agriculture', *Geoforum*, 82(Supplement C): 158–69.

Safransky, S. (2014) 'Greening the urban frontier: race, property, and resettlement in Detroit', *Geoforum*, 56: 237–48.

Safransky, S. (2017) 'Rethinking land struggle in the postindustrial city', *Antipode*, 49(4): 1079–100.

Sbicca, J. (2019) 'Urban agriculture, revalorization, and green gentrification in Denver, Colorado', *Research in Political Sociology*, 26: 149–70.

Schmelzkopf, K. (2002) 'Incommensurability, land use, and the right to space: community gardens in New York City', *Urban Geography*, 23(4): 323–43.

Smith, N. (1996) *The New Urban Frontier: Gentrification and the Ravanchist City*, London: Routledge.

Staeheli, L.A., Mitchell, D. and Gibson, K. (2002) 'Conflicting rights to the city in New York's community gardens', *GeoJournal*, 58(2/3): 197–205.

Stehlin, J.G. and Tarr, A.R. (2017) 'Think regionally, act locally? Gardening, cycling, and the horizon of urban spatial politics', *Urban Geography*, 38(9): 1329–51.

Toews, O. (2018) *Stolen City: Racial Capitalism and the Making of Winnipeg*, Winnipeg: ARP Books.

Tuck, E. and Yang, K.W. (2012) 'Decolonization is not a metaphor', *Decolonization: Indigeneity, Education & Society*, 1(1): 1–40.

Vitiello, D. and Brinkley, C. (2014) 'The hidden history of food system planning', *Journal of Planning History*, 13(2): 91–112.

Voicu, I. and Been, V. (2008) 'The effect of community gardens on neighboring property values', *Real Estate Economics*, 2: 241–83.

Wideman, T.J. (2020) 'Property, waste, and the "unnecessary hardship" of land use planning in Winnipeg, Canada', *Urban Geography*, 41(6): 865–92.

6

Conflicting rationalities and messy actualities of dealing with vacant housing in Halle/Saale, East Germany

Nina Gribat

Introduction: conceptualising urban vacancy

After German reunification, like many other cities in East Germany, Halle/Saale in the federal state of Saxony Anhalt underwent a period of urban decline. It lost a large share of jobs and around 25 per cent of its population[1] between 1990 and 2010. Some people relocated elsewhere for jobs; others moved to a single-family house in the region (something previously impossible due to the German Democratic Republic's [GDR's] strict limitations on suburbanisation). As a consequence, the rate of vacant housing in Halle/Saale and many other East German towns and cities intensified. Urban vacancy eventually became one of the main fields of policy intervention on a local, regional and national level in Germany. In recent years, urban vacancy has received increasing scholarly attention in the field of urban studies. Two main points of reference can be distinguished: post-industrial and post-socialist urban decline and depopulation, often subsumed as 'urban shrinkage' (Haase et al, 2014); and the aftermath of the financial crisis in 2008, often explored as austerity urbanism (Tonkiss, 2013). It can be argued that despite some important differences, in both contexts, urban vacancy is considered as a symbolic marker of urban crises and change. On the one hand, research focuses on identifying causes for urban vacancy, such as exploring links between population change and vacancy (Couch and Cocks, 2013), or between political-economic change and vacancy (Kitchin et al, 2014). On the other hand, scholars examine how urban vacancy is governed in a variety of contexts. Within this strand of research, two sub-fields have developed: research on urban policies (and politics) addressing vacancy (Weiske et al, 2005; Bernt, 2009; Hackworth, 2015); and research on the potential of vacancy leading to alternative (for example, non-capitalist or more sustainable) forms of urban development (Oswalt et al, 2013; Nassauer and Raskin, 2014; Ferreri, 2015; O'Callaghan et al, 2018; see also Part III of this volume). In contributing to these latter strands of literature, I examine in more depth how approaches to governing urban vacancy depend on the type of vacant urban structure, the type of vacant housing and the type of ownership. In particular, I show how different and sometimes contradicting rationalities and practices of governing vacant housing have formed in the context of intersecting local, regional and national policies in Halle/Saale, focusing on two districts: the prefabricated new-town housing district Neustadt; and the old-town predominantly Wilhelminian-style housing district Glaucha.

My approach is based on Foucault's (2001: 171) concept of problematisation: 'how and why certain things (behaviour, phenomena, processes) became a problem'. This involves examining how 'an unproblematic field of experience ... becomes a problem, raises debate, incites new reactions.... [It] is the history of the way people begin to take care of something' (Foucault, 2001: 74). In governmentality studies more broadly, a focus on problematisations is used to analyse situations 'in which the activity of governing comes to be called into question' (Dean, 1999: 27). Problematisations can change over time and, with them, '[r]ationalities are constantly undergoing modifications in the face of some newly identified problem or solution, while retaining certain styles of thought and technological preferences' (Rose et al, 2006: 98). Thus, a focus on problematisation renders explicit transformations of government, which are often accompanied by some form of conflict.

In this chapter, I focus on how vacant housing became a specific problem in Halle/Saale. This focus on conflicting rationalities considers some of the critiques of governmentality studies of not paying enough attention to the 'messy actualities' on the ground (O'Malley et al, 1997). Following this approach, the assumption is that urban policy does not intervene in natural or given spaces, but is involved in constructing these as spaces of intervention (Cochrane, 2007; Dikeç, 2007; Gribat, 2010; Gribat and Huxley, 2015).

The empirical work for this chapter was carried out as part the research project 'Altergrowth' at Université de Strasbourg, funded by the French Research Council (ANR). Between 2015 and 2016, I conducted 21 semi-structured interviews with the planning department, different housing companies and other institutions, civil society groups and activists involved in the process of governing vacancy in Halle/Saale. Interviews and relevant policy documents were analysed, focusing on how vacant housing was problematised in selected areas of the city and how different interventions were justified based on it. Particular attention was paid to conflicting rationalisations of governing vacant housing in order to examine the scope for alternative practices.

The chapter is structured as follows. First, I introduce Neustadt and Glaucha, and the emergence of vacant housing in both districts. Second, I outline the main local, regional and national urban policy interventions that address the issue of vacant housing and the groups of actors that were involved in Halle/Saale. Finally, I contrast the approaches regarding vacant housing in Neustadt and Glaucha, and examine wider sociopolitical implications, such as the shift from public to private housing.

Neustadt and Glaucha in context: the emergence of vacant housing

Vacant housing has existed in Halle/Saale since the end of the Second World War, both in periods of population growth and decline. The location and problematisation of vacancy have changed over time, being connected to urban policy shifts regarding urban form and structure, and related personal and collective preferences, which occurred both after the Second World War and after German reunification.

Halle/Saale has a large old town (which was not bombed as much as other inner cities in Germany in the Second World War) and several housing estates, most of which were built in the GDR. At the time of reunification in 1990, the city as a whole suffered from a housing shortage. The construction of tens of thousands of apartments in the GDR could not satisfy the demand. Halle Neustadt, for instance, was constructed as a separate and independent new town for workers in the nearby chemical industries. In the GDR, Neustadt and other new-town areas of Halle/Saale were very popular among their tenants, with waiting lists for modern apartments. Vacant housing at that time only occurred in the old town areas of Halle/Saale due to war damage, or because of mounting levels of disrepair and lack of modernisations. The focus of GDR housing policy was on constructing new estates according to socialist urban design principles and utilising industrialised construction techniques, such as standardisation and prefabrication. Old-town areas were largely neglected, except for some maintenance of buildings that were considered most significant in terms of heritage. At the time of German reunification, a large number of inner-city vacant housing units were uninhabitable and often could not be quickly remediated, for example, owners of buildings were not known or had been dispossessed after the war. Restitution processes were only carried out after reunification, were lengthy and did not necessarily lead to a reuse of vacant houses. Until 2008/09, the majority of vacant units in Halle/Saale were in the old-town areas: up to 23.5 per cent in Southern Inner City/Glaucha (Stadt Halle [Saale], 2007b) and up to 37.8 per cent in Freiimfelde (von Busse, 2011).

In the large GDR prefabricated housing estates such as Halle Neustadt, vacant housing only started emerging around 1996/97. Thus, the dramatic population loss of Halle/Saale in the early 1990s did not translate directly into the emergence of vacant housing units in the new-town parts. However, when vacancies started occurring there, numbers rose rapidly. By 2002, 20 per cent of the housing units in Neustadt were vacant.

In sum, vacant housing in Halle/Saale already existed during the GDR – albeit in different parts of the city compared to the period after reunification. Different types of owners were affected by vacancy. In the old-town areas, most of the housing is owned by a range of individual owners, most of whom do not own more than one house, whereas in the new-town areas, almost all of the housing is owned by one of the public housing companies. This difference in ownership structure played a role in the problematisations and interventions that were developed.

Different rationalities and messy actualities of vacant housing in Halle/Saale: excess versus opportunity

Before vacant housing emerged as a problem in Halle/Salle in the second half of the 1990s, urban policy interventions focused on renovation of old-town areas and old industrial areas in the centre of Halle/Saale (interview, urban planner). At the end of the 1990s, the public housing companies[2] of Halle/Saale founded the so-called 'Council of 11'. Their aim was to draw attention to their struggle of staying economically viable in light of rising vacancies in their housing stock. Individuals or private companies who owned vacant housing did not join. At that time, there were no urban policies or funding options to address vacant housing at local, regional, federal state or national levels. This changed at the turn of the century, when vacant housing and population loss in East German cities became a national issue due to pressure from the housing sector (Bernt, 2017). After a commission of experts reported that 1 million apartments were empty in East Germany (Pfeiffer et al, 2000), the federal state set up an urban policy to deal with the issue of vacant housing called Stadtumbau Ost ('Urban Renewal East') in 2002. The programme included public funding for demolitions and for urban upgrading. Following the focus on problematisation outlined in the introduction, a field that was considered unproblematic before and during the 1990s, such as vacant housing, prompted new action (Foucault, 2001), and previous forms of governance were questioned (Dean, 1999).

In order to qualify for the Stadtumbau Ost programme, Halle/Saale (and other participating cities in East Germany) was required to develop an *Integriertes Stadtentwicklungskonzept* ('integrated urban development concept' [ISEK]), a strategic urban policy document, which is based on a cross-sectoral negotiation of the key areas of development in the city. In the ISEK,[3] different parts of the city are categorised into three groups: conservation areas; areas to be restructured with priority; and areas to be restructured without priority (Stadt Halle [Saale], 2007b). Areas to be restructured with priority are, in effect, demolition areas. These areas are to be abandoned as urban areas or they are to be cleared for future redevelopment. Areas to be restructured without priority are more heterogeneous but requiring investment. Demolition funds from Stadtumbau Ost are only to be spent in areas to be restructured with/ without priority. Upgrading funds can be spent in all areas. In Halle/ Saale, most of the old-town areas that were selected for the Stadtumbau Ost programme were categorised as conservation areas, whereas areas to be restructured with priority were concentrated in the new-town areas. Following the arguments of Dikeç (2007) and Cochrane (2007), spaces of intervention were constructed in these policy documents based on distinct forms of problematisation of vacant housing.

In the course of implementing Stadtumbau Ost in Halle/Saale, a change of the symbolic value of housing and, in particular, vacant housing can be observed. The distinction is based on the type of housing and the location in old or new areas of Halle/Saale. In Neustadt, vacant housing was problematised largely as excess, whereas in Glaucha, vacant housing was considered an opportunity.

Neustadt: vacant (public) housing as excess

The symbolic shift from a desired housing area in the GDR to the main location of population loss and demolition of housing around ten years after reunification also applies to other new towns that were built in the GDR (Gribat, 2010; Gribat and Huxley, 2015). Neustadt is a particular case because it was the only planned and constructed *independent* new town, which is also recognised in the ISEK:

> Halle-Neustadt has been designed as an urban ensemble, the architectural spatial structure is recognisable as a composition of buildings constructed in industrial style and thus differs clearly from the appearance of the neighbouring organically grown old town. Large-scale prefabricated concrete slab structures characterise the district, a high-rise backdrop that can be experienced from afar provides a characteristic city view. The high-rise buildings along the Magistrale accentuate the street space. (Stadt Halle [Saale], 2007b: 95, all translations from German by the author)

Despite this acknowledgement of the qualities of Neustadt, it was delineated as one of the Stadtumbau Ost areas and the processes that were followed align with those of the other new-town areas. The main goals of Stadtumbau Ost for Neustadt were defined as follows (Stadt Halle [Saale], 2007c): (1) to demolish starting from the periphery in order to improve links to the surrounding landscape and to prevent sprawl; (2) to maintain and support central parts; (3) to achieve less dense urban development by extending green areas and building new structures on the external ring; and (4) to create different landscape axes to structure the district from outside. In short, a 'rightsizing' approach (Hackworth, 2015) was followed.

Where demolitions are actually carried out is dependent on negotiations between the housing providers, the planning department and the urban service infrastructure providers (interview, network of urban development). In Halle/Saale, these stakeholders are organised in a network that has the public housing companies at its centre.[4] Based on Neustadt's ownership structure, the conditions for implementing the aims of the ISEK were conducive. At the time of reunification, four public housing companies – one communal and three associations – owned all the housing stock in Neustadt, around 35,000 units in total. Due to forced privatisations of some of the public housing stock after reunification, there were additional private owners who refused to demolish parts of their housing stock (as is the case in Halle-Neustadt Südpark [Bernt et al, 2017]). However, even public housing companies sometimes do not want to (or cannot) demolish certain buildings, following the aims outlined in the urban policy (Bernt, 2005).

Housing companies, for instance, are likely to prioritise demolition of less valuable units within their portfolios of vacant stock. Some of the buildings that were to be demolished on the outskirts of Neustadt had been renovated, and the housing companies had outstanding mortgages. Others were particularly popular because of the views to the surrounding countryside. In addition, priority for demolition was given to high-rise housing because it was considered less popular. The demolition of high-rise buildings was also more profitable for the housing companies because of the higher number of units. In terms of the ISEK's aim to maintain a recognisable skyline, many of the high-rise buildings were supposed to remain. In short, the planning department had set out aims for Stadtumbau Ost based on urban design and planning principles adhering to urban form, whereas the housing companies focused on economic viability based on their own portfolio – a clear case of conflicting rationalities of governing vacant housing, even among the stakeholders forming the network of Stadtumbau Ost.

Other actors who were not part of the Stadtumbau Ost network posed more fundamental questions regarding the symbolic devaluation of Neustadt and the lack of consultation of its inhabitants in the Stadtumbau Ost process. Cultural initiatives drew attention to the potential of vacant housing and started working with inhabitants to formulate alternative development scenarios. Some of these initiatives, such as Kolorado,[5] were even funded by the first years of the Stadtumbau Ost programme. At around the same time, one of the theatres in Halle reused an empty office block in the centre of Neustadt as a hotel, performance and gathering space for one summer:

> The creation of the hotel-city circumvented studies and planning, and plunged straight into self-generating informal urban strategies that thrive on participatory interaction between artists and the populace, outsiders and locals, and bottom-up and top-down movements. Resembling a high-rise favela HOTEL NEUSTADT also questions the technocracy, or the appearance of urban order. (Park, 2004: 121)

In these projects, urban vacancy was considered as a potential way to reinvent how people could relate to the city in non-commercial ways. Thus, vacancy was problematised differently – as space to be appropriated and reimagined by inhabitants rather than to be demolished. According to a critic, the implementation of cultural and artistic initiatives could have eventually led to a different course of development for Neustadt: "After Hotel Neustadt and the actions of the ZfZK [Centre for Contemporary Art],[6] Halle Neustadt was able to take off culturally, but this failed due to the disinterest of the … town hall" (interview).

In the ISEK, these conflicts over Neustadt's value and the reuse of vacant housing are also mentioned, yet the emphasis lies on not disrupting the Stadtumbau Ost process:

> In recent years, Neustadt has become a place of symbolic confrontation with the GDR prefabricated housing estates, largely supported by young creative people.... However, extreme positions, such as the protection of historical monuments for the entire urban ensemble, even without residents if necessary, are of little help in coping with the challenge of an *orderly urban retreat* from the once aspired big city role of the socialist model city of the 60s and 70s. (Stadt Halle [Saale], 2007b: 94–95, emphasis added)

After an initial period of experimentation with artistic and cultural initiatives, the Stadtumbau Ost process in Neustadt has followed largely a business-as-usual 'rightsizing' approach – an 'orderly urban retreat'. Vacant housing was mostly problematised as excess, the demolition of which was to be managed efficiently by ongoing negotiations with stakeholders such as housing companies, infrastructure providers and the city of Halle. In Glaucha, such a relatively straightforward implementation of Stadtumbau Ost was impossible from the start. A more experimental approach was therefore adopted based on a different problematisation of vacant housing.

Glaucha: vacant housing as an opportunity for urban change

Glaucha is an old urban quarter of Halle that was built during the Wilhelminian period of industrialisation at the end of the 19th century. It comprises an area of about 42 hectares of four-storey perimeter block development, located in close proximity to the city centre of Halle. In the 1970s and 1980s, different urban renewal measures were carried out in Glaucha. At the margins of the urban quarter, several old housing blocks were demolished. New streets and high-rise buildings were constructed on the empty lots and six-storey prefabricated blocks were built adjacent to the old Wilhelminian blocks. Some of the old buildings were also modernised. After the reunification of Germany, there was relatively little investment in Glaucha, which was partly down to modernisations carried out in the GDR. Vacancies rose during the 1990s. The image of the quarter worsened (BMVBS, 2012). In 2007, the rate of vacant housing units in Glaucha was 24.7 per cent (769 of 3,114 units) (KARO architekten, 2009).

When the urban policy Stadtumbau Ost was set up, Halle/Saale delineated an area of 340 hectares in the southern inner city as Stadtumbau Ost, which was largely categorised as a conservation area, including Glaucha. However, in the early years, none of the funding was spent in Glaucha. This changed in 2007 when the urban upgrading aspects (in addition to demolition) of Stadtumbau Ost became more important in Halle/Saale. The pressing needs for support in Halle Glaucha were noted: 50 per cent of the buildings were not modernised; 25 per cent of all apartments were vacant; and 20 per cent of all buildings were at risk of collapse. The middle class had left the area and the image was considered the worst in the whole city (Stadt Halle [Saale], 2010). In addition to being part of Stadtumbau Ost, Halle Glaucha was chosen when the municipality decided upon the 'action areas' for the International Building Exhibition Urban Renewal Saxony-Anhalt (IBA)[7] – a regional project addressing urban decline and vacancy. Different streams of available funding were bundled in Glaucha in order to achieve a reversal of 'a downward spiral of population loss, growing social problems, housing vacancy and the threat of losing cultural heritage' (BMVBS, 2012: 96). In short, based on the problematisation of vacant Wilhelminian housing as threatened cultural heritage, a strategy of conservation was developed: consultancy was offered for the private owners of old buildings; public subsidies to support upgrading measures were made available through Stadtumbau Ost; and local initiatives financed through the IBA were invited to carry out temporary use projects in vacant buildings, with the aim of improving the image of the area.

A total of 50 per cent of all buildings were privately owned in Glaucha, which is why the mobilisation of the owners was seen as a central task. In 2007, an 'owner consultant' was introduced. His task was to provide individual support for the modernisation or the sale of houses in Glaucha and to coordinate all the upgrading measures. This included support with administrative issues, such as getting all the necessary permits, as well as funding. The owner consultant was paid from the upgrading fund of Stadtumbau Ost.

The owner consultant organised events such as the 'Discovery Day Open Glaucha' in October 2008, which aimed to change the area's image: "In order to find people who were willing to invest, it was important to create a good atmosphere in the area: first artists, then students, then [investors]" (interview, owner consultant). The local initiative Postkult – a non-profit organisation that was founded by students – played a particularly active role in establishing temporary use projects. In 2009, Postkult started an urban garden on one of the wasteland sites in the area, organising concerts, parties and sports activities for youths. Several bars, cafes and other initiatives were also set up based on temporary use contracts.

The experimental strategy of the city – to raise interest in the area via temporary use – paid off. The area was soon considered desirable. It attracted people willing to invest in vacant derelict houses, who received support from the owner consultant during the upgrading process. Eventually, this threatened the continuation of temporary use initiatives, as less vacant housing was available and the city focused on redevelopment: "There was freedom back then; Postkult had the feeling of being able to make a real difference in terms of urban development. But the motivations were different from the beginning: Postkult wanted co-determination; the city wanted development. Of course, the two do not go together completely" (interview, activist).

As a result of these conflicting rationalities, temporary use initiatives looked to establish their own long-term perspective by becoming owners. Postkult, for instance, bought a derelict building 'Stadthof Glaucha' in 2011, which they modernised.

In sum, vacant housing in Glaucha was – from the beginning – problematised in terms of an opportunity for urban change rather than being considered as excess, like vacant housing in Neustadt. Funding and an experimental approach of temporary use initiatives to activate interest in the area were dedicated to reviving vacant housing. After four years of intensive interventions in the area of Glaucha, between 2007 and 2011, the city administration of Halle considered its work as almost finished (BMVBS, 2012). In 2015, when I carried out fieldwork, the owner consultant presented the following statistics of success. A total of €3.2 million of public funding had been invested in Glaucha, while €35 million of private capital was spent, accounting for a quota of public funding per project of 8–10 per cent. A total of 46 houses were renovated with the help of funding and 25 without funding. As a result, half of the identified 'problem buildings' in 2008 have been upgraded and are in use again (interview, owner consultant). The rest, he concluded, could be left to the market. The approaches developed in Glaucha were subsequently transferred to other Wilhelminian areas of Halle/Saale as best practice.

Conclusions: contrasting approaches and their wider sociopolitical implications

The cases of Neustadt and Glaucha in Halle/Saale represent contrasting approaches to governing vacant housing through a federal urban policy and targeted regional projects. Whereas vacant housing in Neustadt was problematised as excess, which was to be demolished in order to save public housing companies from bankruptcy, in Glaucha, it was considered an opportunity for urban change. The urban policy Stadtumbau Ost was implemented in Neustadt largely as business-as-usual, following a rightsizing approach. In Glaucha, however, an experimental and far more individualised approach was developed, involving several temporary use initiatives, an owner consultant and funding to support those willing to invest in order to reuse and conserve vacant derelict buildings. In practice, most upgrading funds have been spent in the centre of Halle – a part of town that is largely categorised as a conservation area – while the demolition funds have been mostly spent in areas to be restructured with priority, such as the different new-town areas that were built in the GDR. This demonstrates distinct constructed spaces of intervention (Cochrane, 2007; Dikeç, 2007) and problematisations (Foucault, 2001) of vacant housing emerging through the Stadtumbau Ost process.

The different approaches are largely based on the symbolic shift in valuing certain urban structures and forms of ownership of housing, which occurred after reunification in East Germany (Gribat, 2010; Gribat and Huxley, 2015). Neustadt, a new town built in the GDR following standardised and industrial building methods, was highly popular among tenants until reunification, when this type of housing and urban structure was radically *de*valued. Glaucha, a centrally located old-town part, was far less popular during the GDR but gained cache because of a general *re*valuation of old-town areas after reunification. What contributed to this was the increasingly idealised vision of private ownership that was encouraged and subsidised after reunification, whereas public housing, particularly when vacant, could turn into a liability for communal and other public bodies.

Different rationalities were at play in the assessment of vacant housing:

• The national state, together with the federal states, addressed the issue on a structural level by setting up a new urban policy programme. Vacancy, in this context, is mainly considered as a problem of the public housing providers, threatening their economic viability, as well as that of cities and towns. Reducing public housing stock by publicly subsidising demolitions has two premises: it prevents public housing providers and cities/towns from going bankrupt; and it keeps local exchange values in terms of rents and sale prices of housing stable by limiting oversupply through demolitions.

- Several regional/local initiatives, such as the IBA and Stadtumbau Ost, address vacant housing as an issue that fundamentally questions planning, urban policies and politics-as-usual. These more experimental initiatives emphasised the need to innovate and sometimes even called for more serious explorations of urban development without growth.
- The urban planning department largely considers vacant housing as something to be overcome, with a mix of strategies based on exploiting various streams of available funding – for demolitions in the new-town areas and to initiate redevelopment in the old-town areas.
- Public housing providers largely assess vacant housing based on a portfolio management logic. Blocks that are economically less viable are most attractive for demolition.
- Local civil society groups recognise vacancy as an opportunity for the (temporary) reuse of buildings. Vacancy provides a chance of doing something beyond economic utility, emphasising the use rather than exchange value of buildings. In addition, for some, vacancy provided an opportunity to reimagine the city according to their own ideas, which led to frustration when this contribution was not acknowledged by the city.

These conflicting rationalities have contributed to the development of the range of sometimes contradictory practices addressing vacant housing outlined earlier. The messy actualities of governing vacancy come to the fore as a result, such as a significant shift from public to private ownership. Between 2000 and 2005, the total housing stock of Halle/Saale was reduced by roughly 5,500 units (from 149,969 to 144,584 units), yet the share of reduction or increase of housing stock was distributed unevenly. Communally owned housing, for instance, was reduced by almost 10,000 units (from 44,649 to 34,988 units) and housing associations also lost around 7,500 units (from 43,213 to 35,599 units). In contrast, private ownership of housing (including large-scale private owners) rose by over 12,000 units (from 59,192 to 71,393 units) (Stadt Halle [Saale], 2007a: 31). The Stadtumbau Ost process has thus resulted in a significant redistribution of housing stock from public housing companies to private owners. This redistribution was enabled largely by the state subsidies for demolition and related urban policies.

Increasing social segregation appears as an (un)intended consequence of these Stadtumbau Ost practices. Tenants with lower incomes are increasingly concentrated in low-rent areas, either in not-upgraded housing owned by large-scale private owners such as in Halle–Südpark (which is part of Neustadt) (Bernt et al, 2017), or in areas that are categorised as to be restructured with priority (in effect, demolition areas). In addition, communal and other public housing providers also tend to charge higher rents in central parts of the old town, which means that tenants with lower incomes concentrate in the new-town areas. These tendencies of segregation are not dissimilar to the experiences in other East German shrinking cities (Großmann et al, 2015).

In this context, governing vacancy in Halle/Saale appears as a strangely depoliticised process, as there is little debate regarding the shift from public to private ownership and its social impacts. This chapter suggests that examining more closely the conflicting rationalities relating to distinct problematisations of vacant housing in different districts, as well as of the messy actualities resulting in practice, can offer an avenue to address the politics of governing vacancy.

Notes

[1] Different phases of population loss can be distinguished in Halle/Saale. Between 1990 and 2000, the city lost more than 60,000 inhabitants – almost 20 per cent of its population. Between 2000 and 2010, population loss in Halle/Saale slowed down. The city lost around 10,000 inhabitants from 2000 to 2005, and around 5,000 from 2005 to 2010. In 2012, Halle/Saale had the lowest number of inhabitants, and since then, the population has been growing (2012 = 231,440; 2015 = 238,321) (all data for numbers of inhabitants were obtained from Statistisches Landesamt Sachsen-Anhalt).

[2] Public housing companies in Halle/Saale are either communal companies or associations. All of them were part of the state-owned housing sector in the GDR.

[3] The first ISEK in Halle/Saale was published in 2001 (Stadt Halle [Saale], 2001) and the second in 2007 (Stadt Halle [Saale], 2007a, 2007b, 2007c). In recent years, the planning department of Halle/Saale has developed a new ISEK (*ISEK Halle 2025*) (Stadt Halle [Saale], 2017), based on the publication of a strategic paper of urban development (Stadt Halle [Saale], 2012).

[4] In 1999, a Platform for Housing Economy Halle was founded, which was renamed as 'Network Stadtumbau' in Halle in 2002 after service provision and transport sectors were integrated. In 2008, the network was renamed as 'Network of Urban Development', which shows that the stakeholders of the network are committed to urban development beyond Stadtumbau Ost.

[5] See: http://raumlabor.net/kolorado-neustadt/

[6] The ZfZK wanted to reuse a derelict train station in Neustadt but never got the necessary support of the city and Deutsche Bahn.

[7] In parallel with the implementation of the Stadtumbau Ost policy, a range of regional and local programmes was set up to address urban shrinkage more broadly. The IBA, for instance, ran from 2003 to 2010. It aimed at developing individual strategies for each of the participating 19 towns and cities in the federal state of Saxony-Anhalt.

References

Bernt, M. (2005) 'Stadtumbau Im Gefangenendilemma', in C. Weiske, S. Kabisch and C. Hannemann (eds) *Kommunikative Steuerung Des Stadtumbaus. Interessensgegensätze, Koalitionen und Entscheidungsstrukturen in Schrumpfenden Städten*, Wiesbaden: VS Verlag für Sozialwissenschaften, pp 109–30.

Bernt, M. (2009) 'Partnerships for demolition: the governance of urban renewal in East Germany's shrinking cities', *International Journal of Urban and Regional Research*, 33(3): 754–69.

Bernt, M. (2017) '"Keine Unklugen Leute". Die Durchsetzung Des "Stadtumbau Ost"', *Sub\urban. Zeitschrift Für Kritische Stadtforschung*, 5(1/2): 41–60.

Bernt, M., Colini, L. and Förste, D. (2017) 'Privatization, financialization and state restructuring in Eastern Germany: the case of Am Südpark', *International Journal of Urban and Regional Research*, 41(4): 555–71.

BMVBS (Bundesministerium für Verkehr, Bau- und Stadtentwicklung) (ed) (2012) '10 Jahre Stadtumbau Ost – Berichte Aus Der Praxis', BMVBS.

Cochrane, A. (2007) *Understanding Urban Policy: A Critical Approach*, Oxford: Blackwell.

Couch, C. and Cocks, M. (2013) 'Housing vacancy and the shrinking city: trends and policies in the UK and the city of Liverpool', *Housing Studies*, 28(3): 499–519.

Dean, M. (1999) *Governmentality: Power and Rule in Modern Society*, London: Sage.

Dikeç, M. (2007) 'Space, governmentality, and the geographies of French urban policy', *European Urban and Regional Studies*, 14(2): 277–89.

Ferreri, M. (2015) 'The seductions of temporary urbanism "saving" the city: collective low-budget organizing and urban practice', *Ephemera*, 15(1): 181–91.

Foucault, M. (2001) *Fearless Speech*, New York, NY: Semiotexte.

Gribat, N. (2010) 'Governing the future of a shrinking city: Hoyerswerda, East Germany', PhD thesis, Sheffield Hallam University, UK.

Gribat, N. and Huxley, M. (2015) 'Problem spaces, problem subjects: contesting policies in a shrinking city', in E. Gualini (ed) *Planning and Conflict: Critical Perspectives on Contentious Urban Developments*, London: Routledge, pp 164–84.

Großmann, K., Arndt, T., Haase, A., Rink, D. and Steinführer, A. (2015) 'The influence of housing oversupply on residential segregation: exploring the post-socialist city of Leipzig', *Urban Geography*, 36(4): 550–77.

Haase, A., Rink, D., Grossmann, K., Bernt, M. and Mykhnenko, V. (2014) 'Conceptualizing urban shrinkage', *Environment and Planning A: Economy and Space*, 46(7): 1519–34.

Hackworth, J. (2015) 'Rightsizing as spatial austerity in the American Rust Belt', *Environment and Planning A: Economy and Space*, 47(4): 766–82.

KARO architekten (2009) *IBA-Projekt Sozialraum Glaucha. Das Leben Spielt Hier*, Stadt Halle (Saale).

Kitchin, R., O'Callaghan, C. and Gleeson, J. (2014) 'The new ruins of Ireland? Unfinished estates in the post-Celtic Tiger era', *International Journal of Urban and Regional Research*, 38(3): 1069–80.

Nassauer, J.I. and Raskin, J. (2014) 'Urban vacancy and land use legacies: a frontier for urban ecological research, design, and planning', *Landscape and Urban Planning*, 125: 245–53.

O'Callaghan, C., Di Feliciantonio, C. and Byrne, M. (2018) 'Governing urban vacancy in post-crash Dublin: contested property and alternative social projects', *Urban Geography*, 39(6): 868–91.

O'Malley, P., Weir, L. and Shearing, C. (1997) 'Governmentality, criticism, politics', *Economy and Society*, 26: 501–17.

Oswalt, P., Overmeyer, K. and Misselwitz, P. (eds) (2013) *Urban Catalyst: The Power of Temporary Use*, Berlin: Dom Publishers.

Park, K. (2004) 'Moving cities, moving nations', in Halle Thalia (ed) *Hotel Neustadt*, Berlin: Alexander-Verlag, pp 120–3.

Pfeiffer, U., Simons, H. and Porsch, L. (2000) *Wohnungswirtschaftlicher Strukturwandel in Den Neuen Bundesländern: Bericht Der Kommission*, Berlin: empirica, im Auftrag des BMVBW.

Rose, N., O'Malley, P. and Valverde, M. (2006) 'Governmentality', *Annual Review of Law and Social Sciences*, 2: 83–104.

Stadt Halle (Saale) (2001) *Integriertes Stadtentwicklungskonzept*, Stadt Halle (Saale).

Stadt Halle (Saale) (2007a) *Integriertes Stadtentwicklungskonzept: Gesamtstädtische Entwicklungstendenzen Und Entwicklungsziele*, Stadt Halle (Saale).

Stadt Halle (Saale) (2007b) *Integriertes Stadtentwicklungskonzept. Stadtumbaugebiete*, Stadt Halle (Saale).

Stadt Halle (Saale) (2007c) *Stadt Halle (Saale): Integriertes Stadtentwicklungskonzept. Stadtumbaugebiet Neustadt*, Stadt Halle (Saale).

Stadt Halle (Saale) (ed) (2010) *Stadtumbau. Internationale Bauausstellung Stadtumbau Sachsen-Anhalt 2010 in Halle an Der Saale. Balanceakt Doppelstadt – Kommunikation Und Prozess. Bilanz!*, Stadt Halle (Saale).

Stadt Halle (Saale) (2012) *Strategiedialog Zur Stadtentwicklung Halle 2025: Integriertes Strategiepapier*, Stadt Halle (Saale).

Stadt Halle (Saale) (2017) *Integriertes Stadtentwicklungskonzept, ISEK Halle 2025*.

Tonkiss, F. (2013) 'Austerity urbanism and the makeshift city', *City*, 17(3): 312–24.

Von Busse, H. (2011) 'Spiel mit der Leere. Situationistische Stadtvision am Beispiel von Urban Art zur partizipativen Stadtgestaltung', Fallstudie Halle (Saale), diploma thesis, TU-Dortmund, Germany.

Weiske, C., Kabisch, S. and Hannemann, C. (eds) (2005) *Kommunikative Steuerung Des Stadtumbaus. Interessensgegensätze, Koalitionen und Entscheidungsstrukturen in Schrumpfenden Städten*, Wiesbaden: VS Verlag für Sozialwissenschaften.

7

Post-disaster ruins: the old, the new and the temporary

Sara Caramaschi and Alessandro Coppola

Introduction

Structural housing vacancy and abandonment occur in many circumstances and are phenomena that generally happen when something disturbs the overall 'equilibrium' of a given area. Urban scholarship has often considered these forms of housing emptiness in relationship to processes of urban decline, suburbanisation, deindustrialisation, financial crises and the collapse of local housing markets (Keenan et al, 1999; Glock and Haussermann, 2004; O'Callaghan et al, 2018). Indeed, in certain contexts, processes of economic and social restructuring have led to declining or collapsing demand, resulting in housing underuse, disuse and eventual abandonment (Power and Mumford, 1999; Couch and Cocks, 2013; Wang and Immergluck, 2019). Far from being natural, these processes are often closely linked to the political economy of uneven development and to the action of discrete actors in the realms of the state, the real estate industry and finance (Coppola, 2019).

However, although there is a growing literature on housing emptiness associated with issues of spatial restructuring and urban shrinkage (see Gribat, this volume), its connections to natural disasters have been largely ignored. Disasters dramatically impact the stability of territories, resulting in places that are suddenly shut off and collapse socially and economically (Myers, 2002; Black et al, 2013; Drolet, 2015). Great natural disasters may exceed the ability of communities to recover, especially when pre-impact conditions make the emergency response and reconstruction difficult and costly. Indeed, the combination of damages and territories already experiencing forms of urban decline or contraction leads to longer-lasting socio-spatial impacts. In these cases, the territorial and social breakdown provoked by shocks is magnified, and processes of vacancy, abandonment and ruination occur on a very large scale, making public policy and governmental intervention both crucial and highly problematic. In fact, while housing oversupply can represent an opportunity for the setting up of post-emergency shelter and temporary housing operations (Comerio, 1997), over the long run, it will likely prove to be challenging in terms of reconstruction choices and long-term market viability.

Looking at the government response following the immediate shock, the main urgent issue is the mobilisation of variably defined temporary housing solutions to provide shelter to evacuees. In the meanwhile, the planning operations for the long-term recovery of the built environment are launched, based on highly localised governance conditions and arrangements, trans-scalar state relations and risk protection and compensation regimes. By bringing together different actors and areas of expertise, recovery and reconstruction programmes are supposed to insure a quick return to the pre-shock conditions, allowing evacuees to go back to their homes while taking advantage of the 'window of opportunity' represented by the disaster in terms of promoting safer structures and better spatial strategies (Coppola, 2018).

However, it is highly unlikely that the different phases moving from relief to long-term recovery succeed in a linear sequence; rather, the temporality of post-disaster environments can be more realistically represented as a dramatic, nested intermingling of elements of these phases and their reciprocal legacies. Temporary dwellings may be occupied for long periods, threatening the experience of home as permanent, as reconstruction plans can be severely delayed, both in design and in implementation. Some households may not return to their homes, being unable to cope with, and recover from, stress and trauma, while others may decide to move to less vulnerable areas, leaving their properties empty, especially if located in marginal territories where life trajectories and economic realities prove to be at odds with a possible return.

Against this backdrop, this chapter investigates conditions, actors and factors involved in the spread of vacancy, abandonment and ruination in L'Aquila, an Italian city hit by a devastating earthquake in 2009. We argue that in such post-disaster contexts, a different perspective is needed on emptiness, dramatising and deepening the dimensions of time and space as key factors in understanding these processes. As total territorial facts (Coppola, 2018), disasters and the responses to them tend to rapidly unfold out of certain political-economic arrangements, and distinctive temporal and spatial fixes. Such regimes, which are clearly connected to prevailing understandings of the situation, the strategies of certain actors and established procedures, become readable by observing the conditions and trajectories of distinct elements within the housing stock.

L'Aquila, a post-disaster city

L'Aquila, a regional capital city located in Central Italy, was hit by a severe earthquake on the night of 6 April 2009, extensively damaging its dispersed, sprawling territory, composed of a core city, 58 hamlets and 15 towns. In all, 309 people died, an estimated 65,000 were left homeless and around half of the entire building stock was declared partially or completely uninhabitable. The debate over the reconstruction of the city and the best temporary housing strategy to be implemented developed immediately after the impact and was soon polarised. In particular, based on previous failures in this domain, speed and quality in providing temporary accommodations became the major issues and drivers of public policy. As the entire city was evacuated, people were first moved to tent cities, hotels and available private homes within the region, while the government and the local administration were involved in negotiations regarding the character and location of the temporary housing solutions. Eventually, a decentralised, longer-term temporary housing strategy was agreed upon, with the setting up of settlements on a series of green fields at the margins of the core main city and hamlets.

These settlements have been built based on a model already available to the authorities, the so-called 'sustainable and eco-compatible anti-seismic complexes' (CASE), for a total of 4,448 dwellings in 185 buildings (Erbani, 2010; Frisch, 2018), and were presented as a considerable improvement on more than a century of failing post-emergency housing solutions. Undoubtedly, they offered safe, high-quality homes characterised by a new concept of durability, an 'enhanced temporariness', where the evacuees were provided with all the essentials, from utensils to furniture. Additionally, more traditional temporary prefabricated dwellings, the so-called 'provisional habitation module' (MAP), were installed by the state once it became clear that CASE would not satisfy the demand, while a controversial city decision allowed citizens to build temporary small houses on their own land, regardless of established zoning provisions. Solutions involving existing housing assets were mobilised as well, as the state issued housing vouchers – the so-called 'contribution of independent accommodation' (CAS) – to up to 13,000 families to be freely used on the market and supported the creation of a financial vehicle – the Europa Risorse fund – aimed at acquiring recently built, unsold housing to be rented to evacuees (for an overview, see Figure 7.1).

In the meantime, reconstruction efforts started. While in the city's post-Second World War expansion areas, the recovery advanced

Figure 7.1: Post-emergency solutions in L'Aquila

POST-EMERGENCY SOLUTION	IMPLEMENTATION	CAPACITY	CURRENT STATE	
CASE [Sustainable and Eco-Compatible Anti-Seismic Complexes]	Spring 2010	19 complexes 185 buildings 4,449 housing units ~ 12,000 households	Data from November 2019 indicate that only **2,941** housing units are occupied. Around 838 housing units have been evacuated due to safety reasons, **three** complexes have been abandoned, 668 units are vacant.	
MAP [Provisional Housing Modules]	Winter 2009	28 settlements 1,179 modules ~ 2,500 households	Data from November 2019 indicate that 869 modules are occupied, 156 units are condemned and 154 units vacant.	
Temporary small houses [DCC. 58/09]	Spring 2009 Winter 2010	1,048 regular dwellings Thousands of unauthorized dwellings ~ 2,000–3,000 households	The temporary small houses, both legal and illegal, are still in place. Many of them are used as primary housing solutions, others as second homes, others sit empty with no plans to be dismantled.	
Europa Risorse fund [Europa Risorse S.G.R.]	Winter 2009 – Winter 2018	320 housing units ~ 800 households	Due to disagreements over payments and a trial against the general director, apartments have been either evacuated or left unoccupied starting from 2015.	
CASE [Contribution of Independent Accommodation]	Spring 2009 – Spring 2015	~ 13,000 families	Soon after the quake, this solution was adopted by over 30,000 citizens. At the end of the lifespan of the policy, around 600 dwellers were still using the contribution.	

Source: Figure and photographs by the authors

rapidly, as many buildings just needed repairs, the situation in historical centres was very different. Evacuated, closed off to the inhabitants and guarded by the army, the core of L'Aquila had to wait several years before becoming a worksite; as of today, reconstruction is projected to be completed by 2025. The city saw the launch of a programme of virtually integral reconstruction, based on the principle that whoever owned a damaged dwelling – with minor differences between first and second homes, and between residents or not – had the right to publicly funded reconstruction, inclusive of a certain degree of anti-seismic retrofitting.

Some 11 years after the earthquake, one of the most obvious outcomes of the breadth of the temporary housing and reconstruction programmes is an oversupply of housing that has caused levels of emptiness that increasingly challenge the future use, value and marketability of many buildings, with possible risks of rising structural vacancy, abandonment and ruination. Indeed, the expansion of the overall building stock of the city has not followed a trend of population growth. If the resident population[1] appears to be stable – although many argue that many residents no longer live in the city – key groups of temporary and often unregistered inhabitants that made up a relevant component of the pre-earthquake population have been in decline. Exemplary is the trajectory of the student population that used to live in the historical centre. As official data show a gradual decline in academic enrolment,[2] and there is a lack of reliable data regarding how many of them actually live in the area, it is absolutely clear that this group is far from pre-earthquake figures.

Besides the overall demographic reality, a key dimension is the spatiality of the post-disaster city. Despite the significant benefits in local economic reboot, the strong state-led post-emergency management and reconstruction agenda has caused a dramatic increase in sprawl and the relocation of people, services and public institutions, aggravating the decline of certain areas, leading to overwhelming forms of emptiness and contributing to the production of a dramatised geographical unevenness. The increasing availability of rebuilt homes of a widely upgraded quality is gradually contributing to the emptying of other solutions, including the 'temporary' stock. Also, many permanent dwellings could likely remain vacant or unused in the long term, as large components of the stock were already experiencing filtering and marginalisation before the earthquake.

The discourse on the new urban ruins of L'Aquila is rooted in these tensions. The emergency required people who found themselves suddenly dispossessed to be mobile, and the urban system to accommodate the building up of temporary solutions, the tearing down of damaged buildings and the transformation of large areas into long-term worksites. This complex process has included not only the construction of new dwellings and the reconstruction of old ones, but also the abandonment and decay of those areas where buildings are still waiting to be demolished or rebuilt, as well as an increase in vacancy and underoccupancy rates.

Reconstruction stories: the good, the bad and the ugly

The analysis that follows sheds light on the stratification of the complex and folded temporality and spatiality of the housing stock in this post-disaster city. By advancing a classification of different processes of housing emptiness and ruination based on the current conditions, main factors and actors involved, this contribution explores three situations. The first path focuses on newly rebuilt private dwellings located in the historical centre that fail to find immediate marketability and will likely remain empty for a protracted period. The second path relates to the state-funded temporary housing, their undetermined future and their precipitous fall. The third path concentrates on public housing buildings that were heavily damaged by the earthquake but that the state failed to rebuild. Taken together, these cases show different trajectories of emptiness in this post-disaster city, where the overall reconstruction is turning dramatically into levels of disuse that, under certain conditions, will likely turn into structural vacancy and spreading abandonment.

To sum up, housing emptiness in L'Aquila responds to several processes and meanings, both symbolic and physical, of individual fears and collective angst, state-led decisions, and local challenges. In some situations, people have chosen to leave their properties empty or to abandon certain areas to move elsewhere, while in others, housing emptiness is the outcome of the politics and policies that intensify loss in confidence and trust, as well as of obsolescence and decay. What follows is an essential taxonomy of situations based on which we have identified the three stories that are more extensively addressed in the subsequent sections (see Figure 7.2).

All the conditions illustrated in the scheme set out in Figure 7.2 are variably but closely related to the realities of the reconstruction itself. In this context, different processes contribute to the production of housing emptiness, in terms of ruination, abandonment, vacancy and underoccupancy.

The first process concerns ruination and the distribution of pre-earthquake ruins in the territory, which, based on the invisibility of these assets in a property-based reconstruction system, might have a significant impact on people's decisions as to whether to leave or to stay in certain areas. The second process concerns abandonment, particularly in terms of lack of public intervention or of coordination between actors, both public and private, who contribute to a slower recovery by leaving certain sections of the housing stock un-rebuilt or in an advanced state of deterioration. The third process concerns vacancy and underoccupancy of dwellings, with a great difference among units rebuilt during the reconstruction phase and those that were not damaged in 2009 or built as temporary solutions after the disaster. Here, the main factors are housing oversupply, which impacts prices and demand, and the overall lack of temporal and spatial coordination in the availability of the stock.

Out of this larger taxonomy made of interrelated processes and context-specific impacts on the housing stock, we have identified three stories that represent significant cases (see Figure 7.3), especially in the perspective of the latter two processes that we have just mentioned: the rebuilding of the historical centre; the evacuated and forgotten CASE complexes; and the yet to be rebuilt abandoned public housing. In these

Figure 7.2: Taxonomy of the conditions, the actors involved and the factors and impacts that result in different forms of vacancy, abandonment, underoccupancy and ruination of the stock

	CONDITION	FACTORS	ACTORS INVOLVED	PROCESS
Pre-earthquake ruined dwellings [*mostly located in historical hamlets*]	Progressed ruins	Unknown owners Lack of owners' interest	Private owners City government	ADVANCED RUINATION
Pre-earthquake derelict dwellings [*mostly located in historical hamlets*]	Ruins	Lack of owners' interest Unknown owners	Private owners City government	RUINATION
Un-rebuilt post-earthquake dwellings [*mostly located in historical centres*]	New ruins	Institutional/financial issues Delays/failures in the reconstruction Lack of agreements among owners	Private owners Public Housing Agency City government State agencies Special Office for the Reconstruction	ADVANCED ABANDONMENT
Evacuated post-emergency temporary solutions [*mostly located in the rural-urban fringe*]	New derelicts	Lack of upkeep Physical decline Dysfunctional governance Lack of resources	City government	ABANDONMENT
Non-retrofitted available dwellings [*located in the whole territory*]	Voids	Housing oversupply Filtering-down processes	Private owners	STRUCTURAL VACANCY
Habitable post-emergency temporary solutions [*located in the whole territory*]	Voids	Progresses in the reconstruction Housing oversupply Dysfunctional governance	City government	UNOCCUPANCY
Retrofitted available dwellings [*located in the whole territory*]	Voids	Housing oversupply Lack of spatial and temporal planning	Private owners	VACANCY
Retrofitted unavailable dwellings [*mostly located in historical centres*]	Voids	Owners' choices Unhabitability Lack of spatial and temporal planning	Private owners City government Special Office for the Reconstruction	UNDER-OCCUPANCY

Source: Figure produced by the authors

Figure 7.3: Case studies and location map

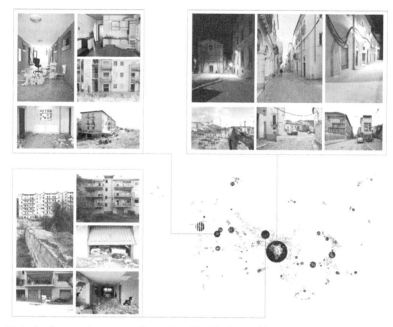

Note: On the map, the case studies analysed in this chapter (the city centre, the public housing complex located in Amiternum and the abandoned CASE complexes); the location of the remaining CASE complexes; and the location of the MAP.

Source: Map and photographs by the authors

situations, the 'weakness of the local institutions' (Frisch, 2018: 22) has accidentally produced and legitimised uneven processes of elected decline, structural vacancy and underoccupancy.

The bothersome emptiness of newly rebuilt historical dwellings

The postponement of the reconstruction of the historical city centre has brought serious impacts on its current status by entrenching trajectories of vacancy, underoccupancy and abandonment. Earlier commentators believed that the rapid reparation of the post-war urban areas would have kept in place households and activities, as the implemented temporary housing strategy was, at the same time, aimed at establishing within the city limits a 'virtual L'Aquila' able to lobby for the reconstruction of the real one. Notably, the city centre was heavily damaged and its recovery was soon considered more difficult, costly and lengthy compared to that of buildings from the 1950s–1970s. Indeed, the nature of the planning tools to be used for its reconstruction and restoration was rather unclear, including considering the imperatives of heritage preservation. Once clarified, the terms of the 2009 national legislation and the approved reconstruction plan in 2012 put the recovery of the city centre in the hands of the Special Office for the Reconstruction, the city and newly formed owners' organisations, called consortiums, essentially encompassing urban blocks.

Despite the acceleration of the reconstruction, processes that took roots in previous years deeply affected the historical centre's dynamic. The decentralisation of services and households has hit not only the image of the centre itself, but also the centrality of every other urban activity. People have been reluctant to move back to a centre largely deprived of its shops and public life, as traditional functions could not return to the main axes until recently. Furthermore, some key symbolic activities are yet to return, as in the case of the public open-air market, still located in the outskirts. Additionally, public spaces and public buildings appear physically deteriorated due to the presence of construction sites, the movement of heavy equipment or delays in their reconstruction. Together with the undesirability of walking into a city visibly empty and gloomy – where streets might be interrupted and closed off at all times, and many buildings are still wrapped up or just reinforced – these issues have been endemic to a post-disaster community facing massive changes and personal tragedy.

Apart from this, the reconstruction of many parts of the city centre is far from being finalised. There are situations in which none of the buildings of a block has been repaired because construction works could not be procured due to both the failures of private owners to reach agreement and the delays associated with implementing works on buildings in public ownership. In other situations, fully refurbished homes are located in desolate or in-progress areas, where occupancy cannot be authorised due to safety reasons or to the impossibility to connect them to utilities networks. Additionally, there are areas where many dwellings that may seem completed from the outside are actually still waiting for interior renovations, which are only partially covered by public funds. Altogether, these issues make life in many parts of the historical city of L'Aquila problematic. Households mostly live where reconstruction has finished because of the comfort of conducting their daily life where everyday activities, grocery stores and services are back, or where their life is not touched by the feeling of living in an unfinished, still traumatic, noisy environment.

A key component of the political economy of the city, which has been further strengthened by the reconstruction, is the fact that L'Aquila has always been a city of homeowners and small landlords. Many residents have multiple properties, both in the city and in the region, marking the fact that, in the past, many units were rented or kept unoccupied for several reasons. Families that own one or more properties in the historical centre have waited years to start applying for the reconstruction funds and, in some cases, cannot inhabit or rent these units due to delays or impracticability. Tenants have also changed their preferences, first being moved to temporary solutions (or other cities) and then, with the advancement of the reconstruction, settling in completed neighbourhoods. Some households may have also bought a new property, taking advantage of the low-cost housing market, or have never returned to L'Aquila. Furthermore, an estimated 448 private houses and units acquired by the city in exchange for financial support for buying new properties now sit empty while reuse programmes have not yet been finalised.

Clearly, the post-disaster housing market has deeply changed, with an evident misalignment between the historical city and the outskirts. This is a contested process because it can be argued that, once completed, the historical centre would attract households again, while some commercial activities – largely subsidised – have already opened. This expected capacity may produce negative impacts on the surroundings, though it is naive to assume that a still-empty city could easily compete in the near future with areas where households are already back to their routines. Therefore, resolving the bothersome emptiness and abandonment of historical centres, both the one of L'Aquila and those of the hamlets, will depend on both the advancement of the reconstruction and the particular scope assigned to local decisions over relocation and revitalisation.

The predictable abandonment and obsolescence of the 'enhanced temporariness' complexes

The future of the CASE complexes is among the most pressing issues of the 'post-reconstruction' phase. Although the official rationale was to preserve pre-existing localised social bonds, the actual implementation of the programme rapidly became controversial as a source of dislocation and social disorganisation (Calandra, 2013). Some 11 years after the disaster, and as rebuilt homes become available, residents are gradually leaving the complexes, the future of which is uncertain. In 2019, only 2,941 units were still occupied, while 668 were vacant and more than 800 were condemned due to structural failures or had been the object of a judicial intervention. The 'durability' of these post-disaster housing assets is ostensibly turning into permanence, both in popular perceptions and in concrete city actions, as new forms of use for these dwellings are being offered and practised.

First, in 2015, with the ending of the mentioned CAS programme, the city has channelled some of its recipients to the CASE complexes. Later, since 2016, it has promoted public calls for potential users, among which figure low-income families, 'fragile' social groups and specific categories of public employees. These appointments have also involved associations and non-governmental organisations (NGOs), and, at times, have happened in a very discretionary way. More recently, in agreement with the city, universities have announced the institution of a foundation whose aim will be renting some units to students. Despite the oversupply of public units,[3] the appointment of new tenants has become a source of political controversy as the new right-wing Mayor cancelled the results of a 2016 public call promoted by the previous administration, based on concerns that the selection criteria were favouring migrants over natives.

Meanwhile, the management of the complexes is proving quite costly for the city administration; it has attempted to revalue rents and ensure that energy and water costs are regularly paid by tenants, as a large debt has been piling up in the recent past. Still, discussions and controversies involve just a portion of the original stock since some of the complexes have been evacuated and are currently in an evident state of decline, while others sit vacant with no chances to be occupied in the near future.

The challenges posed by these assets are manifold. While the evacuated complexes, currently in an evident state of neglect, require structural maintenance works as well as measures to protect them from vandalism, those currently empty are not available to potential renters. Indeed, if these buildings represented a home for many at the beginning of the post-emergency and reconstruction phases, their role today, both in terms of practical and affective state, has radically changed. The habitable dwellings are mostly perceived as merely transitory, barely adequate or inferior solutions, with a lower material engagement for the actors involved. In most of the cases, care practices, essential for their long-term management and use, have been short-term, state-enabled and intended to minimise the impacts on residents, facilitating their relocation as soon as possible. After 11 years, these attempts to secure the local community after a natural disaster reveal themselves to be unsustainable because they have challenged the very same assumption that maintenance has to be a public or collective practice. Indeed, the inability to plan a future and manage the CASE complexes also seems to depend on the fact that the city of L'Aquila relied on the state – which received European Union (EU) funding – to provide these solutions, while the municipality is waiting for state support in order to plan its reuse or decommissioning.

Without a proper strategy and a public entity capable of managing the operation, care, conservation and selective demolition of this de facto massive public housing project, the future of the complexes is uncertain and critical. Households residing in the remaining units will decreasingly feel the need to mobilise their attachment towards these complexes because they risk being forced out due to safety concerns and because of the lack of a body in charge. The buildings that have been evacuated will become derelict, with no solution other than demolition, the massive costs of which local authorities will not be able to bear; the empty buildings might remain so for too long, accelerating their obsolescence and future abandonment. In brief, their chances for reuse as housing solutions appear to be quite illusionary: with an oversupply of housing in the territory, the lack of urbanity and of nearby activities or connections, and the perception of vulnerability that these structures present, the CASE complexes are likely destined to stay unoccupied, exacerbating their rapid decline.

The ruination of damaged public housing

While the so-called private reconstruction has made significant progress, the reconstruction of public assets appears to be far behind in its implementation. This is mainly due to the overall private property-centred orientation of the reconstruction strategy and to the procedural conundrums related to public action. In fact, an essential difference between private and public reconstruction is that although they are both state-funded, public reconstruction is subject to tight procurement rules, while in private reconstruction, professional services and construction works can be granted with greater discretion by buildings' private owners. For these reasons, essential public services are still mostly located in temporary structures – the so-called 'provisional school use module' (MUSP) – as many monumental buildings located within the historical centre are also either in miserable condition or in the early stages of the procurement process. A good example of such misalignment is the ruination of the un-rebuilt public housing inventory.

Government funding aimed at rebuilding public housing was activated soon after the earthquake, with major actors in the process being the regional housing authority, a national public works authority and the municipality. However, the implementation of the public housing reconstruction programme has proved to be quite cumbersome. Some of the developments are still in the dire state in which they were following the 2009 disaster. At the end of 2019, the reconstruction of 200 dwellings belonging to Azienda Territoriale per l'Edilizia Residenziale (ATER), plus 36 located in buildings with a majority of individual owners, was still to be procured. Since the months following the earthquake, a committee of tenants and owners has been set up with the aim of pressuring public institutions, signing petitions, sending letters to newspapers, employing the courts and putting protest signs around the ruins of some of the complexes. Among the reasons for this extreme delay, public officials have mentioned the lack of human resources, complex procedures and the uncertainty regarding the effective availability of funds, with politicians responding to evacuees' mobilisations with 'high-level meetings' and grand announcements.

In a few cases, reconstruction has failed to materialise because public housing buildings are located in areas that the municipality planned to rebuild differently from the pre-earthquake state. In this instance, the lack of reconstruction depends on lengthy and difficult negotiations involving different owners and the design of detailed plans. However, in the majority of cases, the failure to advance the recovery of public housing takes place in a context where reconstruction has been mostly completed, making the presence of these 'new ruins' particularly evident and controversial.

The most blatant case is a series of low-rise apartment buildings located within the city's 1970s' expansion area of Pettino, comprising 56 units. The dwellings were heavily damaged and residents were relocated to temporary housing programmes. Since the disaster, inter-institutional relations and procurement processes regarding the reconstruction proved to be extremely slow, with the site becoming the object of local attention as a context of degradation, working site materials, illegal dumping and squatting. As ground floors appear to be breached by the quake, former dwellers' possessions and signs of recent informal living are in full view, while small piles of debris are spread out in the common spaces between the buildings. As they are in close proximity to completely repaired and inhabited residential buildings, a public park and temporary school complexes, they appear to be ostensibly hidden within this environment, being no more than a backdrop to a fully normalised everyday life.

Discussion

The post-emergency response and the overall reconstruction have led to the stratification of an impressive array of tools and regulations aimed at assessing the conditions of the built environment and at ordering its repair and return to use. At different moments in time, these complex layers have comprised the whole built environment, equally involving the individual housing trajectories of the entire local population and deeply restructuring the use and exchange of real estate assets. Processes of housing vacancy, abandonment and ruination are mediated by the stratification of these regulations, and appear to be a structural by-product of how emergency and recovery have been conceived and implemented in the post-disaster period. In particular, the establishment of ownership rights as a key principle in the political economy of the reconstruction, and the high investment in 'durable' temporary housing, have created the conditions for the amplification of structural emptiness, and eventually ruination, in a territory that was already experiencing a decline in the use of its housing stock. Within this context, by looking at the three stories, we can distinguish a variety of factors that produce and reproduce different, interrelated processes of housing emptiness.

In the case of historical centres, voids seem the outcome of combined processes of vacancy and underoccupancy of different relevance and temporality. It appears to be the exacerbation of pre-earthquake trends that already marked the decline of the historical centre as a place of residence and its evolution into the locus of temporary populations – mostly students, now a presence in decline – and professional activities. The overall inability of public action to acknowledge and address pre-existing and post-disaster trends is in this sense a major factor of the current situation. Furthermore, weak spatial and temporal coordination, and a series of implementation problems with the ownership-based governance of the reconstruction, are apparently worsening the situation. The still-ruinous environment, with ongoing massive reconstruction activities that often cause structural delays and limited liveability, is largely the by-product of the lack of an active management strategy and is among the main reasons for the overall emptiness. In other words, housing vacancy, underoccupancy, abandonment and ruination mark the choice of preserving property images and abstract value expectations, rather than formulating a spatially relevant collective strategy for the reactivation of historical centres in the new post-disaster conditions.

In the example of the CASE complexes, the turning of post-emergency temporary solutions into a de facto long-term mass housing programme, with no organised decommissioned strategy, points to current and future realities of both obsolescence and abandonment. The public authority has minimised maintenance expenditure, if any, on the existing units, resulting in processes of downward 'filtering' associated with the reduction in the number of residents and physical decline. Here, abandonment and underoccupancy are the outcomes of the original programme's misconception and of the lack of a clear, shared strategy among the different agencies involved. This is a quite paradoxical trajectory given that such complexes had been presented by hegemonic actors as a key innovation in terms of effectiveness and efficiency at times of emergency response, as opposed to previous experiences. As these sites may become, both formally and informally, housing solutions for the marginal sections of the population and a perceived liability for the values and living conditions of nearby environments, these assets will likely become increasingly controversial objects. Indeed, the housing surplus, the decentralisation of amenities, the movement of services and the overall condition and stages of obsolescence will have a significant impact on people's decisions to leave or inhabit them. Likewise, these factors and the concentration of socially disadvantaged households will inhibit their attractiveness for other social groups. While currently abandoned units and desolate complexes might be demolished or removed – even though the local authority has no plans or budget for this – renovations of empty stock will be difficult too.

Finally, in the case of public housing, despite routine public declarations regarding the engagement to rebuild and the availability of the funding to do it, these complexes represent the weakest segment of the residential reconstruction programme. Although it does not seem to be an intentional strategy to remove affordable housing, but rather mostly the outcome of governance coordination challenges, it points to the apparent paradox of a fully state-funded programme that fails in reconstructing public assets. As they were mostly inhabited by renters who have been relocated in CASE complexes – being moved, in a sense, from one public housing supply to another one – public housing has not attracted great attention from politicians and policymakers. This case further underlines how property can play a highly exclusionary role in the context of an ownership-based local society and reconstruction strategy, as it critically contributes to making certain claims stronger, and ultimately more legitimate, than others. The advanced state of abandonment of public housing and the relocation of households in long-term temporary solutions outline the implications of the disaster in terms of quality, recovery and safety for the different strata of society.

Planning efforts following natural disasters have often been seen as opportunities to promote new spatial strategies, embedded in wider development visions. Under certain circumstances, they have entailed selective rebuilding strategies aimed at repositioning affected cities in terms of class and housing supply. By limiting post-emergency housing support to certain social groups and by purposefully deciding not to rebuild certain components of the stock – for example, public housing and rentals – disasters have represented an opportunity to foster highly exclusionary agendas. Similarly, shrinkage situations have been seen as opportunities in this regard, with rightsizing strategies promoting demolition programmes aimed at re-naturalising the most disinvested, socially troubled and minority neighbourhoods, while concentrating development in 'sound' and 'stable' – and often white – neighbourhoods (Coppola, 2019). Strategies of this sort, especially when actively encouraged and facilitated by planning or development schemes, have attracted widespread criticism for promoting the interests of real estate and of certain groups of homeowners, thereby excluding and expelling the poor and disadvantaged (Smith, 1996; Atkinson and Bridge, 2005). In these peculiar contexts, ruination processes appear to be the outcomes of clear political strategies and rationales, as they tend to prepare and reinforce the legitimacy of final demolition or non-reconstruction decisions aimed at 'getting rid' of what, and who, are no longer considered in line with the new vision of the recovered city.

What happened in L'Aquila seems not to be the direct outcome of highly intentional strategies, but more of a set of consequences of the lack of an overall spatio-temporally selective strategy and of an ever-powerful, (over)building coalition composed of a network of widespread interests, sustained by the generous financial mobilisation of the Italian state. This circumstance further underlines how, in these contexts, the centrality of the state per se is not a guarantee of protection, neither of the public interest, nor of the most vulnerable sections of the population. In L'Aquila, as the entire post-disaster city is being rebuilt and the remnants of what had been presented as temporary housing is inscribing itself into permanence, processes of vacancy, abandonment and ruination are at work within the internal fractures of this model, fractures that will be increasingly evident, if not destabilising, for the time being. Overall, while the reconstruction was supposed to solve problems of equity, ensuring the integral rebuilding of the city, the lack of realistic collective visions may lead, in later stages, to the emergence of differentiation processes that will affect the ways in which certain social groups will access housing.

Conclusion

In this chapter, we have presented and discussed processes of housing emptiness and ruination in the context of three different stories about post-disaster L'Aquila. This has allowed us to read vacancy, underoccupancy, abandonment and ruination as largely the outcomes of the specific political economy of the reconstruction. We have argued that such processes also widely respond to the temporalities and spatialities put in motion by the post-emergency response and reconstruction strategy that, being based on a very narrow understanding of property rights, has led towards an oversupply of housing.

The trajectory of discrete components of the stock clearly points to a differentiated reality. As we have underlined, it is the outcome not so much of an intentional filtering strategy, but rather of the lack of a binding strategy for the reconstruction of the city. Post-disaster situations require complex planning frameworks addressing temporal and spatial dimensions, as temporal decisions may prove to have spatial effects and vice versa. In the lack of such a planning rationale, spatio-temporal fixes will be spontaneously and incrementally produced, powerfully contributing to the determination of the trajectory of discrete components of the built environment.

Besides what we have observed in the present time, we can assume that in the upcoming years, a combination of market forces and variably intentional or remedial public actions will largely preside over the production and reproduction of housing emptiness and ruination. Based on their position within the set of conditions and factors we have described, parts of the housing stock may experience filter-down processes, others may be abandoned and others may eventually experience forms of ruination. In this perspective, the case of L'Aquila offers more evidence of how the temporalities and spatialities of post-disaster cities are open-ended processes that stretch throughout the years after both the shock and what is generally considered the recovery from it. Likewise, it shows how they are related to the political economy of places and overall reconstruction strategies, and how these trajectories of housing emptiness offer tremendous opportunities to make sense of this reality.

Notes

[1] By residents, we mean people who formally reside within the limits of a given commune. Residents' numbers may be currently inflated given certain requirements associated with the reconstruction process.

[2] Students numbered 24,699 in 2009, while only 19,552 in 2018 (statistics from MIUR, 2019, http://ustat.miur.it/ [accessed 15 January 2020]).

[3] The city also has to deal with the future of the 450 units as the outcome of another post-earthquake procedure and the approximately 1,000 remaining temporary dwellings of the MAP initiative.

References

Atkinson, R. and Bridge, G. (2005) *Gentrification in a Global Context*, London: Routledge.

Black, R., Arnell, N.W., Adger, W.N., Thomas, D. and Geddes, A. (2013) 'Migration, immobility and displacement outcomes following extreme events', *Environmental Science and Policy*, 27(1): S32–43.

Calandra, L. (2013) 'Cultura e territorialità: quando l'abitare diventa multitopico. Esempi da L'Aquila post sisma', in M. Pedrana (ed) *Multiculturalità e territorializzazione. Casi di studio*, Roma: IF press, pp 7–32.

Comerio, M. (1997) 'Housing issues after disasters', *Journal of Contingencies and Crisis Management*, 5(3): 166–78.

Coppola, A. (2018) 'Crisis and transitions. L'Aquila and the window (Of lost?) opportunity of its reconstruction', in A. Coppola, C. Fontana and V. Gingardi (eds) *Envisaging L'Aquila. Strategies, Spatialities and Sociabilities of a Recovering City*, Trento: ProfessionalDreamers, pp 165–87.

Coppola, A. (2019) 'Projects of becoming in a right-sizing shrinking city', *Urban Geography*, 40(2): 237–56.

Couch, C. and Cocks, M. (2013) 'Housing vacancy and the shrinking city: trends and policies in the UK and the city of Liverpool', *Housing Studies*, 28(3): 499–519.

Drolet, J. (2015) 'Disasters in social, cultural and political context', in J.D. Wright (ed) *International Encyclopedia of the Social & Behavioural Sciences* (vol 6), Amsterdam: Elsevier, pp 478–84.

Erbani, F. (2010) *Il disastro. L'Aquila dopo il terremoto: le scelte e le colpe*, Roma-Bari: Laterza.

Frisch, G.J. (2018) 'An inertial reconstruction. The challenges and failures of governance and planning', in A. Coppola, C. Fontana and V. Gingardi (eds) *Envisaging L'Aquila. Strategies, Spatialities and Sociabilities of a Recovering City*, Trento: ProfessionalDreamers, pp 13–24.

Glock, B. and Haussermann, H. (2004) 'New trends in urban development and public policy in Eastern Germany: dealing with the vacant housing problem at the local level', *International Journal of Urban and Regional Research*, 28(4): 919–29.

Keenan, P., Lowe, S. and Spencer, S. (1999) 'Housing abandonment in inner cities – the politics of low demand for housing', *Housing Studies*, 14(5): 703–16.

Myers, N. (2002) 'Environmental refugees: a growing phenomenon of the 21st century', *Philosophical Transactions of the Royal Society B: Biological Sciences*, 357(1420): 609–13.

O'Callaghan, C., Di Feliciantonio, C. and Byrne, M. (2018) 'Governing urban vacancy in post-crash Dublin: contested property and alternative social projects', *Urban Geography*, 39(6): 868–91.

Power, A. and Mumford, K. (1999) *The Slow Death of Great Cities?*, York: Joseph Rowntree Foundation.

Smith, N. (1996) *The New Urban Frontier: Gentrification and the Revanchist City*, London: Routledge.

Wang, K. and Immergluck, D. (2019) 'Housing vacancy and urban growth: explaining changes in long-term vacancy after the US foreclosure crisis', *Journal of Housing and the Built Environment*, 34(2): 511–32.

8

The post-crisis properties
of demolishing Detroit, Michigan

Michael R.J. Koscielniak

Placing and planning demolition

Between 2005 and 2015, nearly 140,000 homes in Detroit faced mortgage or tax foreclosure. The Great Recession obliterated black wealth, shattered neighbourhoods and intensified economic uncertainty in US metropolises already weakened by decades of institutionalised segregation and population loss (Kurth and MacDonald, 2015). Over the course of just a few years, residents of Detroit fled in numbers bested only by New Orleans, LA, during the post-Hurricane Katrina flight. In May 2014, Motor City Mapping – a project of the public–private Detroit Blight Removal Task Force (DBRTF) – identified 78,000 buildings in some state of disrepair. DBRTF leaders concluded over 40,000 of these structures needed immediate demolition (Clark, 2014). The largest residential demolition programme in US history began awarding contracts that summer (Dolan, 2014).

For many, smashing these empty structures was common sense to escape the aftermath of the Great Recession and, like online mortgage impresario Dan Gilbert and Mayor Mike Duggan, most did not baulk at the billion-dollar price tag of a blight-free city. They shared the belief that vacant land was Detroit's competitive advantage. In 2013, Gilbert – the Chairman of Quicken Loans and a staunch defender of his company's poor record of mortgage foreclosures – said empty parcels would attract interests that 'are going to develop them and develop them in mass as soon as we get the structures down and maybe we don't have to worry about raising peas or corn or whatever it is you do in the farm' (McGraw, 2013). Since 2014, the Detroit Demolition Programme (DDP), along with public and private partners, have spent over US$500 million to demolish over 20,000 abandoned houses (Stafford, 2019a). Drawing on federal funds initially earmarked for anti-foreclosure programmes (Mallach, 2014), Detroit is one of several US cities cleaning up the mess of subprime mortgage lending that sank the country's economy for nearly a decade (Immergluck, 2009).

Brian Farkas, a Detroit Building Authority (DBA) director and Duggan lieutenant, echoed this in a 2016 presentation to the Detroit City Council, stating: 'The reason we're tearing down is to rebuild' (Farkas, 2016). One neighbourhood activist has gone so far as to claim the city should demolish residential blight and then 'the capitalists will take care of this rest' (Hackman, 2014). The *rest* is a rebuilt and redeveloped Detroit where profit is the primary objective and vacant public land achieves its higher purpose by becoming valuable private property.

The capitalist's enthusiasm for demolition-dependent redevelopment is matched only by the critic's enmity for its role in shaping cities and regions. Whether as a signal to investors that a declining city is open for business (Rosenman and Walker, 2015) or as the elimination of landscapes connected to social problems (Goetz, 2010), demolition makes it possible for public and private interests to shape the built environment. The National Demolition Association (NDA) slogan 'making way for a better world' is unambiguous in connecting wreckage to renewal (NDA, 2019). Even in times of progressive idealism, demolition served to displace black and low-income communities (Ammon, 2016). Today, demolition is treated as a local response to the global challenge of economic restructuring (Ryan, 2012; Grossmann et al, 2013). As a tool of austerity, demolition can drive the final nail in the coffin of a disposable neighbourhood (Rhodes and Russo, 2013; Hackworth, 2016). As a tool of neighbourhood preservation, demolition can harden boundaries around affluent areas and stigmatised neighbours (Mallach, 2011). As a tool of gentrification, demolition enables capital to flood into property markets with high potential values (Weber et al, 2006). In each case, demolition clears the way for the future by materialising a variation on spatial difference (Akers et al, 2020). As an expression of this uneven development, the muscle of demolition narrows possible futures – gentrification or social death – by intensifying historic geographies of class and anti-black racism (see also McClintock, this volume).

Disassembling demolition-dependent redevelopment

By unlocking development and preserving exclusion, demolition remains rooted in the ideology of the growth machine. The bulldozer is a collaborator in the land-use intensifications that convert use values to exchange values (Logan and Molotch, 1987). Foreclosure, speculation, blight and demolition combine to dispatch the social dimension of undervalued neighbourhoods and transform them into markets accessible to outsiders. That cycle of neglect creates new rent gaps and new opportunities for re-valuation (Smith, 1987). Decline is a stage in the ordinary exploitation of the built environment. The machine chews up communities and spits out commodities. Rentiers and development officials work hand-in-glove to configure land to maximise values, regardless of costs to incumbent inhabitants. In these entrepreneurial conjunctures, gentrification is almost an inevitable outcome of the factors of production. The growth coalition spatialises its ideology by developing land, marginalising labour, accumulating capital and extracting its income.

In Detroit, blight removal abets a back-to-the-city movement by capital (Cwiek, 2019). By eliminating the physical barriers to reinvestment, demolition is the state's blunt instrument for smoothing space and allowing capital to realise its practical purpose of returning to exploit the city's prior period of decline (Larsen, 2017). The refrain delivered by boosters and critics of demolition remains unaltered: the production of vacant land is a precondition to the class and racial restructuring of Detroit (Neavling, 2013). Newly cleared of ruins and the reminders of past abandonment, this land can now attract investors (Williams, 2019). The demolished post-crisis city becomes the blank canvas for capital's imagination.

While this explanation is useful in Detroit's central-corridor neighbourhoods, where major institutions and developers can preordain redevelopment, other property practices around occupancy, speculation and eviction dominate the city (Akers, 2013b; Safransky, 2014; Seymour and Akers, 2021). Notwithstanding the optimism in public, private and philanthropic circles, a queue of venturesome investors jostling for prime real estate is not snaking around the block. Demolition has not opened land markets or changed the roster of the development elite. Powerful landholders – among them Ford Motor Company (Reindl, 2018), trucking tycoon Manuel Moroun (Reindl and Gallagher, 2018), Dan Gilbert (Pinho, 2018) and developer Tony Soave (Gross, 2019) – have doubled down on positions that make them compulsory partners in land deals. Despite arguments that Detroit is in the middle of a frenzied 're-everything' process, where gentrification drives displacement (Jay and Conklin, 2020), land and property in much of the city have proven less growth-oriented than decline-oriented (Dewar et al, 2014; Seymour, 2020). Most vacant land remains in the Detroit Land Bank Authority (DLBA) inventory and the majority of property sales involve neighbours looking to reuse an adjacent cleared lot. These side-lot sales for gardens or recreation represent the majority of post-demolition transactions (Clifford, 2018).

Home financing remains hard to come by in places without anchor institutions, official historical significance or intact commercial strips. Land contracts remain the default instrument in the absence of conventional mortgages (Gross, 2018). These predatory arrangements entice potential occupants with homeownership, but research has established associations with eviction and housing insecurity (Akers and Seymour, 2018). Throughout Detroit, unconstitutional property tax assessments continue to drive tax foreclosures that force out low-income occupants and, in turn, produce the next wave of blighted properties demanding demolition (MacDonald and Bettancourt, 2019). Between 2005 and 2015, Detroit spent US\$34 million demolishing properties owned and then abandoned by speculators (Akers and Seymour, 2019). None of these structural challenges, however, have softened the city's stance on the merits of publicly funded destruction. In late 2019, Detroit's Chief Financial Officer remarked: 'When you look at all the different capital investments we make, no other capital has the same return on investment as demo' (Frank, 2019).

Given those outcomes, simplifying the DDP as 'demolition for development' (Mah, 2012) enabling lucrative land-use intensification obscures the land-use *debasements* that produce value without rebuilding (see also Gribat, this volume). While *demolition* may be an on-demand delivery of destruction at a discrete address, *demolishing* is a process embedded in regional property relations, supply chains, industrial systems and forms of valuation. The existing scholarship has overlooked this process and its geographic relationship to decline. One way out of this reliance on future redevelopment to ground critique of demolition is to link demolishing to rentiership. Andreucci et al (2017) distinguish between relations of capital and relations of rent. They argue rent is a form of income generation separate from capital accumulation that is dependent on capturing and redistributing surplus value rather than its production. As a companion to accumulation, they argue this appropriation can 'shed light on the hidden, depoliticised processes at work by which surplus value is distributed between different classes and fractions of classes' (Andreucci et al, 2017: 43). Therefore, it is not that residential demolition is failing to improve the city's neighbourhoods and reset Detroit's real estate market. Rather, as an exemplar of value grabbing, demolishing Detroit is enacting a concurrent land regime irreducible to accumulation and gentrification, or austerity and disinvestment. The relationship of decline to devaluation should remain an open question. Within that process, rent is not simply lurking in the shadows of value (Knuth et al, 2019). Instead, destruction provides new mechanisms for valuation.

A backfill-to-the-city movement

As a budget item, demolition may oblige a dichotomy of success or failure, but as a political-economic project, it has so far succeeded in transforming demolition contractors into potent city builders. Prior work has relegated these contractors to beneficiaries of changes in land regimes rather than an essential part of a coalition effecting those changes (Highsmith, 2015). In that binary of renewal or decay, the wrecker creates the raw material of redevelopment but remains incidental to value extraction. However, this narrow attention to redevelopment disguises the potency of demolishing to shape the built environment. Demolishing is part of a sprawling supply chain moving 10 million y^3 of dirt to fill holes created by demolition. Demolishing has not simply produced land; it has transformed the purpose of the land. Beyond use and exchange, beyond public and private, is a geography of extraction, rentiership and regulatory capture taking shape as a *backfill-to-the-city movement.*[1] Backfilling is a counterpart to the funding, labour, machinery and fuel that makes demolishing possible. Despite its perceived ubiquity, dirt, like any other commodity, has a price. It is a price embedded in a market vulnerable to and shaped by scarcity. However, supply and demand are part of the performance of value that disguises how power enacts and controls price (MacKenzie, 2006). Each of the planned 40,000 demolitions in Detroit will need 250 y^3 of material. Taken together, this represents a flow of material that exceeds the volume removed by the construction of the Channel Tunnel. At the onset of the DDP in 2014, officials ignored environmental consultants who warned that their Hardest Hit Funds (HHF) demolition goals – 1,800 in four months – would strain and exhaust available backfill supplies. DDP officials disregarded the advice and awarded contracts to three major firms. The DDP did not incorporate backfill costs into these agreements because administrators anticipated contractors would draw from free material created by two infrastructure projects: a new downtown National Hockey League arena and the rebuild of a federal highway (Stafford, 2019b). The decision proved fiscally disastrous when tests concluded these supplies contained disqualifying levels of chloride. Backfill became an essential resource and secondary market upon which demolition depended.

The DDP realised these miscues and pursued an agenda transforming the backfill problem into a programme. By the beginning of 2015, the DDP contracted AKT Peerless to manage the new Backfill Material Programme. Backfill, as they had discovered, was vital to Detroit recovering its land and competing with suburbs. AKT and

149

the DDP developed guidelines for approval, established monitoring processes and launched an online platform. New procedures required contractors to submit a profile of each source to AKT before dumping the material at a demolition. AKT and the DDP required these to be original sources of material. Backfill sources could fall into one of six categories depending on the type of source site: residential construction; commercial landscape material yard; non-residential construction; industrial construction; dredge sites; and other. The DDP prohibited material from the last three sources. For each transaction, contractors submitted the volume of material, destination (demolition site) and source site. AKT reviewed Google Earth imagery to confirm material originated from residential sites and by rule approved the transaction within hours of submission. The second category had a 24-hour turnaround. The majority of backfill originated from these two categories. In the event of non-residential construction sources, AKT required soil testing if the volume exceeded 2,000 y^3.

Properties of demolishing: 18410 Stout Street, Detroit, Michigan

On 2 March 2015, Adamo Group demolished 18410 Stout Street in North-west Detroit. The DLBA – a quasi-governmental entity independent of city government and serving as the fiduciary agent for the DDP – held the deed and awarded the US$12,995.35 contract. The DBA – another quasi-governmental entity but housed within city government – administered the contract. Adamo – a regional demolition firm with a national reputation in commercial and industrial structure removal – made quick work of the vacant 813 square foot home. 18410 Stout Street was just one of the 3,861 vacant houses demolished in the city by the end of 2015. Adamo, like the dozen other contractors working in Detroit, had rendered the tiny parcel vacant and developable.

The DLBA assumed control of 18410 in 2014 after Mayor Mike Duggan and the Detroit City Council arranged a transfer of 16,399 properties to its growing inventory. Formerly staffed by five employees, the DLBA reached 75 full-time workers in 2015 and over 150 in 2019. The expansion in personnel paralleled the receipt of US$258,656,459 from the federal HHF to wreck abandoned houses in Detroit. In 2010, the US Congress authorised US$7.6 billion in relief for 18 state governments to assist owner-occupants struggling with mortgage payments after the collapse of the US housing market. However, HHF eligibility rules proved too strict for many desperate homeowners coping with the consequences of delinquency. Facing the prospect of underutilisation, congressional members from the US Midwest persuaded the Treasury to permit state agencies to steer hundreds of millions in HHF foreclosure prevention towards residential demolition. Blight removal became neighbourhood stabilisation. In early 2013, the US Treasury gave permission to the Michigan State Housing Development Authority (MSHDA) to divert part of its share of HHF to demolition. Programmes based in Flint, Michigan and Detroit would be the primary recipients. Money earmarked for stabilising owner-occupancy mutated into the public sector's broom for sweeping away evidence of prior predatory lending.

The modest house at 18410 Stout was one such chunk of evidence. Between 1991 and 2007, 18410 had only three owners. In the seven years prior to its demolition, 13 different owners held the deed. This property gauntlet allowed 18410 to ride the wave of the Great Recession – occasionally occupied, always transferable. Banks, investors, speculators and institutions each took their turn neglecting the property. In 2007, just as the first waves of foreclosures began to rattle the US economy, the Wayne County Sheriff seized 18410 from Redell Salter (the owner-occupant since 2001) and sold it to Argent Securities for US$65,064.00. Less than a year later, Argent conveyed the deed to REO Nationwide Inc., which proceeded to sell the vacant home to Izair Skender for just US$3,000. Private ownership of the property culminated with California-based Stone Crest Income & Investment Opportunity Fund 1 selling to California-based Stonecrest Income & Investment Opportunity Fund 1 for US$1,000 – representing a US$64,064.00 loss of value in just three years. In 2012, Wayne County Treasurer foreclosed for unpaid property taxes. From there, 18410 Stout Street entered the inventory of the Detroit Planning and Development Department where it lingered until the City Council approved a property transfer to the newly invigorated DLBA. The DDP placed the property into HHF-funded demolition in July 2014.

An HHF-financed demolition includes seven stages. Contractors wreck a structure and bill the MSHDA for inspections, abatement structure removal, lot maintenance, grading, backfill, seeding and project management. As of March 2015, the DDP operated on an advance fund that would replenish with later HHF reimbursement. Using MSHDA records, Table 8.1 shows what Adamo sought reimbursement for after demolishing the structure at 18410 Stout Street.

The final HHF stage includes assigning a lien to the demolished property equal to the demolition cost: US$15,008.35. The lien discounts 20 per cent annually and expires after five years. This

Table 8.1: Reimbursement sought by Adamo after demolishing the structure at 18410 Stout Street

Task	Cost
Inspection	US$763.00
Removal	US$8,771.15
Lot maintenance	US$750.00
Grade	US$309.57
Backfill dirt	US$1,135.09
Seed	US$103.19
Project management	US$500.00
Demolition miscellaneous	US$2,676.35
Total	**US$15,008.35**

Source: The author

was a vestigial provision the MSHDA adopted from its prior anti-foreclosure efforts. In that programme, the lien served the purpose of discouraging owner-occupants from flipping their property after receiving public mortgage assistance. With the inception of the blight removal programme, MSHDA administrators determined it was easier to maintain those lien provisions rather than overhaul rules. In the case of 18410 Stout Street, the DLBA could only sell the vacant property if the buyer agreed to pay the lien plus a 'fair market value' determined by DLBA staff. Although the DDP's official demolition data portal lists the demolition cost as US$12,995.35, the lien represents the MSHDA's own cost figure. Therefore, the lien would discount along the terms outlined in Table 8.2.

Adamo demolished 18410 Stout Street within this regulatory and valuation environment. However, no record exists for the backfill transaction. The contractor reported US$1,135.09 in backfill costs but nothing describing the source or volume. In early 2019, Brian Farkas, the DBA director, claimed the lack of records for 2,389 HHF demolitions was a data-retrieval glitch and not a recordkeeping issue. He dismissed the omissions as an inefficiency of paper records and 'not as a reflection of our work in the field to ensure the use of clean dirt' (Ferretti, 2019). However, obtaining clean material is not a synonym for regulatory compliance. Farkas could not explain the 151 incorrect addresses (including the proper noun of 'Detroit' misspelled at least seven times) in available records, nor why contractors used paper recordkeeping during a period (2015–18) when AKT and the DPP made the soil-management platform a requirement for backfill

Table 8.2: Hardest Hit Fund lien annual discount

Date	Lien
10/15/2015	US$15,008.35
10/15/2016	US$12,006.68
10/15/2017	US$9,005.01
10/15/2018	US$6,003.34
10/15/2019	US$3,001.67
10/15/2020	US$0.00

Source: The author

approval. The transaction for 18410 Stout Street may be missing but contractors submitted 48 other transactions on Stout Street for approval.

The absence of 18410 Stout Street from the record of backfill destinations should serve as the definitive word on its hereafter of emptiness – another casualty of neighbourhood disinvestment and local regulatory dysfunction. However, demolition backfill does not belong solely to destinations. In 2016, Adamo reported 18410 Stout Street as the backfill source for two demolitions: 17147 Ferguson and 19211 Curtis. AKT approved 18410 Stout Street as a source 17 months after Adamo demolished the house on the site. Adamo knocked down 19211 Curtis on 27 June 2016 and billed US$9,763.00. A day later, Adamo demolished 17147 Ferguson and billed US$9,201.00. Adamo submitted the two transactions reporting 18410 Stout Street as the backfill source on 29 August 2016. The contractor used 72 y^3 of material to fill 17147 Ferguson and 168 y^3 to fill 19211 Curtis. For the backfill moved to Ferguson, Adamo billed US$528.73; for the other, it billed US$591.07. Somehow, Adamo had transformed a vacant lot into a key asset within its demolition process.

The formal approvals that appear in DDP records disguise the backfilling process but, more importantly, conceal the interests that command and benefit from that process. The parcel of 18410 Stout Street was never the original source for demolition backfill. No evidence suggests Adamo excavated one of its 2015 demolition sites to obtain backfill for two demolitions in 2016. The DLBA never surrendered ownership to Adamo or an outside party. The parcel did not need to change hands from public to private to generate income. Instead, Adamo used the residential address to meet the letter of regulation by embedding its backfill source in a neighbourhood. By doing so, neither the DDP nor AKT required additional monitoring.

Rather than an origin, aerial imagery from summer 2016 confirms Adamo used 18410 Stout Street as a stockpile site for staging its other demolitions. As one regional contractor familiar with demolition stated, "source washing" is standard operating procedure for firms that prioritise wider margins over public welfare. Within the backfill market, the supply of approvable sources exceeded the supply of approvable materials. Contractors recognised the vulnerabilities within an accelerated residential source approval process and anticipated AKT would register backfill's location in space as a sensible substitute for its origin. Rather than a gap in compliance, Adamo's approach to backfill signals the forms of land use and control that compliance with the DDP regulation enables.

The dirt on Detroit

The parcel of 18410 Stout Street is one of 444 approved sources feeding backfill to demolishing Detroit. AKT and the DDP elected to categorise these sites as technical or topographic features of the region (residential, commercial; landscape yard, quarry; industrial, road). Backfill, however, is not a geological outcrop that fortunate contractors stumble across while conducting their ordinary business of wrecking the city. As a commodity, backfill is as much an expression of social and economic relationships as the physical embrace between excavator and land. As David Harvey (2001: 51) explains, 'Resources can only be defined in relationship to the mode of production which seeks to make use of them.' By the middle of 2019, the DDP has paid out over US$15,000,000 to contractors for backfill material. Like coal, natural gas or precious metals, backfill excavation and management are shot through with the exploitative operations of land and capital (Mezzadra and Neilson, 2019). The technical categories used by the DDP and AKT do not capture the people, property and processes that produce the commodity. A narrow understanding of demolition – the practical convergence of equipment and labour at the precise intersection of latitude and longitude – neglects the productive, geographic and relational dimension of demolishing, and obfuscates how the production of demolition transforms land use and enables contractors, haulers, suburban developers and excavators to extract remaining value from the city's built environment. Categorising backfill by zoning designation flattens the relationship between Detroit's property market and contradictions of land and logistics.

An alternative categorisation centres those relations and represents backfill as a socio-environmental product instead of a topographic feature with technical importance. My analysis of the 444 backfill sources reveals eight types, each illustrating real estate practices that trouble the self-evidence of demolition-dependent redevelopment in Detroit. These categories reveal geographic links between demolishing and value grabbing. The categories are: expansive; speculative; destructive; extractive; new construction; illusive; infrastructural; and unknown. As of early 2019, destructive source sites contributed the largest volume of backfill material. Destructive sources entail the manufacturing of backfill material from road and residential debris. Expansive sources are graveyards, parking lots and commercial construction projects that generated material as waste. Extractive sources are quarries, sand pits, mines and mineral yards. Infrastructural sources are bridge, surface street, highway and sewer projects that generated waste material. Unknown sources either did not exist as addresses in the Detroit region or the process that produced the material could not be identified from either aerial imagery or property records. Table 8.3 illustrates the variation in these backfill source category types. The remainder of this section examines speculative, new construction and illusive sources.

Speculative source sites represented the largest portion of sources. At the 125 speculative sources, demolition contractors purchased material that was removed to construct basements at speculative residential construction sites. Contractors used HHF funding to haul this material to demolition holes in Detroit neighbourhoods. By relocating the waste of suburban speculation to Detroit, contractors converted the material into a commodity. In June 2016, DMC Group, one of the second-tier

Table 8.3: Backfill source sites by category

Category	Backfill volume (y³)	Source sites
Destructive	573,219	5
Extractive	182,126	12
Expansive	210,031	25
Illusive	170,862	52
New construction	140,247	125
Speculative	145,640	124
Infrastructural	108,116	35
Not available	28,986	66
Grand total	1,559,227	444

Source: The author

contractors working on HHF contracts, sourced 3,100 y³ of material from the construction of 1015 S. Bates in Birmingham, Michigan, a wealthy suburb of Detroit with 21,322 residents and a median household income of US$114,537. The suburb of 1015 S. Bates is a 4,199 square foot speculative build currently listed for US$1,859,000. By paying the builder US$29,299.78 in HHF for backfill, DMC subsidised the construction of 1015 S. Bates with money set aside to stabilise Detroit's property market. The 124 other speculative sources share the profile. Whether a single property or subdivision, contractors used millions in HHF to purchase backfill from projects equal to over US$66,413,937.00 in real estate sales for affluent municipalities. Combined with new construction source sites – those that I could link to a new owner or occupant – sources of material that served regional wealth account for over 56 per cent of all backfill sources.

Finally, the 48 illusive backfill sources illustrate that Adamo's Stout Street source washing is not an anomaly within the DDP. AKT and the DDP demonstrated a pattern of approving a residential address despite no evidence corroborating its source credentials. These sources present the illusion of a residential source. These misleading records implicate both large-scale apartment developments and DLBA-owned vacant land like 18410 Stout Street. To wit, 18410 is not the only address on Stout Street turned into a logistical asset by Adamo. Seven other sources with a Stout Street address appear in the DDP backfill records. The street illustrates how contractors captured the DDP regulatory apparatus and shaped land use without redevelopment. In sum, Adamo claimed that Stout Street addresses contributed 2,072 y³ of backfill to complete 13 demolitions. The contractor billed HHF US$8,893.86 to cover the costs of material. While small in scale, these transactions along Stout Street are instructive for understanding how vacant land in Detroit takes on new potency in a city facing ubiquitous abandonment.

Conclusions: towards the production of demolition

The DDP seeks to rebuild the city. In 2016, the Legislative Policy Division, the research arm of the Detroit City Council, summed up the significance of backfilling: 'The intentional creation of even greater economic and physical barriers to such redevelopment would be wasting of the City's potentially greatest assets in the form of its abundant open space of undervalued urban real estate available for building and redevelopment' (Legislative Policy Division, 2016: 3). As I have argued, the abundance of cleared land has not culminated in redevelopment for the majority of Detroit. However, in the absence of those investors, the hundreds of millions in HHF have enabled regional contractors to appropriate value and occupy land on the back of the city's crippled built environment. Although the liens have frustrated conventional city building, they opened space for a parallel set of interests to exploit the built environment by other means. In turn, Detroit is less defined by use or exchange value, or capitalised and potential rent; at the centre is a land regime that does not depend on redevelopment to realise value.

Such a land regime has an important place within refreshed approaches to decline. As Akers (2013a) argued, decline is not a withdrawal of capital and an interruption in accumulation, but a shift in practices. Along with Akers, Seymour (2020) has dubbed this the *production of decline* and focused on the pipelines and pathways that drive destruction. Decline is not a process occurring within Detroit, but a process happening to Detroit with local, regional, national and global dimensions. Backfilling Detroit is a local and regional mechanism of decline that helps sustain value grabbing. Demolishing did not trigger development, but siphoned the remaining value of Detroit's built environment into the hands of a few well-positioned actors. The relationship of demolishing to property relations inside the city and within the region has produced a labyrinth of rents where destruction debases land use but ensures income for contractors, haulers, suburban homebuilders and excavators. Rather than a local response to a global challenge, the logistics of the DDP served as a local and regional driver of decline in which demolishing Detroit revalued properties for capture by these parties. Ruins are not waiting for the new phase of development to provide opportunities for value. In cities like Detroit, Michigan, an urban process driven by rentiership suggests room for refreshing the study of uneven development by moving it from a seesaw consequence of capital mobility to the prevailing material condition.

Note

[1] The measurements used in this chapter are listed in yards. This is in keeping with the industry standard used in the US, and from which the case study and research materials are drawn.

References

Akers, J. (2013a) 'Decline industry: the market production of Detroit', PhD dissertation, University of Toronto, Canada.

Akers, J. (2013b) 'Making markets: think tank legislation and private property in Detroit', *Urban Geography*, 34(8): 1070–95.

Akers, J. and Seymour, E. (2018) 'Instrumental exploitation: predatory property relations at city's end', *Geoforum*, 91: 127–40.

Akers, J. and Seymour, E. (2019) 'The eviction machine: neighborhood instability and blight in Detroit's neighbourhoods', Poverty Solutions White Paper. Available at: https://poverty.umich.edu/files/2019/07/Akers-et-al-Eviction-Machine-Revised-June-18.pdf (accessed 26 July 2020).

Akers, J., Beal, V. and Rousseau, M. (2020) 'Redefining the city and demolishing the rest: the techno-green fix in postcrash Cleveland, Ohio', *Environment and Planning E: Nature and Space*, 3(1): 207–27.

Ammon, F.R. (2016) *Bulldozer: Demolition and Clearance of the Postwar Landscape*. New Haven, CT: Yale University Press.

Andreucci, D., Garcia-Lamarca, M., Wedekind, J. and Swyngedouw, E. (2017) '"Value grabbing": a political ecology of rent', *Capitalism Nature Socialism*, 28(3): 28–47.

Clark, A. (2014) 'Will "blexting" help with Detroit blight?', *Next City*, 28 July. Available at: https://nextcity.org/daily/entry/detroit-blight-blexting-houses-motor-city-mapping (accessed 26 July 2020).

Clifford, T. (2018) 'Detroit Land Bank's $100 side-lot programme hits 10000 purchases', *Crain's Detroit*, 17 September. Available at: www.crainsdetroit.com/real-estate/detroit-land-banks-100-side-lot-programme-hits-10000-purchases (accessed 26 July 2020).

Cwiek, S. (2019) 'Demolitions are transforming Detroit. Some wonder: what comes next', *Michigan Radio*, 17 October. Available at: www.michiganradio.org/post/demolitions-are-transforming-detroit-some-wonder-what-comes-next (accessed 26 July 2020).

Dewar, M., Seymour, E. and Druta, O. (2014) 'Disinvesting in the city: the role of tax foreclosure in Detroit', *Urban Affairs Review*, 51(5): 587–615.

Dolan, M. (2014) 'Mayor aims to reverse Detroit exodus', *The Wall Street Journal*, 22 June. Available at: www.wsj.com/articles/mayor-mike-duggan-aims-to-reverse-detroit-exodus-1403480663 (accessed 26 July 2020).

Farkas, B. (2016) 'Safe demolition at scale', Detroit Building Authority, 26 April. Available at: www.michigan.gov/documents/deq/deq-oea-tou-Farkas-safety_523538_7.pdf (accessed 26 July 2020).

Ferretti, C. (2019) 'Soil records under scrutiny in Detroit demolitions', *The Detroit News*, 7 March. Available at: www.detroitnews.com/story/news/local/detroit-city/2019/03/08/soil-records-under-scrutiny-detroit-demolitions/2768976002/ (accessed 26 July 2020).

Frank, A. (2019) 'Duggan unveils $250 million bond plan to rid Detroit of blight in 5 years', *Crain's Detroit*, 16 September. Available at: www. crainsdetroit.com/government/duggan-unveils-250-million-bond-plan-rid-detroit-blight-5-years (accessed 26 July 2020).

Goetz, E.G. (2010) 'Gentrification in black and white: the racial impact of public housing demolition in American cities', *Urban Studies*, 48(8): 1581–604.

Gross, A. (2018) 'Detroit real estate game creates chaos in neighbourhoods', *Detroit Free Press*, 17 August. Available at: www. freep.com/story/news/local/michigan/detroit/2018/08/17/detroit-home-values-real-estate/921453002/ (accessed 26 July 2020).

Gross, A. (2019) 'Questions raised about Soave Enterprise land purchases in Detroit before Jeep deal', *Detroit Free Press*, 21 May. Available at: www.freep.com/story/news/local/michigan/detroit/2019/05/21/soave-bought-two-key-parcels-talks-fca-expansion-starting/3752311002/ (accessed 26 July 2020).

Grossmann, K., Bontje, M., Haase, A. and Mykhnenko, V. (2013) 'Shrinking cities: notes for the further research agenda', *Cities*, 35: 221–5.

Hackman, R. (2014) 'Detroit demolishes its ruins: "The capitalists will take care of the rest"', *The Guardian*, 28 September. Available at: www.theguardian.com/money/2014/sep/28/detroit-demolish-ruins-capitalists-abandoned-buildings-plan (accessed 26 July 2020).

Hackworth, J. (2016) 'Demolition as urban policy in the American Rust Belt', *Environment and Planning A: Economy and Space*, 48(11): 2201–22.

Harvey, D. (2001) *Spaces of Capital: Towards a Critical Geography*, Edinburgh: Edinburgh University Press.

Highsmith, A. (2015) *Demolition Means Progress: Flint, Michigan, and the Fate of the American Metropolis*, Chicago, IL: The University of Chicago Press.

Immergluck, D. (2009) *Foreclosed: High-Risk Lending, Deregulation, and the Undermining of America's Mortgage Market*, Ithaca, NY: Cornell University Press.

Jay, M. and Conklin, P. (2020) *A People's History of Detroit*, Durham: Duke University Press.

Knuth, S., Potts, S. and Goldstein, J.E. (2019) 'In value's shadow: devaluation as accumulation frontier', *Environment and Planning A: Economy and Space*, 51(2): 461–6.

Kurth, J. and MacDonald, C. (2015) 'Volume of abandoned homes "absolutely terrifying"', *The Detroit News*, 24 June. Available at: www.detroitnews.com/story/news/special-reports/2015/05/14/detroit-abandoned-homes-volume-terrifying/27237787/ (accessed 26 July 2020).

Larsen, R. (2017) 'Detroit: the most exciting city in America', *The New York Times*, 20 November. Available at: www.nytimes.com/2017/11/20/travel/detroit-michigan-downtown.html (accessed 26 July 2020).

Legislative Policy Division (2016) *Demolition Standards and Land Use*, 6 July, Detroit: Detroit City Council.

Logan, J. and Molotch, H. (1987) *Urban Fortunes: The Political Economy of Place*, Berkeley, CA: University of California Press.

MacDonald, C. and Bettancourt, M. (2019) 'Effort to stave off Detroit foreclosures leaves many deeper in debt', *Detroit Free Press*, 4 December. Available at: www.detroitnews.com/story/news/local/detroit-housing-crisis/2019/12/05/detroit-foreclosures-effort-wayne-county-treasurer-puts-many-residents-into-deeper-debt/1770381001/ (accessed 26 July 2020).

MacKenzie, D. (2006) *An Engine, Not a Camera*, Cambridge: MIT Press.

Mah, A. (2012) 'Demolition for development: a critical analysis of official urban imaginaries in past and present UK cities', *Journal of Historical Sociology*, 25(1): 151–76.

Mallach, A. (2011) 'Demolition and preservation in shrinking US industrial cities', *Building Research & Information*, 39(4): 380–94.

Mallach, A. (2014) 'Hardest Hit Funds demolition policy change on track to become a boon for distressed communities', Center for Community Progress blog, 1 July. Available at: www.communityprogress.net/blog/federal-policy-change-leads-results-ground-hardest-hit-funds-demolish-derelict-houses (accessed 26 July 2020).

McGraw, B. (2013) 'Dan Gilbert is planning to tear down every single abandoned building in Detroit', *Deadline Detroit*, 1 October. Available at: www.deadlinedetroit.com/articles/6587/dan_gilbert_is_planning_to_demolish_every_last_abandoned_building_in_detroit (accessed 26 July 2020).

Mezzadra, S. and Neilson, B. (2019) *The Politics of Operations: Excavating Contemporary Capitalism*, Durham: Duke University Press.

NDA (National Demolition Association) (2019) 'Making way'. Available at: www.demolitionassociation.com/News-Media (accessed 26 July 2020).

Neavling, S. (2013) 'Bring on more gentrification, declares Detroit's economic development czar', *Motor City Muckraker*, 16 May. Available at: http://motorcitymuckraker.com/2013/05/16/bring-on-more-gentrification-declares-detroits-economic-development-czar-george-jackson/ (accessed 26 July 2020).

Pinho, K. (2018) 'Hudson's site tower details revealed in city documents', *Crain's Detroit*, 9 October. Available at: www.crainsdetroit.com/real-estate/hudsons-site-tower-details-revealed-city-documents (accessed 26 July 2020).

Reindl, J.C. (2018) 'Could abandoned Detroit train station be Ford's millennial magnet?', *Detroit Free Press*, 24 March. Available at: www.freep.com/story/money/cars/ford/2018/03/24/detroit-train-station-ford-millennial-magnet/449500002/ (accessed 26 July 2020).

Reindl, J.C. and Gallagher, J. (2018) 'Ford buys landmark train station that symbolized Detroit's decay', *Detroit Free Press*, 11 June. Available at: www.usatoday.com/story/money/cars/2018/06/11/ford-detroit-train-station/690064002/ (accessed 26 July 2020).

Rhodes, J. and Russo, J. (2013) 'Shrinking "smart"? Urban redevelopment and shrinkage in Youngstown, Ohio', *Urban Geography*, 34(3): 305–26.

Rosenman, E. and Walker, S. (2015) 'Tearing down the city to save it? "Back-door regionalism" and the demolition coalition in Cleveland, Ohio', *Environment and Planning A: Economy and Space*, 48(2): 273–91.

Ryan, B. (2012) *Design after Decline: How America Rebuilds Shrinking Cities*, Philadelphia, PA: University of Pennsylvania Press.

Safransky, S. (2014) 'Greening the urban frontier: race, property, and resettlement in Detroit', *Geoforum*, 56: 237–48.

Seymour, E. (2020) 'From REO to ruin: post-foreclosure pathways and the production of decline in Detroit, Michigan', *Housing Policy Debate*, 30(3): 431–56.

Seymour, E. and Akers, J. (2021) 'Building the eviction economy: speculation, precarity, and eviction in Detroit', *Urban Affairs Review*, 57(1): 35–69.

Smith, N. (1987) 'Gentrification and the rent gap', *Annals of the Association of American Geographers*, 77(3): 462–65.

Stafford, K. (2019a) 'Detroit demolition programme mismanaged, riddled with problems, auditor says', *Detroit Free Press*, 8 November. Available at: www.freep.com/story/news/local/michigan/detroit/2019/11/08/detroit-demolition-auditor-general-report/2522761001/ (accessed 26 July 2020).

Stafford, K. (2019b) 'Was contaminated dirt used to fill Detroit demolition holes? Feds ask', *Detroit Free Press*, 11 February. Available at: www.freep.com/story/news/investigations/2019/02/11/detroit-land-bank-federal-demolition-dirt-probe-sites-across-detroit/2796355002/ (accessed 26 July 2020).

Weber, R., Doussard, M., Bhatta, S.D. and McGrath, D. (2006) 'Tearing the city down: understanding demolition activity in gentrifying neighbourhoods', *Journal of Urban Affairs*, 28(1): 19–41.

Williams, C. (2019) 'Vacant land becoming asset as development returns to Detroit', *Associated Press*, 28 April. Available at: https://apnews.com/89bfa6aa9167480dbf2568674ce560d2 (accessed 26 July 2020).

9

Guarding presence: absent owners and the labour of managing vacancy

Lauren Wagner

Introduction

The environs of Tangier, Morocco, are a patchwork of cleared lots and new construction, staggered in age and size. Walking through one of these neighbourhoods can feel disjointed: turn in one direction and a whole neighbourhood of rectangular apartment blocks are evenly spaced, separated by paved roads; turn in another direction and a rocky expanse of ground appears, often with further neighbourhoods of apartments at a distance.

Shortly after dark one evening during the summer of 2016, I was walking in one of these areas in the process of collecting data about housing and vacancy in the city. At the corner of one of the rectangular apartment buildings, I approached a man sitting in a chair positioned to see the surrounding streets – a guardian, watching over parked cars and street activity for the budding neighbourhood. We chatted about the expanding housing developments in Tangier, including the buildings he was guarding and another set visible in the distance across a cleared field (see Figure 9.1). To me, the distant buildings appeared oppressively dark, still-unfinished constructions, at most partially occupied by dwellers, but the guardian says all of those apartments, like all the ones near his position, are 'full'.

This chapter explores how both of us, myself and the guardian, formulated an impression of what makes housing 'full' or 'empty'. Our contradictory impressions bring into relief how vacancy can be partial or temporary, somewhere between housing that is owned, occupied and in use, and housing that is abandoned. Using the case of Tangier, I examine some of the ways that cyclical vacancy can be recognised and conceptualised by actors connected with it. This exploration is partly epistemological – questioning how 'vacancy' can be observed by different methods and different observers – as well as partly conceptual, calling upon problems related to vacancy that have come forward in strands of research that touch on housing dynamics – like migratory and

Figure 9.1: View of houses across a field, near Tangier Boukhalef, 2015

Source: Photo by the author

touristic mobilities – but are not often incorporated into housing studies (Melly, 2010; Lopez, 2014; Mata-Codesal, 2014). In this example, I consider different kinds of ordinary owner mobilities – of vacationing second homes intermingled with labour migrations, interspersed with circulating residents – and how such mobilities might make vacancy more complex than simply 'empty'.

While, in some ways, these mobilities and the vacancies they produce in Tangier pre-date the global shift in housing financialisation (Guyer, 2015), they are also linked with problems of absent owners that have arisen when housing is more functional as capital than as dwelling space. Although Tangier is not in the same realm of the global marketplace as some other sites for speculative housing investment (see the chapters by Ferreri and by Di Feliciantonio and O'Callaghan, this volume), the city has nevertheless experienced its own version of crisis. As with prominent global cities that have become the focus of research in housing vacancy – or, more concretely, the absence of dwelling owners – these absences have had palpable effects on the lives of residents and the fabric of the city. Yet, Tangier arguably presents a more complex case, composed of nested ownerships, dwellings and mobilities that include forms of cyclical and partial dwelling performed by middle-class owners alongside elites. Furthermore, it extends historically, with forms of occupancy and absence by mobile residents that have laid groundwork for current formulations. In this sense, Tangier presents a case that does not hinge immediately upon the global housing crisis as its primary catalyst, yet integrates that event within longer histories of housing dynamics that have incorporated dweller mobilities as part of their normative operation.

Through fieldwork in which I was seeking to observe vacancy and its effects in Tangier, I came to the epistemological problem of what makes housing observable as 'full'. Taking as a point of departure the problem of how the guardian and I might perceive the same housing as being simultaneously empty and full, I discuss how I learned to observe 'vacancy' through the kinds of actors and activities that intervene to 'fill' housing when it may be left inconsistently occupied. To do so, I first contextualise the city of Tangier and its geographical and historical position for mobile dwellers, then situate owner and dweller mobilities in relation to the problematics of ownership and vacancy as conceived across literatures in housing, tourism and migration. Finally, I evaluate some key observations from fieldwork, which largely indicate that what fills the gap between owner and vacancy are actors like the guardian himself, who 'occupy' property on behalf of owners, with or without their permission. These activities, I contend, become a way to recognise the work of occupancy through what kind of labour is required when housing lies 'vacant'.

Housing dynamics in Tangier

Tangier's position as the African tip at the mouth of the Mediterranean has rendered it historically significant in international geopolitics and trade. That positioning brings many new residents into the city but equally attracts temporary and transient dwellers to its resources, both economic and physical. Housing provision in Tangier has fluctuated along with these mobilities, and along with the city's integration in international governance of housing. These forces have exercised influence on how housing works in Tangier and the particular forms of vacancy they have left behind.

Tangier may be most well known for its 20th-century period as an international zone governed by a collection of European powers as a neutral waypoint between the Mediterranean and the Atlantic Ocean, and made famous by the global literati who stayed there. Yet, it was a significantly international city for a century before that. During the 18th- and 19th-century expansion of European imperialism, the Sultanate of Morocco remained an independent state, for which Tangier served as the diplomatic outpost from the early 19th century (Abitbol, 2009). It was one of the only places Europeans (as Christians) were permitted to reside in the Islamic territory. As a site for many diplomatic households, it attracted European travellers touring through Spain (Howard-Vyse, 1882; Thomas, 1892; Liberty, 1908), as well as European entrepreneurs and professionals 'modernising' the city (Miller, 2001; Viehoff, 2009). While many of these 'foreign' residents became 'Tangerois' – integral to the city's fabric (Bialasiewicz and Wagner, 2015) – they often remained somehow partial residents, with access to dwellings elsewhere or recourse to other laws.

These partial and passing dwellers enabled certain paradoxes of occupation and vacancy to emerge. For example, some residences, though physically located in Tangier, could be subject to international governance under Tangier International Zone management. Journalist Rom Landau recounted an anecdote of an 'American-protected' property owner who extended his house higher than the local laws prescribed, claiming that he was governed by US law that did not recognise the height limit. Later, when his tenants would not pay rent, 'the authorities informed him that so far as they were concerned the applicant and his house did not exist, and it was impossible to give police assistance to non-existent entities' (Landau, 1952: 138). Inversely, some residences continue to be recognised as 'owned', though the owners and their extended families have been absent for generations. Anecdotes from fieldwork for this project attributed some of these absences to the departure of many Moroccan Jews for Israel during the tumultuous decade after 1948, which saw both the independence of the Kingdom of Morocco from French protection in 1952 and the disbanding of the international city in 1955 (Hillali, 1996). When descendants with a rightful claim to the property cannot be located, it may remain in indefinite limbo without a legal way to be reclaimed by the city. In short, Tangier's history as internationally fluid in its residents and its legal status makes for additional complexity in the landscape of occupancy and vacancy.

Likewise, as a zone on the border of Morocco and Spain, Tangier and the surrounding region have long served as a destination for passage of migratory and touristic flows. Currently, the most dominant mobility is that of migrants from Morocco and elsewhere in Africa reaching the Moroccan coastline and getting stuck searching for a means to cross into Europe (Driessen, 2007). These mobilities bring many to the city as clandestine dwellers, often without legal or economic means to establish residence. Simultaneously, the northern coastline of

Morocco, including Tangier, has long been a site of Spanish tourism and second-home investment, as well as more recent investments by Spanish developers in the entrepreneurial city centre (Kanai and Kutz, 2011; Therrien, 2019). Both the South to North migration and the North to South tourism bring mixtures of visitors for unpredictable durations, seeking housing that may fall beyond the ordinary owner-occupancy framework.

Finally, mobility within Morocco towards Tangier is linked both to its touristic desirability as a cosmopolitan city on the sea and to the recent creation of a large international port – Tanger Med – and free-trade zones oriented towards European manufacturing. Since the free-trade zones became active in 2000, the population of the city has increased sharply. Comparing the 2004 and 2014 censuses, the annual population increase was 3.26 per cent – more than double any other Moroccan city (Recensement Général de la Population et de l'Habitat 2014, 2015: 8). Alongside that, testimonials from previous research and in news reporting indicate that Tangier has become increasingly desirable as a holiday location, as well as for the purchase of vacation homes by both domestic and diasporic tourists (Wagner, 2014; Abjiou, 2018). Concomitantly, the pressure on housing has increased, rendering prices per square metre in Tangier on a par with Europe.

These flows of people have intersected with national efforts to fundamentally restructure housing stock for the whole of Morocco. In the context of a 2004 initiative Villes sans Bidonvilles ('Cities without Slums'), the housing authorities have used a combination of tax rebates and public–private partnerships to enable households with low or intermittent incomes to qualify and be able to pay for new, more secure housing (Toutain, 2014; Lam and Feather, 2016). The housing units for them to buy are composed of new developments (see Figure 9.2), numbering in the hundreds of thousands nationally, built by private developers working in partnership with the Housing Ministry (Jeffreys, 2012). This initiative included opening 3,200 hectares of land for urban development to extend the city of Tangier (Ghannam, 2006) and thousands of new units of housing.

Yet, according to the 2014 census, the region containing Tangier trails only behind the region of the largest city, Casablanca, in numbers of unoccupied and second-home housing units (Maaroufi, no date). Ten years after the initiation of the programme, many cities have been declared 'slum-free' but the fate of the housing that was built is less clear. Its occupancy, and vacancy, was the core subject of the research project that is recounted in the fieldwork stories that follow.

Figure 9.2: On-site advertising for an apartment complex under construction, Tangier 2015

Note: The government subsidy initiative set standard prices for introductory units at 250,000 Dirham (about €25,000).

Source: Photo by the author

These trends that colour housing and its occupancy in the city of Tangier provide some context through which to observe how vacancy is understood there. As a city characterised by the passage of internationally mobile people, unoccupied housing is necessary to accommodate those populations, whether migrant or tourist. Simultaneously, as a city that is growing in population and in its footprint, its housing capacity is increasing in ways that may not match directly with the influx of people. These conditions lead back to the conceptual problem of vacancy, that is, in how it might be understood when observing that it is not simply a matter of the presence or absence of users or dwellers, but also the presence of 'dwellers in absence'.

Conceptualising vacancy through circulatory mobilities

Vacancy has largely emerged in geographies of the built environment in relation to abandonment. From post–crisis places where housing construction is halted and left unoccupied due to the flight of capital (Kitchin et al, 2014), to the incremental decline of buildings from purposeful to ruin (Chelcea, 2015; Lorimer and Murray, 2015), these forms of vacancy are presented as effectively linear transitions from utility to dereliction, sometimes with a distant or uncertain possibility for resuscitation (Dawney, 2020). Yet, some of the current practices of vacancy – particularly those that have sparked more interest in the consequences of when housing is treated as capital more than as dwelling space (Guyer, 2015) – reflect circulations rather than linear transitions. They involve circulations of capital, which may hold housing in limbo as owned but perennially unused for dwelling (Fields, 2015; Fernandez et al, 2016; Forrest et al, 2016; Rogers and Koh, 2017). They also involve the periodic and predictable circulations of middle-class dwellers becoming more mobile between work and home locations (Nadler, 2014; Hilti, 2016), or even non-elite investors becoming 'dual tenure' households, owning and dwelling across more than one property (Hulse and McPherson, 2014). In contrast to vacancy as a linear timeline of abandonment, these owners maintain ties to multiple locations in circulatory mobility, thereby always leaving one location temporarily and periodically vacant.

These emerging forms of circulatory presence and absence simultaneously violate assumptions about how owners 'occupy' as fixed and permanent, and challenge the idea of vacancy as dereliction or abandonment. Circulatory mobilities mean an owner cannot always be present, fulfilling the duties of a good citizen and neighbour in a community (Valverde, 2015). Rather, they index an owner who is active, even if they are absent, in keeping a property maintained and usable against forces of decay. This active absence emerges as 'managing', calling into practice forms of controlled temporary occupancy like property guardianship (Ferreri et al, 2017), or the care work and monitoring needed for second homes and vacation homes (Coppock, 1977; Paris, 2010) in order to keep a house materially functional and prevent unauthorised occupancy.

Many of these problems and strategies for managing periodic presence and absence are evoked in literature on 'remittance houses' (Lopez, 2014), built and owned by migrants in their country of origin. Research on such houses within migration studies indicates how ownership by the absent migrant can function similarly to speculative capital, rendering property as 'full' and unavailable to the dwelling community around it in the long stretches between moments when the owner visits – which range from frequent and regular circulation to indefinite and unfulfilled intentions to 'return'. While these houses are sometimes allocated to family members as dwellers, they have been characterised as 'empty', 'inside-out' and 'wasted' (Agoumy, 2007; Melly, 2010; Mata-Codesal, 2014). These colloquialisms describe their lack of occupancy or their incompleteness as a structure, while still recognising that they are 'owned' property, often being cared for through networks of friends and relatives (Schaab and Wagner, 2020). They become palpably vacant both through their presence as built investments of capital and through the management interventions they require from the surrounding community between the periodic returns of an owner-occupier.

In short, similarly to how Doron (2000) observed the transgressive occupations that filled what were labelled 'dead', 'wasteland' or 'void' spaces, circulatory vacancies are inhabited by something that fills them. The central distinction is that the timescale for an owner's return matters in recognising what might inhabit them: structures marked as abandoned or locked in a limbo of uncertainty become open to transgressive occupations, while housing that is a node in circulatory mobilities – like those of mobile workers, migrants or vacation homeowners – is monitored and protected for its future planned use (see Part III, this volume). The examples I observed of how housing was being 'filled' in Tangier indicate some of the different forms of protection and monitoring that arise for managing vacancy on the shorter timescale of circulatory mobilities.

Fieldwork lessons: the problem of operationalising vacancy

In the summer of 2015, funded by the American Institute of Maghrib Studies, I spent eight weeks doing fieldwork in Tangier to investigate dynamics of property ownership and occupancy. While the main focus of the project was on migrant-owned housing and how cyclical and temporary presences and absences of migrants might be visible in neighbourhoods, I quickly found that the variety of housing vacancies in Tangier made it very difficult to isolate one kind of absence from another. Although I had chosen to come during the summer in order to observe the transition from absence to presence – as many diasporic Moroccans 'return' to use their houses during summer holidays – the transition was not as readily observable as hoped.

Instead, I pursued avenues of observation that would allow me to record how the absence of occupants might be visible and palpable to residents, and, more specifically, which properties were in some way left vacant. On these lines, I performed transect walks in several neighbourhoods known for different eras of housing development, recording impressions about occupancy and vacancy through photography and fieldnotes, while I also inserted myself as a participant observer in housing vacancy as a person seeking to rent a home. This latter method – of seeking housing – led me to the conversations that are recounted and collated in this chapter. These conversations are not comprehensive or conclusive in describing how vacancy is managed in Tangier, but sketch three forms of management labour that become visible in this city of many modes of vacancy: professional guardians, precarious guardians and circulating owners.

Professional guardians

The first form of vacancy management that appeared during this fieldwork was the presence and activity of guardians as observers and nodes of information about vacancy within a neighbourhood (see Figure 9.3). In Tangier, as in Morocco more broadly, it is not uncommon for larger apartment buildings to have a live-in guardian or concierge, part of whose job is knowing the residents and being aware of which apartments may be vacant. Alongside concierges are parking guardians, who monitor and manage a small territory of public

Figure 9.3: The post of guardian, Tangier 2015

Source: Photo by the author

street parking. Beyond these, neighbours may combine resources to employ a street guardian for extra security. As guardians, all of these (almost universally) men spend most of their time as 'eyes on the street' (Jacobs, 1961), keeping track of the activity of the neighbourhood. As I learned through the process of seeking an apartment, some parking guardians use their knowledge of housing vacancy to double as rental agents. Through their perpetual, professional presence, they become a reliable initial point of contact for those seeking to temporarily 'fill' an apartment in the city block where they guard, as they manage vacancy that would otherwise be unadvertised.

Precarious guardians

The second form of vacancy management I found in Tangier was the presence, and absence, of property guardianship not unlike the precarious rental structure now found in some Global North cities (Ferreri et al, 2017), but specific to the forms of housing vacancy found in Tangier. Primarily, these included guardians, like friends or family members, who were invited by an owner, usually a Moroccan citizen resident in Europe, to occupy their home in their absence. In some cases, these were homes that were only partially constructed, so part of the precarity of that living situation lay in navigating the unfinished, sometimes unsafe, parts of the house, alongside a risk of being evicted at short notice – though this was lessened because of their intimate connection to the owner.

In addition, I encountered cases of undocumented migrants from sub-Saharan Africa occupying housing, both in completed developments and unfinished structures. These migrants in particular were the subject of police attention during the summer of my fieldwork, when several apartment blocks were evacuated of their sub-Saharan residents, many of whom were arrested as illegal occupants (RFI, no date). Yet, their role in squatting these apartments is not clear; in an interview, a group of migrants explained to me that, in some cases, their peers would be let into these apartments by a Moroccan person and even charged rent for living there, not knowing that their gatekeeper may not have the right themselves to take ownership. In other words, the lack of guardianship over the empty apartment means that someone on site can take advantage of both the owner and the migrant occupant in 'filling' them. Furthermore, I was unable to determine who the owners might be of these apartments – such as Moroccan citizens living in Morocco, Moroccan citizens living elsewhere or foreigners investing in them as capital or as second homes, among many other possibilities.

The numbers of migrants expelled, along with my observations of and discussions with residents in similar apartment blocks, indicate that a large proportion of the new housing developments have apartments that remain uninhabited by owners. In this case, vacancy is managed through exploitation of unguarded property, which becomes an opportunity for occupancy by those in need of housing.

Circulating owners

Finally, several participants in this fieldwork were examples of dual-tenure owners within the same city. While looking for rental apartments for my own use, I encountered three different owners who were living in Tangier across multiple apartments – meaning that they kept more than one home as furnished and semi-inhabited, which was occasionally rented when possible. In two of these cases, this dual tenure was made possible by the recent housing boom and accompanying subsidies, through which they were able to buy a second apartment even while already having access to a stable first home. Their management of vacancy in these second homes required visiting to check up on them from time to time, which was relatively easy as they were resident in the same city. Yet, unlike what might be expected elsewhere, these properties were not completely turned over to the rental market to be occupied and (hopefully) profitable, though in all three cases, the owners were firmly established as resident in one of their apartments and not the other. Instead, these owners seemed to prefer occasional, short-term, cash-only renters for their alternate dwellings, indicating that part of the reluctance to formally rent them may be related to legal or tax implications. This form of dual tenure – within the same city and without extracting significant profit from the second home – challenges the common rationalities behind the ownership of second homes as vacation homes (in another place), as investment properties or even as a multi-sited household. It creates a peculiar semi-vacancy of housing, being partially dwelled and monitored by an owner that is nearby but only periodically occupying it.

In general, all of these examples involve some kind of active labour to manage vacancy, even when that labour is simply 'being present' as a mechanism of surveillance. I also observed, and was advised by participants, that webcams and other remote technologies are becoming more common to fill that role. Yet, in line with Jane Jacobs' observations about the role of community 'eyes on the street', in these examples, the cases of active guardians – such as the concierges, the authorised dwellers and even the dual-tenure owners – fill more complex roles

Figure 9.4: Being shown around an apartment complex by a security guard, Tangier 2012

Note: The security guard said these are largely already purchased.

Source: Photo by the author

through their guarding activities beyond simply 'surveillance' (see Figure 9.4). These observations are too limited at this point to draw concrete conclusions about the impact or breadth of their multiple roles but – to put it simply – those homes would not be able to be occupied by squatters. Their surveillance would involve not only watching, but also the protection that comes with physical presence of an occupant.

Between ownership and occupancy: an economics of care

These three examples, though only briefly described here, flesh out forms of periodic vacancy that arise from owners who circulate between presence and absence. They illustrate how, in between normative owner–occupancy and total abandonment, some kind of guardianship or surveillance becomes necessary to protect property as an asset, whether or not it is a 'finished' dwelling and safe for habitation. They also demonstrate how guardianship can take different forms with different actors involved: owner and agent, professional and semi-professional, and authorised and unauthorised. These observations open potentially fruitful alternate perspectives on vacancy as a site of productive and informal labour activity within a city's landscape of housing rather than as dereliction or abandonment.

The specificity of Tangier provides a counterpoint to the majority of emerging literature on post-crisis financialisation of housing as an example of non-elite homeowners and the activity their cyclical absence can produce. Some of these pre-date the housing crisis as part of the range of mobilities cutting through Tangier, while others may have been exacerbated by the global push towards buying housing. Inasmuch as the expansion of subsidised developments in Morocco intended for lower-income citizens coincided with the trend towards housing financialisation, these examples of vacancy are not divorced from how housing has increasingly mobilised as capital. Yet, simultaneously, they are not fully explained without considering the role of migration in this city – international out-migration, domestic in-migration and passage of migrants en route to Europe – and how actors involved in these overlapping flows may have intersecting patterns of occupancy in housing that become visible through practices to manage vacancy.

Most pertinently for this volume, these examples show diverse perspectives on what can make a home observable as 'full' when it is enmeshed in circulatory mobilities. Through experimenting with ways of observing vacancy, I learned to focus on the labour required – and actors engaged – in actively managing vacancy through guardianship. Initially, I was inclined to interpret perceived absence as vacancy, as indicated by my conversation with the guardian described in the introduction. However, taking his perspective seriously has meant considering how timescales of absence and presence create different forms of management to fill vacancy. In short, dereliction and transgressive occupations might index properties that are to remain indefinitely vacant, while forms of guardianship, monitoring and surveillance mark the cyclical absence of mobile owners.

References

Abitbol, M. (2009) *Histoire du Maroc*, Paris: Perrin.

Abjiou, A. (2018) 'Tourisme: Tanger tient ses promesses', *L'Economiste*, 31 October. Available at: www.leconomiste.com/article/1035821-tourisme-tanger-tient-ses-promesses (accessed 17 October 2019).

Agoumy, T. (2007) 'The transformative impact of transfer originating from migration on local socio-economic dynamics', in S. Gupta and T. Omoniyi (eds) *The Cultures of Economic Migration: International Perspectives*, London: Ashgate, pp 77 85.

Bialasiewicz, L. and Wagner, L.B. (2015) 'Extra-ordinary Tangier: domesticating practices in a border zone', *GeoHumanities*, 1(1): 131–56.

Chelcea, L. (2015) 'Postindustrial ecologies: industrial rubble, nature and the limits of representation', *Parcours Anthropologiques*, 10: 186–201.

Coppock, J.T. (ed) (1977) *Second Homes: Curse or Blessing?*, Oxford: Pergamon Press.

Dawney, L. (2020) 'Decommissioned places: ruins, endurance and care at the end of the first nuclear age', *Transactions of the Institute of British Geographers*, 45(1): 33–49.

Doron, G.M. (2000) 'The dead zone and the architecture of transgression', *City*, 4(2): 247–63.

Driessen, H. (2007) 'Coping with "Fortress Europe": views from four seaports on the Spanish–Moroccan border', in W. Armstrong and J. Anderson (eds) *Geopolitics of European Union Enlargement*, London: Routledge, pp 94–105.

Fernandez, R., Hofman, A. and Aalbers, M.B. (2016) 'London and New York as a safe deposit box for the transnational wealth elite', *Environment and Planning A*, 48(12): 2443–61.

Ferreri, M., Dawson, G. and Vasudevan, A. (2017) 'Living precariously: property guardianship and the flexible city', *Transactions of the Institute of British Geographers*, 42(2): 246–59.

Fields, D. (2015) 'Contesting the financialization of urban space: community organizations and the struggle to preserve affordable rental housing in New York City', *Journal of Urban Affairs*, 37(2): 144–65.

Forrest, R., Wissink, B. and Koh, S.Y. (eds) (2016) *Cities and the Super-Rich*, Basingstoke: Palgrave Macmillan.

Ghannam, F. (2006) 'Les 170 nouvelles zones urbaines qui seront ouvertes en 2007', *La Vie éco*, 12 October. Available at: www.lavieeco.com/economie/les-170-nouvelles-zones-urbaines-qui-seront-ouvertes-en-2007-2151/ (accessed 21 October 2019).

Guyer, J.I. (2015) 'Housing as "capital"', *HAU: Journal of Ethnographic Theory*, 5(1): 495–500.

Hillali, M. (1996) 'Le cosmopolitanisme à Tanger: Mythe et réalité', *Horizons Maghrebins*, 12(31/32): 42–8.

Hilti, N. (2016) 'Multi-local lifeworlds: between movement and mooring', *Cultural Studies*, 30(3): 467–82.

Howard-Vyse, L. (1882) *A Winter in Tangier and Home Through Spain*, London: Hatchards.

Hulse, K. and McPherson, A. (2014) 'Exploring dual housing tenure status as a household response to demographic, social and economic change', *Housing Studies*, 29(8): 1028–44.

Jacobs, J. (1961) *The Death and Life of Great American Cities*, New York, NY: Random House.

Jeffreys, A. (2012) *The Report: Morocco 2012*, London: Oxford Business Group.

Kanai, M. and Kutz, W. (2011) 'Entrepreneurialism in the globalising city-region of Tangier, Morocco', *Tijdschrift Voor Economische En Sociale Geografie*, 102(3): 346–60.

Kitchin, R., O'Callaghan, C. and Gleeson, J. (2014) 'The new ruins of Ireland? Unfinished estates in the post-Celtic Tiger era', *International Journal of Urban and Regional Research*, 38(3): 1069–80.

Lam, A. and Feather, C. (2016) 'Promoting access to affordable housing finance: Morocco's Fogarim guarantee fund and U.S. housing finance', *Cityscape*, 18(2): 189–200.

Landau, R. (1952) *Portrait of Tangier*, London: Robert Hale.

Liberty, A.L. (1908) *A Day in Tangier*, London: A. and C. Black.

Lopez, S.L. (2014) *The Remittance Landscape: Spaces of Migration in Rural Mexico and Urban USA*, Chicago, IL: University of Chicago Press.

Lorimer, H. and Murray, S. (2015) 'The ruin in question', *Performance Research*, 20(3): 58–66.

Maaroufi, Y. (no date) 'Note d'information du Haut-Commissariat au Plan sur le parc de logements au Maroc à l'occasion de la journée mondiale de l'habitat du 2 octobre 2017', Haut-Commissariat au Plan du Royaume du Maroc. Available at: www.hcp.ma/Note-d-information-du-Haut-Commissariat-au-Plan-sur-le-parc-de-logements-au-Maroc-a-l-occasion-de-la-journee-mondiale-de_a2020.html (accessed 17 October 2019).

Mata-Codesal, D. (2014) 'From "mud houses" to "wasted houses": remittances and housing in rural highland Ecuador', *REMHU: Revista Interdisciplinar Da Mobilidade Humana*, 22(42): 263–80.

Melly, C. (2010) 'Inside-out houses: urban belonging and imagined futures in Dakar, Senegal', *Comparative Studies in Society and History*, 52(1): 37–65.

Miller, S.G. (2001) 'Watering the garden of Tangier: colonial contestations in a Moroccan city', in S. Slyomovics (ed) *The Walled Arab City in Literature, Architecture and History: The Living Medina in the Maghrib*, London and Portland, OR: Frank Cass, pp 25–50.

Nadler, R. (2014) *Plug&Play Places, Lifeworlds of Multilocal Creative Knowledge Workers*, Berlin: De Gruyter Open.

Paris, C. (2010) *Affluence, Mobility and Second Home Ownership*, London: Routledge.

Recensement Général de la Population et de l'Habitat 2014 (2015) *Note sur les premiers résultats du Recensement Général de la Population et de l'Habitat 2014*, Rabat: Haut-Commissariat au Plan du Royaume du Maroc. Available at: https://rgph2014.hcp.ma/downloads/Publications-RGPH-2014_t18649.html (accessed 19 October 2019).

RFI (Radio France Internationale) (no date) 'Maroc: arrestations massives de migrants subsahariens à Tanger – Afrique'. Available at: www.rfi.fr/afrique/20150704-maroc-nouvelles-rafles-migrants-subsahariens-tanger-boukhalef-ivoiriens-expulsions-detentions/ (accessed 23 July 2015).

Rogers, D. and Koh, S.Y. (2017) 'The globalisation of real estate: the politics and practice of foreign real estate investment', *International Journal of Housing Policy*, 17(1): 1–14.

Schaab, T. and Wagner, L. (2020) 'Expanding transnational care networks: comparing caring for families with caring for homes', *Global Networks*, 20(1): 190–207.

Therrien, C. (2019) 'Work, love, refuge, and adventure: contemporary Spanish migrants in the city of Tangier', *The Journal of North African Studies*, 24(1): 175–200.

Thomas, M. (1892) *A Scamper through Spain and Tangier*, London: Hutchinson.

Toutain, O. (2014) 'A solution to finance the rehousing of Morocco's slum dwellers', *ID4D*, 25 September. Available at: https://ideas4development.org/en/involving-third-party-partners-to-finance-rehousing-moroccos-slum-dwellers/ (accessed 21 October 2019).

Valverde, M. (2015) *Chronotopes of Law: Jurisdiction, Scale and Governance*, Chicago, IL: University of Chicago Press.

Viehoff, V.A. (2009) 'Engineering modernity: the provision of water for Tangier 1840–1956', PhD dissertation, University College London, UK.

Wagner, L.B. (2014) 'Trouble at home: diasporic second homes as leisure space across generations', *Annals of Leisure Research*, 17(1): 71–85.

PART III

Reappropriating urban vacant spaces

10

Politicising vacancy and commoning housing in municipalist Barcelona

Mara Ferreri

Introduction

In summer 2014, I attended a public gathering in a small square in the Carpenters Estate, an East London council estate slated for demolition. The event was organised by a collective of single mothers called Focus E15 to mark the occupation of four vacant flats to raise awareness about the destruction of social rented housing in the borough of Newham. Within days, both the protest–occupation and the collective gained high visibility in the national media, becoming something of a flagship struggle in London's housing activism, as well as a clear inspiration for other direct actions against displacement, accumulation by dispossession and gentrification (Gillespie et al, 2018). In photographs, the occupation was usually framed by a large green banner, hanging in front of the facade: 'These homes need people, these people need homes.' The slogan drew attention to the need for social rented housing while denouncing a wasteful system. Powerfully and effectively, it presented a clear antithesis: vacant houses and unhomed people are to be brought together to solve a material, as well as rhetorical, tension. The slogan, I later discovered, had been directly inspired by the chant *'gente sin casas, casas sin gente'* ('people without homes, homes without people') of the Platform of People Affected by Mortgages (PAH) in Spain (Di Feliciantonio, 2017; García-Lamarca, 2017). The ease with which the slogan had travelled between the two contexts evidences not only the important work of transnational solidarity and learning post-2008, but also the resurgence of a politicisation of vacant housing through direct action across the world (Dizon, 2019; Ferreri, 2020b; Noterman, 2020), which demands critical attention (see also the remaining chapters in Part III, this volume).

The connection between the needs of unhomed people and residential vacancy is a powerful rhetorical construct, with a long history. The politicisation of urban vacancy through the right of use above and beyond a title to property can be found throughout the histories and geographies of squatting and direct action (Blomley, 2008; Martínez López, 2017; Watson, 2017). In the Spanish context, the slogan powerfully captured the injustice of high levels of empty housing at times of increased precarisation and homelessness caused by the mortgaged-backed housing bubble and crash in 2008. By giving visibility to the chasm between unused homes and unhomed people, high-visibility campaigning made manifest 'that the poor have a right to not be excluded' (Blomley, 2008: 316) in contrast to the 'right to exclude' of property owners and developers. This challenge to property in the name of social use, described by activists as the reclaiming of the '*función social*' ('social function') of housing, embedded itself in urban politics at different scales; in the city of Barcelona, it filtered from social movements and third sector organisations to influence municipal policymaking, as will be explored in this chapter.

Urban vacant spaces, however, are not just an effect of the urbanisation of crises; they are an active element in their *production and reproduction*, pointing to new 'frontiers' of precarisation, dispossession and territorial restructuring, as well as organising (Safransky, 2014). Collective use in direct confrontation with rent extractivism and unfettered housing financialisation and neoliberalisation (Rolnik, 2019) can generate forms of urban commoning against everyday enclosures (Safransky, 2014; Bresnihan and Byrne, 2015). However, while vacant housing has become a key element in the wider politicisation of property after the global financial crisis (GFC) (O'Callaghan et al, 2018), politicising 'vacancy' remains a contested process of symbolic and practical counterclaims. In this chapter, I argue for the need to explore critical questions around conceptualising and politicising vacancy – as a geographically and historically contingent set of 'new urban ruins' given visibility through Spain's housing and mortgage bubble – to gain a deeper understanding of the role of vacant spaces and their (in)visibility in the context of wider urban dispossession (Ferreri and Vasudevan, 2019). Combining critical policy analysis with ethnographic accounts, I analyse proposals to reclaim the social use of private empty houses by transforming them into social housing in Barcelona. Convergences and divergences between performative, direct reclaiming and municipal policy interventions point to the need for a careful analysis of how vacancy is imagined, governed and contested, as well as a rethinking of what its politicisation might entail in the context of rapid processes of dispossession and revalorisation.

'Knowing' vacancy: two empty housing censuses

The rhetoric of use as a performative counterclaim to property expects vacancy to be static and self-evident: an empty house, land or bloc of flats. As powerfully argued by Sara Safransky (2014), however, the discursive and technical treatment of land and property as 'empty' is anything but self-evident, often drawing on the erasure of existing uses and users, as well as a redrawing of territories to designate new frontiers for dispossession and development. Defining and making visible urban vacancy, whether of an individual dwelling, a building or an entire neighbourhood, is a highly political act. The production of data about empty and vacant properties, chiefly through cartography, is mired in power entanglements and competing interests. As in the somewhat famous case of the 'unfinished estates' of post-real estate boom-and-bust Ireland, making vacancy visible can have unforeseen consequences (Kitchin et al, 2014). Discursively, political claims to use, as in the powerful slogan with which I opened this chapter, can also paradoxically act to obfuscate the root causes of vacancy by simplifying the often complex socially and spatially different ownership arrangements that underwrite 'property' in times of housing financialisation, as well as the political processes that have enabled them. A grounded approach thus requires understanding the conditions and politics of knowledge production about vacancy as a political issue.

In Spain, the scale and extension of the issue of vacant properties after the 2008 crisis was long rumoured, but it only became a well-known phenomenon with the publication of the results of the 2011 census, which estimated a total of 3.5 million vacant dwellings across the country (INE, 2011). As early as 2011, scholars were writing of high vacancy rates and high housing costs as 'the Spanish paradox' (Hoekstra and Vakili-Zad, 2011). A distinctive element of the Spanish housing crisis, which find echoes in the Irish case (O'Callaghan et al, 2018), was the very high level of vacancy due to unprecedented overproduction during the 'housing boom' period. It is estimated that between 2001 and 2011, 'there was a 24 per cent increase in the housing stock (to more than 26 million homes) relative to just a 5.8 per cent increase in the population (to approximately 47 million inhabitants)' (Charnock et al, 2014: 98). The geographies of such housing vacancy were inexorably linked to the national and regional geographies of mortgage repossessions and evictions (Gutiérrez and Domènech, 2018). One of most affected regions was Catalonia, where the census estimated approximately 450,000 vacant dwellings. Inevitably, the high number became a hotly debated topic. Vacant homes at times of widespread evictions and repossessions were not just a visible symptom of the crisis; they became a site of intense politicisation at the level of both grass-roots organising and radical municipalist movements, which were to take centre stage in the Spanish municipal elections of 2015.

The results became particularly politicised in the city of Barcelona. The 2011 census had estimated that the number of vacant houses in the city was equal to 10.8 per cent of its total housing stock – a shocking statistic that movements and new citizenship platforms transformed into a key issue of the 2015 campaign of the municipalist platform Barcelona en Comú (BnC), whose protagonists and politics were closely intertwined with those of the PAH, as well as of autonomous urban and housing movements (França, 2018). The result of this politicisation of vacancy became an electoral promise to undertake a detailed census of all the vacant housing in the city, act upon the reasons for its vacancy and mobilise them for the common good. A new census was necessary not only to update the information, but also to create a solid and reliable data baseline for housing policy interventions, which was, at best, patchy up to that date. In answer to this need, the recently elected BnC government created the Barcelona Housing Observatory (O-HB), a cross-institutional coordination of agencies, with the aim to facilitate data and knowledge sharing across different public organisations, as well as data transparency.[1]

The *cens d'habitatge buits* ('vacant housing census') was a key demand of social movements and of other left-wing parties in the city and region, such as the Candidatura d'Unitat Popular ('Candidacy of Popular Unity' [CUP]), a Catalan alliance of left-wing parties that is traditionally seen as representing the position of anti-capitalist urban social movements. In 2016, Maria Rovira Torrens, representative of the CUP branch at the Barcelona Municipal Council, presented a series of formal propositions and objections to the 2016–25 city housing plan, pressing the urgency of this new census, alongside direct interventions by the local government to expropriate empty dwellings and incorporate them into the municipal public housing stock (CUP Capgirem Barcelona, 2016).

From empty houses to social housing

The proposition of reclaiming empty housing as a possible solution to the need for social housing provision, historically less than 2 per cent of all housing stock, was not only mooted from 'anti-capitalist' left-wing quarters; instead, the idea had permeated public debate and policy proposals since the GFC. In local policy debates, the emergence of programmes to bring vacant housing back into use (*Mobilització d'habitatges buits* ['mobilisation of vacant housing']) became an important example of post-crisis 'political innovation' in policymaking regarding the right to housing (Antón-Alonso et al, 2017). The idea of 'mobilising' vacant dwellings to respond to the demand for social housing in the city of Barcelona had already been an item of discussion through the *Acuerdo Ciutadano* ('Citizen Agreement'), a mechanism of participatory policymaking between the local government and representatives of 700 organisations, including community groups, businesses, unions and educational institutions.[2] This led to the establishment of the *Pisos Buits* ('Vacant Homes') programme, alongside other policies aimed at bottom-up social initiatives (García Bernardos and Iglesias Costa, 2015).

While awaiting the results of the census, third sector organisations were also weighing in on the debate on their own terms. The association of third sector housing organisations denounced the close link between mortgage repossession and vacant dwellings in the hands of financial institutions. Based on the *Registre d'habitatges buits o amb ocupants sense títol habilitant* ('registry of vacant housing') of the Generalitat of Catalonia, it was estimated that 47,000 of all the dwellings on the register were owned by financial entities (mostly banks and real estate investment trusts [REITs]) (Taula d'Entitats del Tercer Sector Social de Catalunya, 2017: 6). The number prompted a debate around the question of bank-owned vacant dwellings and a report, published by the Board of Third Sector Organisations in Catalonia, aptly titled 'Banks' vacant houses: a lost opportunity to expand the social housing stock?' (Taula d'Entitats del Tercer Sector Social de Catalunya, 2017). Also in 2017, the CONFABV, the regional confederation of neighbourhood associations, launched the *Omplim els buits* ('Filling the empties') programme to address vacancy through community-led self-refurbishment. Finally, in 2018, the newly formed O-HB established a working group named *D'habitatge buit a habitatge social* ('From empty houses to social housing'). In the expanded housing policy community of Barcelona, the reallocation of 'homes needing people' to 'people needing homes' was becoming a self-evident solution that needed acting upon.

Surprising results and policy responses

The urgency created by pressure from social movements, left-wing parties and third sector housing met with the logistical complexity of a detailed survey of a densely populated territory, characterised by demographic changes and rapid real estate market dynamics, such as the unprecedented growth of the private rented sector to 31 per cent of the total housing stock (O-HB, 2020: 9). To obtain a more up-to-date and accurate picture, the census contrasted data from the municipal registry of people domiciled in the city with the registry of the Barcelona water company to detect dwellings with limited water consumption; this was followed by in-person visits in the city's 73 neighbourhoods. The census took considerable resources and time: it was organised in three research phases, between October 2017 and December 2018, and employed between 15 and 40 researchers (Ajuntament de Barcelona, 2018). It was finally concluded in March 2019, a few months before the end of the first legislature of BnC.

The results of the vacant homes census brought to light two politically significant issues. The first was an important discrepancy between national and local statistics on the accurate total number of the housing stock. In the city of Barcelona, the change amounted to 4.8 per cent fewer homes than noted by the 2011 census (O-HB, 2018). This had implications for the estimated number of vacant dwellings, both in the region and in the city, and debunked the key statistical finding of the 2011 census: instead of 10.88 per cent of the total housing stock, equal to 88,259 dwellings, the total number of vacant dwellings in the city was found to be 1.22 per cent, equal to 10,052 dwellings (Ajuntament de Barcelona, 2019). The difference between the former and latter estimates was both quantitatively and qualitatively significant. In place of yet another proof of the 'Spanish paradox', such a low proportion of vacant housing in the city signalled a 'hot' real estate market and a potential crisis of supply in response to demand.[3] Politically, the first results offered ammunition to those commentators and analysts who bemoaned the obstinate persistence on the question of vacancy as a solution to the need for low-income, secure housing in the city.

The second issue highlighted by the vacant homes census was a different property composition from the one imagined by both politicians and urban social movements. Preliminary results published in 2018 showed that while 25 per cent of vacant properties were indeed in the hands of financial entities and companies, the majority (70.36 per cent) were owned by individuals (*petit propietaris*) (Ajuntament de Barcelona, 2018).[4] Moreover, of the over 5,000 empty dwellings that were identified as suitable for use as social rented housing, over 3,000 required refurbishment or renewal work, and around 650 were destined for unlicensed tourist use (Ajuntament de Barcelona, 2019: 19). These results led the municipality to embark upon a three-pronged programme: to mobilise vacant dwellings owned by individuals through guaranteed social rental contracts (the *Borsa de Lloguer*); to support the refurbishment of dilapidated empty dwellings through the municipal Rehabilitation Services; and to sanction all those dwellings that might be vacant for long periods of time as part of a seasonal tourist offer, often at the margins of official tourist licensing (Cócola-Gant, 2016; Sans and Quaglieri Domínguez, 2016).

The different compositions in property ownership challenged a political analysis of accumulation by dispossession dominated by the idea of a large transfer of asset from small owner-occupiers to financialised real estate investment groups. Nonetheless, financial investors and their agents were still responsible for at least 25 per cent of all vacant housing. To tackle this issue, local policymakers could draw on a progressive legal framework around two regional laws passed by the Catalan Parliament to enshrine the 'right to housing': the Llei pel Dret a l'Habitatge de Catalunya ('Catalan Law for the Right to Housing') in 2007[5] and the Llei 24/2015 (a law created through a people's initiative spearheaded by the PAH). Financial entities such as banks and investment trusts, and their agencies, could be fined if their dwellings were empty for over two years, in accordance with the Catalan Law for the Right to Housing (Llei 18/2007). Additionally, if properties are dilapidated, financial entities can be issued with conservation ordnances. Other policy instruments include the right for preferential acquisition of vacant dwellings, the taxation of owners of vacant dwellings and the possibility of temporary expropriation of vacant housing to include them in the municipal social rented registry (Ajuntament de Barcelona, 2019). Despite these notable legal and policy responses, however, the application of these laws has been limited and often contingent upon the ability of organised residents to apply pressure through protests and occupations. The following two vignettes from the Barcelona district of Sants-Montjuïc illustrate limitations around politicising vacancy, while also outlining the potential for a politics of commoning temporary vacancy as new ruins within a rapidly shifting real estate landscape.

Radical counterclaims

Both public policies and political mobilisations around vacancy are often driven by largely static imaginaries of ruins and vacancy that imply a prolonged period of dilapidation and inactivity. Vacancy is imagined as an easily recognisable long-term condition; the reality, however, tends to be far more complex and dynamic, requiring adapting imaginaries and conceptualisations to rapidly changing conditions.

In the framework of global housing financialisation and real estate expansion, this involves a rethinking of different urban temporalities and their (in)visibilities. Politicising vacancy often involves a performative strategy around such invisibilities. Acts of claims-making can function as powerful connectors between urban processes that appear disparate on the surface, such as evictions and foreign investment into short-term letting. Anti-displacement graffiti in areas affected by high short-term lettings for tourists, for instance, have started deploying different languages for different addressees. The slogan 'People get evicted for your enjoyment' implicates English-speaking foreign visitors into local dynamics of residential dispossession. By its side, a stencil addresses Catalan speakers in a call for collectivising individual struggles: 'If you can't do it alone ... together we can do anything!' (see Figure 10.1). The ladder hints at practical ways of reclaiming home through occupation.

The occupation of vacant housing, and particularly those owned by financial institutions, has become a widely known component of the repertoire of housing movements across Spain (Martínez López and García Bernardos, 2015; García-Lamarca, 2017; see also the chapters

Figure 10.1: Stencil graffiti on a wall, District Sants-Montjuic, May 2019

Source: Photo by the author

by Di Feliciantonio and O'Callaghan and by McArdle, this volume) and 'has converted into a distinguishing mark of the contemporary housing struggles' (García-Calderón Pavón and Janoschka, 2016: 113). In Barcelona, neighbourhood housing assemblies and citywide networks, from people affected by mortgages to new tenants' unions, have increasingly publicly recognised the occupations of vacant dwellings through squatting as a legitimate solution to the inability of local governments to meet urgent housing needs; in 2019, the official waiting list for 'emergency housing' for street homeless households reached 550 (Merino, 2019).

As recently documented by a militant research project into organised mass squatting, at least 26 per cent of housing occupations in Catalonia are the direct result of assembly-based organising (Obra Social Barcelona, 2018: 34). Challenging categorical distinctions between *political* squatting and squatting '*for housing*' (Martinez López, 2018), which reproduce counterproductive hierarchies of needs and motivations, housing assemblies across Catalonia often support squatting directly and indirectly alongside other 'insurgent acts of being-in-common' (García-Lamarca, 2015), such as eviction resistance and street protests. In this sense, the reappropriations of spaces not only meet individual needs, but also function as a form of commoning, 'where possession does not rest on liberal sociality, but rather is collectively enacted' (Noterman, 2020: 12) through processes of self-organisation and the everyday sharing of knowledge and resources. In such a performative reclaiming of collective possession of vacant housing, bundled and individualised notions of legal title to property become unsettled and distributed, even if squatters decide for tactical reasons to engage with individualising processes of institutional recognition as 'persons in housing need'.

Moreover, taking back vacant property through occupations reframes relations of subordination – between the poor and those with resources or title to property – as relations of oppression (Blomley, 2008), such as in the earlier example about short-term letting, touristification and displacement. Occupations thus become a tool to make visible and politicise new dynamics and temporalities of vacancy in the city. Rather than the ruins of a recession, financial investment can be a key driver of vacancy in contemporary cities, for instance, through the operation of REITs (see Power and Risager, 2019). In Spain, REITs usually operate by targeting tenanted blocs of properties, which are purchased with the aim of refurbishing the flats to a higher standard and selling them on the open market. A 2016 investigative report denounced the fact that property purchases by investment funds accounted for 43 per cent of all real estate market transactions in the city of Barcelona (Garde, 2016). Simultaneously, local housing assemblies began protesting against and raising awareness of REITs as a facet of the new real estate boom and an important factor in exacerbating the housing crisis in urban areas (García-Lamarca, 2020).

Of the estimated 76 apartment blocks acquired by investment trusts between 2015 and 2017, 16 were purchased by the Finnish fund Vauras Investment (García, 2019). One of them was a bloc of flats near the popular tourist destination of Plaça d'Espanya and the National Museum of Catalan Art. Tenants on short-term contracts were asked to leave, and the few flats with lifelong rental contracts became empty after the death or relocation of elderly tenants. In response to this, in the summer of 2017, a housing direct action group occupied the six vacant flats to house formerly homeless households, which included four single mothers with children, and created a self-managed assembly, calling themselves Bloc Llavors.[6] The vacant space being occupied was the result not of mortgage repossessions, as in PAH 'recuperations' (Gonick, 2016), but rather by new frontiers of dispossession opened by the global real estate sector, and the widespread residential precarity experienced by individuals and families, as declared by the large banner dropped during an eviction resistance in May 2019, which read 'Thinking, acting and building against the precarisation of our lives' (see Figure 10.2). Some members of the assembly – but by no means all – demanded a formalisation of their stay through social rented contracts mediated by the municipality. In January 2020, after the occupiers had successfully resisted four eviction attempts, officers from the Barcelona city government publicly backed these demands and threatened the investment trust with the use of the city and regional laws available to enforce a negotiation.[7] Despite the resistance and this institutional backing, the occupants were evicted on 3 March 2020, less than two weeks before the announcement of the national lockdown and suspension of all eviction proceedings due to the COVID-19 pandemic.

The two vignettes are examples of politicising urban vacancy that challenge common understandings and enact a wider critique of the effects of global real estate processes. Both cases highlight how the temporalities of vacancy are central to conceptualising the politics of occupation. In the first case, the displacement and vacancy produced by short-term tourist lettings are often temporary, making them invisible to legislators. Nonetheless, they are inscribed in the withdrawal of properties from long-term residential use, ushering in higher rental costs and transience that are permanently transforming neighbourhood composition. Similarly, for the operations of REITs to be profitable,

Figure 10.2: Banner drop at Bloc Llavors, District Sants-Montjuic, May 2019

Source: Photo by the author

the time period between emptying, refurbishing and reselling the properties needs to be short. In both cases, it is unlikely that the conditions of vacancy would have been detected by vacant housing policies designed around ideas of long-term, abandoned or dilapidated housing units. The targeted actions discussed earlier politicised vacancy by addressing the new, heightened temporalities of touristification and investment. Assembly-based neighbourhood self-organisation can be seen to enact both performative and practical forms of collective repossession, reshaping imaginaries of urban vacancy and the possibility of transforming them into commons.

Conclusions

Urban vacant spaces are key to understanding and politicising the urbanisation of crises. In the context of heightened precarisation of urban life, they are clear indicators of rapidly emerging geographies of financialisation and rent extractivism but can also be the focus of plural imaginaries and progressive policy responses. Reflecting on the politics of understanding and politicising vacancy raises the question of what types of urban vacancy – and processes of ruination and abandonment – are privileged or left invisible in critical analysis. As I have argued in this chapter, such an approach necessarily understands urban vacancy in its interconnected spatial and temporal dimensions. A situated and ground-up approach to policy and activist responses can offer a nuanced diagnostic of what kinds of urban politics are possible and what constellations of actors are required to instigate radical counterclaims (Ferreri and Vasudevan, 2019).

The controversy around the rationale and results of the two censuses of empty houses in Barcelona reveals how inadequate definitions and blunt policy instruments can limit progressive responses to post-2008 urban vacancy. While the political insistence on vacant housing was a significant element in the wider politicisation of property after the GFC, from the point of view of a systemic critique, such insistence could be criticised as misguided. In the fast-paced investment circuits of globalised cities, tools designed to detect and address long-term vacancy are inevitably bound to fall short of the needs of unhomed people and of residents at risk of displacement. The symbolic and practical actions undertaken by neighbourhood housing assemblies discussed in the latter part of the chapter offer a reframing of the causes of vacant property that challenges common understandings. These fleeting but highly visible examples of counter-power make a strong bottom–up case for a broader politicisation of (temporary) vacancy in rapid processes of urban dispossession and revalorisation.

I understand 'politicising vacancy' as a contested process of engendering symbolic and practical counterclaims to place and property in dynamic relation to, and against, site-specific forms of displacement and dispossession (Ferreri, 2020a). In such a shifting terrain, engaging with municipalist policymaking and social movements makes it possible to acknowledge the everyday politics of expanding understanding and possibilities for action. The politicisation of urban vacancy inevitably leads to contesting the very legitimacy of private property (O'Callaghan et al, 2018). Such a contestation is powerfully embodied in the occupation and reclaiming of vacant properties as collectively managed commons to 'think, act and build against the precarisation of life'. Beyond calls for reallocating 'housing without people' to 'people without housing', such actions intervene in key spatio-temporal articulations of flows of investment and dispossession, and enact a collective politics of radical emplacement (Ferreri, 2020b). While often short-lived, in Barcelona and elsewhere, these performative occupations function as a much-needed critique of the limits of inadequate understandings and policy instruments, and raise urgent political questions about the wider rhythms of ruination of urban life by financialisation and real estate interests.

Notes

[1]   See: https://ohb.cat/visor/#/23210/2016
[2]   The *Acuerdo Ciutadano* was set up in 2006 (see: www.bcn.cat/barcelonainclusiva/es/que_es html)
[3]   It is widely accepted in policy circles and orthodox housing economics that a 4–5 per cent vacancy of total stock is desirable to support locational mobility and demographic changes, while anything below 4 per cent immediately signals an 'overheated' housing market.
[4]   The remaining under 5 per cent was made up of 'other cases' and data are not available.
[5]   Llei 18/2007, de 28 de desembre.
[6]   See: https://obrasocialbcn.net/bloc-llavors/
[7]   Institutional support draws on a combination of regional laws (18/2007 and 24/2015), aided by a housing emergency decree that had been recently approved by the Catalan Parliament (Decret Llei 17/2019, 23 desembre).

References

Ajuntament de Barcelona (2018) 'Cens d'habitatges buits a Barcelona. Resultats primera i segona fas', press release, 27 March. Available at: http://ajuntament.barcelona.cat/premsa/2018/03/27/el-cens-dhabitatge-buit-de-barcelona-detecta-un-152-de-pisos-sense-habitar-2/ (accessed 7 June 2020).

Ajuntament de Barcelona (2019) *Pla pel Dret a l'Habitatge de Barcelona 2016–2025 Balanç 2018*, Barcelona: Ajuntament de Barcelona.

Antón-Alonso, F., Cruz, H., Porcel, S., Blanco, I., Vidal-Folch, L. and Gomà, R. (2017) *Innovació i Metròpoli: Innovació social i política, densitat institucional i vulnerabilitat urbana a la Barcelona metropolitana*, Barcelona: AMB, IERMB and IGOP.

Blomley, N. (2008) 'Enclosure, common right and the property of the poor', *Social & Legal Studies*, 17(3): 311–31.

Bresnihan, P. and Byrne, M. (2015) 'Escape into the city: everyday practices of commoning and the production of urban space in Dublin', *Antipode*, 47(1): 36–54.

Charnock, G., Purcell, T. and Ribera-Fumaz, R. (2014) *The Limits to Capital in Spain: Crisis and Revolt in the European South*, Basingstoke: Palgrave Macmillan.

Cócola-Gant, A. (2016) 'Holiday rentals: the new gentrification battlefront', *Sociological Research Online*, 21(3): 112–20.

CUP (Candidatura d'Unitat Popular) Capgirem Barcelona (2016) 'Objections to the Right to Housing Plan of Barcelona en Comú (2016–2025)', paper presented at the CUP Jornades 2017 sobre habitatge (December), Barcelona.

Di Feliciantonio, C. (2017) 'Social movements and alternative housing models: practicing the "politics of possibilities" in Spain', *Housing, Theory and Society*, 37(1): 38–56.

Dizon, H.M. (2019) 'Philippine housing takeover: how the urban poor claimed their right to shelter', *Radical Housing Journal*, 1(1): 105–29.

Ferreri, M. (2020a) 'Painted bullet holes and broken promises: understanding and challenging municipal dispossession in London's public housing "decanting"', *International Journal of Urban and Regional Research*, 44(6): 1007–22.

Ferreri, M. (2020b) 'Contesting displacement through radical emplacement and occupations in austerity Europe', in P. Adey, J. Bowstead, K. Brickell, V. Desai, M. Dolton, A. Pinkerton and A. Siddiqi (eds) *The Handbook of Displacement*, London: Palgrave Macmillan.

Ferreri, M. and Vasudevan, A. (2019) 'Vacancy at the edges of the precarious city', *Geoforum*, 101: 165–73.

França, J. (2018) *Habitar la trinxera | Històries del moviment pel dret a l'habitatge a Barcelona*, Barcelona: Fundació Periodisme Plural i l'Editorial Octaedro.

García, G. (2019) 'Veïnes d'un bloc del Poble-sec de Barcelona, en mans d'un inversor finlandés', *La Directa*, 18 January. Available at: https://directa.cat/veines-dun-bloc-del-poble-sec-de-barcelona-en-mans-dun-inversor-finlandes/ (accessed 7 June 2020).

García Bernardos, A. and Iglesias Costa, M. (2015) 'La ciudad en disputa: crisis, modelos de ciudad y políticas urbanas en Barcelona', *Quid*, 16(5): 39–68.

García-Calderón Pavón, I. and Janoschka, M. (2016) 'Viviendas en disputa – ¿espacios de emancipación? Un análisis de las luchas por la vivienda en Madrid', *Historia Actual Online*, 40: 113–27.

García-Lamarca, M. (2015) 'Insurgent acts of being-in-common and housing in Spain: making urban commons?', in M. Dellenbaugh, M. Kip, M. Bieniok, A. Müller and M. Schwegmann (eds) *Urban Commons: Moving Beyond State and Market*, Berlin: De Gruyter, pp 165–77.

García-Lamarca, M. (2017) 'Creating political subjects: collective knowledge and action to enact housing rights in Spain', *Community Development Journal*, 52(3): 421–35.

García-Lamarca, M. (2020) 'Real estate crisis resolution regimes and residential REITs: emerging socio-spatial impacts in Barcelona', *Housing Studies*, online first, DOI: 10.1080/02673037.2020.1769034.

Garde, C. (2016) 'El 43% dels pisos de Barcelona jaels compren inversors immobiliaris', *Nació Digital*, 7 September. Available at: www.naciodigital.cat/noticia/115327/43/dels/pisos/barcelona/ja/compren/inversors/immobiliaris (accessed 7 June 2020).

Gillespie, T., Hardy, K. and Watt, P. (2018) 'Austerity urbanism and Olympic counter-legacies: gendering, defending and expanding the urban commons in East London', *Environment and Planning D: Society and Space*, 36(5): 812–30.

Gonick, S. (2016) 'From occupation to recuperation: property, politics and provincialization in contemporary Madrid', *International Journal of Urban and Regional Research*, 40(4): 833–48.

Gutiérrez, A. and Domènech, A. (2018) 'The mortgage crisis and evictions in Barcelona: identifying the determinants of the spatial clustering of foreclosures', *European Planning Studies*, 26(10): 1939–60.

Hoekstra, J. and Vakili-Zad, C. (2011) 'High vacancy rates and rising house prices: the Spanish paradox', *Tijdschrift Voor Economische En Sociale Geografie*, 102(1): 55–71.

INE (National Institute of Statistics) (2011) 'Censos de Población y Vivienda 2011', press release, 18 April. Available at: www.ine.es/prensa/np775.pdf (accessed 7 June 2020).

Kitchin, R., O'Callaghan, C. and Gleeson, J. (2014) 'The new ruins of Ireland? Unfinished estates in the post-Celtic Tiger era', *International Journal of Urban and Regional Research*, 38(3): 1069–80.

Martínez López, M.A. (2017) 'Squatters and migrants in Madrid: interactions, contexts and cycles', *Urban Studies*, 54(11): 2472–89.

Martínez López, M.A. (ed) (2018) *The Urban Politics of Squatters' Movements*, London: Palgrave Macmillan.

Martínez López, M.A. and García Bernardos, À. (2015) 'Ocupar las plazas, liberar edificios', *ACME: An International Journal for Critical Geographies*, 14(1): 157–84.

Merino, A. (2019) 'L'espera eterna per accedir a un pis d'emergència a Barcelona', *Nació Digital*, 28 September. Available at: www.naciodigital.cat/noticia/188097/espera/eterna/accedir/pis/emergencia/Barcelona (accessed 7 June 2020).

Noterman, E. (2020) 'Taking back vacant property', *Urban Geography*, online first, DOI: 10.1080/02723638.2020.1743519.

Obra Social Barcelona (2018) *¡La vivienda para quien la habita! Informe sobre ockupación de vivienda vacía en Catalunya*, Obra Social Barcelona, Barcelona. Available at: https://obrasocialbcn.net/informe-ockupacio/ (accessed 7 June 2020).

Observatori Metropolità de l'Habitatge de Barcelona (O-HB) (2020) 'L'habitatge a la metròpoli de Barcelona 2019', Barcelona: O-HB.

O'Callaghan, C., Di Feliciantonio, C. and Byrne, M. (2018) 'Governing urban vacancy in post-crash Dublin: contested property and alternative social projects', *Urban Geography*, 39(6): 868–91.

O-HB (Observatori Metropolità de l'Habitatge de Barcelona) (2018) *L'habitatge a la metròpoli de Barcelona*, Barcelona: O-HB.

O-HB (Observatori Metropolità de l'Habitatge de Barcelona) (2020) *L'habitatge a la metròpoli de Barcelona 2019*, Barcelona: O-HB.

Power, E. and Risager, B.S. (2019) 'Rent-striking the REIT: reflections on tenant organizing', *Radical Housing Journal*, 1(2): 81–101.

Rolnik, R. (2019) *Urban Warfare*, London: Verso.

Safransky, S. (2014) 'Greening the urban frontier: race, property, and resettlement in Detroit', *Geoforum*, 56: 237–48.

Sans, A.A. and Quaglieri Domínguez, A. (2016) 'Unravelling Airbnb: urban perspectives from Barcelona', in A.P. Russo and G. Richards (eds) *Reinventing the Local in Tourism: Producing, Consuming and Negotiating Place*, Bristol: Channel View Publications, pp 209–28.

Taula d'Entitats del Tercer Sector Social de Catalunya (2017) *Els habitatges buits dels bancs. Una oportunitat perduda per ampliar el parc d'habitatge social?*, Barcelona: Taula d'entitats del Tercer Sector Social de Catalunya.

Watson, D. (2017) *Squatting in Britain 1945–1955: Housing, Politics, and Direct Action*, London: Merlin Press.

11

Spatio-legal world-making in vacant buildings: property politics and squatting movements in the city of São Paulo

Matthew Caulkins

Introduction

The definition of urban vacancy is fraught with conceptual and practical difficulties. The definitions vary as widely as do the different forms of state intention designed to reduce vacancy. With this in mind, the proposition here is that vacancy is the frontier space where different spatio-legal world-making projects collide. This chapter centres on three conflicting spatio-legal logics and how they relate to persistent vacant spaces in the centre of São Paulo. Recent statistics for the metropolitan region highlight the explosive combination of 595,691 vacant buildings with the potential of being occupied and 639,839 inhabitants left homeless or living in precarious conditions (Fundação Pinheiros, 2018). On the one hand, a market logic values vacancy as a necessary condition for the generation of speculative profits. On the other, the bureaucratic logic of controlled consumption views vacancy as inefficient because it does not provide socially or economically productive uses. Lastly, squatting movements see the potential in these vacant spaces to reduce the astronomical housing deficit and, in particular, the lack of centrally located social housing.

   This chapter argues that vacancy is a socially constructed category (Sack, 1983), both spatially and legally (Delaney, 2010). Ideas of empty property and empty space are entwined and cannot be completely separated. Spaces are considered vacant because they are not deemed economically or socially productive, and because they do not present visible signs of being actively owned. The physical emptiness can facilitate potential sales or being filled with different social uses (Vasudevan, 2015). However, the concept of vacancy is contested. The research this chapter draws on – interviews held at a particular moment in Brazilian politics in 2016 when both federal and municipal administrations were in the hands of the Partido dos Trabalhadores ('Workers Party' [PT]) – focused on a conflict in a space of vacancy, understanding conflicts as privileged moments of social construction that destabilise and potentially realign the social fabric by pitting different spatio-legal projects against each other. The claim of this chapter is that different spatio-legal imaginaries clash in concrete spaces through contact between their distinct lived expressions. In the example discussed here, it is the material experience of a police force that clashes with practices of micro-sovereignty at an occupation. This is the case even though the state's dominant spatio-legal imaginary appears impermeable to the claims of occupations and their counter-projects.

The chapter presents literature highlighting how 'vacancy' is in the eye of the beholder. The following section begins by discussing conflicting interpretations of the vacancy of places undergoing gentrification processes (Smith, 1986), then moves on to distinctions between conceived and lived space, conflicts between official and unofficial legal worlds, and the co-constitutive nature of the spatial and the legal (Delaney, 2010). Then, these concepts are used to discuss the example of conflicting spatio-legal projects in vacant spaces in the city of São Paulo.

Spatio-legal world-making in the urban frontier

Neil Smith's (1986) path-breaking discussion interprets redevelopment in New York as a territorial project following frontier dynamics. Two different spatio-legal imaginaries interpret the process differently. In one explanation of this project, there is a back-to-the-city movement, where people are moving back to an abandoned part of town. Artists and other creative types are interpreted as pioneers 'roughing it' in lofts of downtrodden neighbourhoods. A different version sees capital, rather than people, as setting the key dynamics (Smith, 1979). The state disinvests in certain neighbourhoods (Marcuse, 1985), creating a rent gap that makes investment once more attractive. That same frontier logic was present as European colonial projects visualised socially vibrant Indigenous territories in South America as empty lands (Ugarte et al, 2019). A spatio-legal imaginary founded on the Cartesian notion of empty space inferred the moral imperative for those empty lands to become economically productive (Blomley, 2002). Similarly, run-down, inner-city areas are considered empty of productive uses and ripe for redevelopment. It is this urban real estate development – 'gentrification writ large' (Smith, 2002: 447) – that has now become a global urban strategy. However, local inhabitants see those same 'empty' territories as vibrant places filled with socially productive uses. Furthermore, it is not only distinct imaginaries that collide in these examples; rather, the lived spatio-legal practices of developers clash with the lived experiences of local inhabitants. Architects and planners may draw up plans for redevelopment projects, but it is in concrete places that bulldozers, trucks and construction workers clash with flesh-and-blood local residents. In order to understand these dynamics in more depth, I turn now to the distinction between conceived and lived space in the work of Henri Lefebvre.

Lefebvre (1991 [1974]) distinguishes between the role of conceived and lived space in the social processes that lead to the production of space. Conceived spaces are those created by spatial technicians like architects and engineers. These are technical spaces in the service of the state and capital. Lefebvre does not distinguish between state and capital, presenting the idea of the bureaucratic society of controlled consumption (Butler, 2012). On the other hand, lived space is the space of the subaltern, the space of resistance of the working class. Lefebvre's work seeks to open up space for resistance movements, as he understands that any effective social change depends on social force (Gray, 2018). However, his work suffers from an overly rigid distinction where the working class are equated with lived space and conceived space is equated with capital. Here, I will extend his initial discussion to understand how any socio-spatial project is both conceived and lived. Redevelopment is lived as well as conceived, just as squatters and street protesters not only live, but also conceive, their counter-projects.

In search of the role of the law in these projects, we turn to legal pluralism, occupations and nomos, based on the work of Robert Cover (Matthews, 2017). Cover (1983) discusses the creation of a community-based 'nomos' or system of meaning. These nomoi are world-creating and depend on a common corpus of narratives that educate the individual as part of a community that 'work[s] out the implications of [its] law' (Cover, 1983: 13). In contrast, the imperial law of state institutions rests on weak interpersonal commitments, an 'objective mode of discourse and the impartial and neutral application of norms' (Cover, 1983: 13). Cover's work resonates with the strong utopianism of squatting movements and their struggles with local states. In Cover's discussion of the fertility of nomoi, an excess of law is created by these utopian groups. The jurispathic function of judges, then, is to kill that excess of laws, as they decide to uphold certain nomoi and punish others as deviant. In this vision attuned to the creation of legal worlds by social movements, commitment becomes the test of these home-grown community normative worlds in the face of state coercion. However, Cover's work has been criticised for its lack of attention to the spatial dynamics of normative construction (Delaney, 2010). The remainder of the section seeks to bring the spatial and legal aspects of conflicts over vacancy together.

Delaney's (2010) research programme[1] on *The Spatial, the Legal and the Pragmatics of World-Making* brings together critical geography and critical legal studies to understand the way space and law are co-constructed in everyday situations. This focus allows the work to notice the 'production and maintenance of unremarkableness' (Delaney, 2010: 42). Not only is the law drawn upon in (legal) conflicts, but its meanings are also internalised in everyday life. So, too, with space. Certain events rupture that unremarkableness, bringing to light the spatio-legal settings that constituted the 'nomoscape' in the first place. In Delaney's (2010: 150) words, squats can be understood as 'an embodied performance that disconfirms prevailing and privileged encodings'. The dominant spatio-legal understanding of property and economic productivity forms a coherent project that is promoted by developers and the state. Occupations promote a counter-project linking property to socially productive uses. Finally, 'nomospheric technicians' are the strategically situated actors, such as judges and lawyers in courts, who create, defend and promote spatio-legal understandings. The shortcoming of Delaney's work is its focus on *official* projects and counter-projects created by *official* technicians, such as lawyers and judges. In this way, it misses those unofficial technicians who, at times, are able to harness social movements to promote alternative socio-legal projects (however, for one such analysis utilising Delaney and Cover's work, see Matthews, 2017). Notwithstanding the limitations of each author's work, the bringing together of elements of these three conceptualisations – Lefebvre's forceful description of the production of space, Cover's dynamic view of the creation of law within utopian communities and Delaney's account of spatio-legal world-making – can illuminate spatio-legal projects and counter-projects as they clash in vacant spaces.

The conflict in São Paulo

Brazilian cities provide an unusually fertile test ground for our discussion as decades of activism of the National Forum for Urban Reform resulted in innovative legal doctrines. The 'social function of property' was enshrined in the 1988 Constitution and later in the 2001 City Statute of São Paulo (Fernandes, 2007). The social function of property is a legal doctrine that many Latin American countries share, arguably translated as the 'social obligation norm' in English (Mirow, 2010). In cities, it implies that property must provide a social function and unproductive properties can be expropriated by the state. The city of São Paulo provides further interest for our discussion. There have been extremely high rates of property vacancy in the city as a result of the hollowing out of the centre in the 1960s and cycles of disinvestment (Pereira, 2012). The 2010 census indicated that there were 290,000 vacant residential properties in the city of São Paulo alone (Earle, 2012). At the same time, the city presents a huge housing deficit. Numbers vary widely between the official figure of 133,000 and the insistence by the *movimentos de moradia* ('housing movements') that the number is 809,419 (Pereira, 2012). We can broadly identify two kinds of property activism. One is the quiet property activism of the peripheral favelas, where encroachment works by staying under the radar in hopes of avoiding eviction (Bayat, 2000). Another type is the loud activism of inner-city *cortiços* ('slum tenements') that led to the current strategy of occupying buildings (Earle, 2012). As local activists tell the history, initially, there were only *ocupação denuncia* ('protest occupations') but now all occupations serve the double function of protest and, at least temporarily, *ocupação moradia* ('housing occupations').

In the discussion in the following section, there are not two, but three, spatio-legal logics that can be observed as they move back and forth between relationships of cooperation and conflict: a market logic as the building is bought and sold; the logic of the public administration that was focusing increasingly on vacancy in those years; and the logic of the squatting movement that occupied the building in two waves (2002–07 and 2010–present). The building we will focus on is known as Prestes Maia. This is where I held semi-structured interviews over a six-month period in 2016 with residents and movement coordinators of the Movimento Moradia Luta e Justiça ('Housing Struggle and Justice Movement' [MMLJ]) that occupies the Prestes Maia building. Residents and coordinators are made up of a mix of peripheral favela and central *cortiço* residents, who work in the centre of the city, and homeless people. They are known within the housing movements by the politically generative neologism '*sem-teto*' ('roofless'). The Prestes Maia building was previously a cloth factory that went bankrupt in the 1970s, was repossessed by Citibank in the 1980s and was bought back by the previous owners at auction in the 1990s (Pereira, 2012). The building sat empty until it was occupied by the first squatting movement (from 2002 to 2007). There was a library in the building's basement of hundreds of books salvaged from the rubbish, and cinema functions held on the first floor, where middle-class activists and residents mingled (Melo, 2010). The second occupation began in 2010 and is still in the building.

Interviews were also held with local government officials in a variety of capacities related to housing and occupations in the centre. The city administration had been interested in reducing the excessive property vacancy and renewing the city centre for decades, even remodelling a very small number of buildings as social housing. However, my interest here will focus on the Departamento da Função Social da Propriedade ('Department of the Social Function of Property' [DFSP]), created in 2014, and its complicated relationship with spaces of (property) vacancy. In the next section, I sketch the three spatio-legal imaginaries and their relations on the ground.

Spatio-legal projects in conflict

There are three logics that collide at Prestes Maia. The market logic is heavily imbued with an economic definition of property. The owner insists on his ability to use (or not use) the Prestes Maia building at will. For the past few decades, he has been 'land sweating' (Blomley, 2017) as he waited for the expropriation value to be significantly higher than the unpaid taxes he owed the city. What this means in practical terms is that vacancy is the 'space' owners need in order to play the market. As the 2014 spatial plan defined Prestes Maia as a micro-zone, where the only possible use is social housing, the best option for the owner became negotiating for compulsory purchase with the city administration. However, a coordinator from Frente Luta e Moradia ('Front for the Struggle for Housing') – an umbrella organisation that provides consulting to the smaller occupation movements – insisted on the obscenity of the state negotiating and paying an inflated market price for what should technically be a 'compulsory acquisition'. The architect working with Prestes Maia in anticipation of state-financed remodelling also insisted the valuation was erroneous. Even market price, he insisted, would be much lower, considering the building is zoned exclusively for social housing and only the structure is functional, having been gutted decades ago of lifts, windows and so on.

The public administration logic is heavily imbued with Weberian formality. The most iconic formality appears in judges' insistence that the social function of property is not specified in the Constitution and can thus only be implemented when specified by administrative law (Bedeschi, 2018). Judges deploy formalism to avoid any significant involvement with a controversial law. Commentators on the official

Brazilian spatio-legal imaginary have insisted that the judicial view of property is heavily slanted in favour of powerful landholders (Holston, 1991; Maricato, 2003). In Brazilian law, there are two routes to evict squatters and these are distinguished by the common judicial interpretation of the distinction between property and possession. One is called '*reivindicatória de propriedade*' ('property claim') and the other '*reintegração da posse*' ('repossession'). According to legal advocates of housing movements, abandoned buildings would have to follow the more tedious route of *reivindicatória de propriedade*, with its onus on the owner to prove ownership, call in witnesses and so on. This is because the building was vacant and the owner was not occupying (literally, in possession of) the building at the moment the squat was produced. Judges, on the other hand, accept the speedier *reintegração da posse*, with its lower demands in terms of proofs. They promote a view of possession as automatically included in property ownership and accept the presentation of proofs of this 'possession', such as copies of paid bills. Yet, in fact, these only prove ownership, not physical possession and occupation of the building at the moment the movement broke in and entered.

In contrast, the São Paulo spatial plan of 2014, which was written by the progressive local PT administration, (re)defines property as socially productive by giving the constitutional doctrine of the social function of property administrative teeth. In essence, though, the legislation is only able to open a small but important space for activism. The definition insists that property must be used but only as defined formally. This does not defend squatting, but rather justifies the serving of notices to owners of vacant properties by the municipal administration. Notified properties will then pay double property taxes up to a ceiling of 15 per cent of the land value. Interviews with officials working for the DFSP, however, did uncover a small nod in favour of the locally well-known squatting movements. The DFSP did not serve notices to those vacant properties that were 'used' by squatters, as they did not want to contribute arguments that owners might use to speed evictions of movements in local courts. However, even this non-formal reasoning was defended in formal legal rhetoric of not wanting to deviate the *função social da propriedade* from its stated objective. It is defined as an instrument to increase use of vacant properties, not the improvement of their legal situation from informal to formal uses.

The squatting movement follows a different logic that is deeply influenced by their lived experience of the vacant spaces they occupy. The movement understands property by drawing on the moral justification of the social function of property written into the Brazilian

Constitution in 1988. Although the social function does not technically justify squatting, morally, they insist on the need of property to be used in order to be socially acceptable. As the top coordinator of MMLJ understands it, property rights are not open to being used, but *have* to be used. By implication, the coordinator also presents the previous owner as immoral for having maintained the building vacant for so many decades. Vacancy is central to the spatio-legal imaginary of the squatting movement. The search for possible sites for occupations is defined by vacancy indicators. These are buildings that present markers of relatively long-term abandonment by their owners (broken windows, weeds, unpaid bills, a history of unpaid property taxes and so on). As these buildings were vacant for prolonged periods of time, a huge amount of work is needed to clean them and make them inhabitable again. As one floor coordinator explained, the building was so full of rubbish that each day for weeks they had to cart out 10–20 truckloads for the city to take away.

This is just the first action for the movement to be able to use these buildings to provide decommodified housing for residents. The effective ability to provide temporary housing for members depends on their success in postponing evictions. As Roy (2017) puts it, the politics of emplacement of poor people's movements is also a politics of postponement. Thus, their project is only possible as long as they are able to keep the police out. Here, the material spatial configuration becomes important. The single entrance of the building helps make evictions more difficult. According to a lawyer from a local legal advocacy office, the police are reluctant to evict huge movements like Prestes Maia, with its 400-plus families, out through a single front door.

The movement prolongs their temporary hold on buildings in hopes of negotiating with the city for the purchase and remodelling of the building as social housing units. They attempt to force the city administration into negotiation by protesting on the streets. All residents have to participate in protests as part of their obligations to the movement. This is the pedagogy of confrontation (De Carli et al, 2015), where residents arrive at the movement to satisfy their individual housing needs but are educated into a shared struggle. Di Feliciantonio (2016) presents a similar discussion of collective subjectification processes in Italian squatting in times of austerity. Individuals become part of a political collective as a result of the action/gesture of squatting and the deconstruction of identities of indebtedness. Residents at Prestes Maia also have to participate in the constant cleaning of common areas on each floor and the 20-plus floors of stairs. Residents' participation is registered in a carrot-and-stick point system. Residents aspire to get a state-financed social housing unit and know they must keep their points up in order to be among the top 295 families of the total 400 plus that the remodelled building is planned to accommodate.

These vacant spaces are transformed from abandoned buildings into spaces of a tense imaginary of sovereignty. The movement is able to control the borders when the doorman asks for identification from newcomers. The coordination polices the inside of the building, deciding who stays and who leaves. For example, wife beaters are expelled on the spot. Later, they are called back and their case is reviewed by the coordination. Drinking in common areas is also considered an infraction. Similarly, the coordination maintains internal welfare policies of providing food boxes for families suffering unemployment and those who have children with disabilities. In light of this, the coordination insists on their autonomy in relation to the city administration. The top coordinator was adamant that they are not cooperating with the city administration: "the movement does not work for and does not work with [the city]. The movement is an opposition to claim the rights of the worker, the *sem-teto*."

Yet, the coordination depends on the city administration, as their ultimate goal is to gain social housing units for members of the movement. In fact, the movement's point system is held on the city's social housing roster website, Prohabit. Those with the most points are already registered with the city. This speaks volumes about the interplay between the autonomy and engagement of these movements (on Spanish housing movements, see Gonick, 2016). This is important for residents, who know waiting times are impossibly long in normal conditions. Remodelled buildings are given directly to movements to allocate to their own members rather than to individual families on the city's generic waiting list. Membership in squatting movements allows residents to jump the queue as long as the squat is successful. The next section presents a discussion of how these conflicting spatio-legal projects contribute to housing and property politics in the city.

Property politics

There are two important impacts of the spatio-legal counter-project of these housing movements on the city's housing politics. First, as discussed earlier, the occupation of vacant spaces allows movements the possibility of influencing the sequencing of formal social housing rosters. Second, they also influence the location of these housing solutions. The movements work in an interstitial space between autonomy and engagement, that is, between autogestion and the city's point system (in Prohabit) for the social housing roster. This shows that vacancy is the space of contact between the spatio-legal project of movements and of the state. On the other hand, decades of activism by squatting movements have brought small adjustments to the federal Minha Casa Minha Vida ('My House My Life') social housing programme. That programme, described elsewhere as a countercyclical policy (Santo Amore, 2015), places tenants in social housing units in extremely distant locations due to lower peripheral land prices. Due to activism by these movements, there have been some concessions that facilitate building units in central locations. The gains have been an increased allowance for remodelling budgets and inclusion of permission for *autogestão* ('self-management of construction'). The first is important because remodelling prices are higher than newbuild in favelas, and the second allows the movements to lower costs and improve quality by managing the remodelling process themselves. However, these innovations were put on hold by the impeachment of PT President Dilma and the incoming President's moratorium on social spending.

A small but important impact of the spatio-legal project of the movements on the city's property politics was in the informal treatment afforded them by the DFSP. The PT administration's policy of improving the use of vacant properties focused on central areas first, as these presented high rates of vacancy. The movement's material presence in the space of the centre meant they were considered an important player in the rolling out of the policy. As discussed earlier, this impacted the practice of serving notices to vacant properties. The DFSP decided not to serve notices to occupied buildings in order to avoid contributing to their eviction. However, when the PT was voted out in 2018, the change in administration meant the DFSP was de-staffed and the policy was effectively abandoned before any concrete results could become apparent (Bonduki, 2017). The DFSP was not able to impact the official spatio-legal project in an ongoing manner beyond this one administration.

Also in relation to property politics, the spatio-legal projects of the movements have been less interested in contesting the privileged imaginary of private property. In fact, movements only focus on gaining remodelled units from the federal financing programme Minha Casa Minha Vida, which are offered in private property (Santo Amore, 2015). This echoes other literature that points to the slippery slope between property activism and formalisation (Porter, 2014). It seems the widespread uptake of de Soto's (2000) recommendations for developing nations to solve their problems regarding informality primarily through formalisation has severely limited the imagined options for activists. Surely, this also has to do with the experience of precarity the housing movement and their members are materially subjected to on a daily basis (Blomley, 2019). More transformative is the pedagogy of confrontation in educating citizens into a shared struggle (De Carli et al, 2015). The lived experience of the occupation, with its requirements of participating in street protests and collective cleaning, means individuals are educated into a shared spatio-legal world-making project.

Conclusions

Urban vacancy is not a singular, stable phenomenon that can be understood in a simple and straightforward manner; rather, it is constructed through innovative conceptions, as well as through distinct lived experiences. In order to illuminate its meaning, the spatial and legal aspects of vacancy must be held together and analysed in tandem. Careful attention must also be paid to the way distinct spatio-legal projects vie for control of specific places.

This chapter reviewed how three projects clash in the vacant space known as the Prestes Maia building. The owner mobilises a spatio-legal imaginary of free disposition of property supported by current judicial practice. The city administration defends the social function of property enshrined in the Constitution in seeking to activate sub-utilised properties. Finally, echoing Vasudevan (2015), the housing movement views vacancy as a space of radical potential that can contribute to the alleviation of the housing needs of hundreds, if not thousands, of the urban poor.

Urban vacancy, then, can be understood as an empty signifier simultaneously inhabited by conflicting projects. In specific confrontations, urban vacancy is put to work by the different spatio-legal projects that contingently inhabit it. There is no single definition of vacancy or non-vacancy; rather, spatio-legal worlds are mobilised precisely in order to uphold specific descriptive and normative views of the same spaces. Furthermore, it is through such mobilisations that speculators are vindicated, vacant properties are activated for the market by 'progressive' legislation or squatters are evicted. Research into spatio-legal projects matters because these confrontations can lead to such divergent results for those involved. Our understanding of housing and property politics can be greatly enhanced by increasing our focus on vacant spaces and the political antagonism that occurs in and around them.

It is in vacant spaces such as the Prestes Maia building, immersed as it is in the frontier of urban renewal of the centre of São Paulo, that the legal is enmeshed in the spatial in an especially intense manner. Tensions have again increased greatly of late with the swing of Brazilian politics towards the far right (Paolinelli and Canettieri, 2019). This chapter suggests the need for further research into how different spatio-legal world-making projects fill the empty signifier of property vacancy during right-wing administrations to help find leverage points that might support the precarious position of poor people's movements in the deepening housing crisis of the current global pandemic. The importance of urban vacancy as an infrastructure and resource is too great to leave it to be filled by whoever gets there first.

Acknowledgements

This research was supported by the Australian Research Council (DP140102851).

Note

1 Although, in his book, Delaney created and utilised the somewhat cumbersome neologism 'nomosphere', I have preferred the more straightforward adjective 'spatio-legal' that he uses less frequently.

References

Bayat, A. (2000) 'From "dangerous classes" to "quiet rebels": politics of the urban subaltern in the Global South', *International Sociology*, 15(3): 533–57.

Bedeschi, L. (2018) 'Limites do sistema possessório: Conhecimento e prática do princípio constitucional da função social da propriedade no Tribunal de Justiça de São Paulo', PhD thesis, Universidade Federal do ABC, Brazil.

Blomley, N. (2002) 'Mud for the land', *Public Culture*, 14(3): 557–82.

Blomley, N. (2017) 'Land use, planning, and the "difficult character of property"', *Planning Theory & Practice*, 18(3): 351–64.

Blomley, N. (2019) 'The territorialization of property in land: space, power and practice', *Territory, Politics, Governance*, 7(2): 233–49.

Bonduki, N. (2017) 'Em meio a imóveis ociosos, prefeitura quer arranha-céus sobre os quintais', *Folha de São Paulo*, 14 November. Available at: www1.folha.uol.com.br/colunas/nabil-bonduki/2017/11/1935230-em-meio-a-imoveis-ociosos-prefeitura-quer-arranha-ceus-sobre-os-quintais.shtml (accessed 29 January 2020).

Butler, C. (2012) *Henri Lefebvre: Spatial Politics, Everyday Life and the Right to the City*, Abingdon: Routledge-Cavendish.

Cover, R. (1983) 'The Supreme Court, 1982 term – foreword: nomos and narrative', *Harvard Law Review*, 97: 4–68.

De Carli, B., Frediani, A., Barbosa, B., Comarú, F. and Moretti, R. (2015) 'Regeneration through the "pedagogy of confrontation": exploring the critical spatial practices of social movements in inner city São Paulo as avenues for urban renewal', *DEARQ: Revista de Arquitectura de la Universidad de los Andes*, 16: 146–61.

Delaney, D. (2010) *The Spatial, the Legal and the Pragmatics of World-Making: Nomospheric Investigations*, Abingdon: Routledge-Cavendish.

De Soto, H. (2000) *The Mystery of Capital: Why Capitalism Triumphs in the West and Fails Everywhere Else*, New York, NY: Basic Books.

Di Feliciantonio, C. (2016) 'Subjectification in times of indebtedness and neoliberal/austerity urbanism', *Antipode*, 48(5): 1206–27.

Earle, L. (2012) 'From insurgent to transgressive citizenship: housing, social movements and the politics of rights in São Paulo', *Journal of Latin American Studies*, 44(1): 97–126.

Fernandes, E. (2007) 'Constructing the right to the city in Brazil', *Social & Legal Studies*, 16(2): 201–19.

Fundação Pinheiros (2018) *Déficit Habitacional no Brasil – 2015*, Belo Horizonte: Fundação João Pinheiros.

Gonick, S. (2016) 'Indignation and inclusion: activism, difference, and emergent urban politics in postcrash Madrid', *Environment and Planning D: Society and Space*, 34(2): 209–26.

Gray, N. (2018) 'Beyond the right to the city: territorial autogestion and the Take over the City movement in 1970s Italy', *Antipode*, 50(2): 319–39.

Holston, J. (1991) 'The misrule of law: land and usurpation in Brazil', *Comparative Studies in Society and History*, 33(4): 695–725.

Lefebvre, H. (1991 [1974]) *The Production of Space*, Oxford: Blackwell.

Marcuse, P. (1985) 'Gentrification, abandonment, and displacement: connections, causes, and policy responses in New York City', *Washington University Journal of Urban & Contemporary Law*, 28: 195–240.

Maricato, E. (2003) 'Metrópole, legislação e desigualdade', *Estudos avançados*, 17(48): 151–66.

Matthews, D. (2017) 'The nomos of Hong Kong's Umbrella Movement', in B. Jones (ed) *Law and Politics of the Taiwan Sunflower and Hong Kong Umbrella Movements*, Abingdon: Routledge, pp 100–14.

Melo, C. (2010) 'Performing *sem-teto*: the transversal tactics of *artivismo* and the squatters' movement', *Journal of Latin American Cultural Studies*, 19(1): 1–21.

Mirow, M. (2010) 'The social-obligation norm of property: Duguit, Hayem, and others', *Florida Journal of International Law*, 22: 191–226.

Paolinelli, M. and Canettieri, T. (2019) 'Dez anos de ocupações organizadas em Belo Horizonte: radicalizando a luta pela moradia e articulando ativismos contra o urbanismo neoliberal', *Cadernos Metrópole*, 21(46): 831–54.

Pereira, O. (2012) 'Lutas urbanas por moradia: o centro de São Paulo', PhD thesis, Universidade de São Paulo, Brazil.

Porter, L. (2014) 'Possessory politics and the conceit of procedure: exposing the cost of rights under conditions of dispossession', *Planning Theory*, 13(4): 387–406.

Roy, A. (2017) 'Dis/possessive collectivism: property and personhood at city's end', *Geoforum*, 80: A1–11.

Sack, R.D. (1983) 'Human territoriality: a theory', *Annals of the Association of American Geographers*, 73(1): 55–74.

Santo Amore, C. (2015) '"Minha Casa Minha Vida" para iniciantes', in C. Santo Amore, L.Z. Shimbo and M. Rufino (eds) *Minha Casa … E a Cidade? Avaliação do Programa Minha Casa Minha Vida em seis estados Brasileiros*, São Paulo: Observatório das Metrópoles, pp 11–28.

Smith, N. (1979) 'Toward a theory of gentrification: a back to the city movement by capital, not people', *Journal of the American Planning Association*, 45(4): 538–48.

Smith, N. (1986) 'Gentrification, the frontier, and the restructuring of urban space', in N. Smith and P. Williams (eds) *Gentrification of the City*, Boston, MA: Allen & Unwin, pp 15–34.

Smith, N. (2002) 'New globalism, new urbanism: gentrification as global urban strategy', *Antipode*, 34(3): 427–50.

Ugarte, M., Fontana, M. and Caulkins, M. (2019) 'Urbanisation and Indigenous dispossession: rethinking the spatio-legal imaginary in Chile vis-à-vis the Mapuche nation', *Settler Colonial Studies*, 9(2): 187–206.

Vasudevan, A. (2015) 'The autonomous city: towards a critical geography of occupation', *Progress in Human Geography*, 39(3): 316–37.

12

(Im)Material infrastructures and the reproduction of alternative social projects in urban vacant spaces

Cesare Di Feliciantonio and Cian O'Callaghan

Introduction

> The city is still empty, few days since the eviction of Communia…. Many people involved in the project have come back to the city from their holidays, from their family homes, several meetings are being organised. People from the neighbourhood, other squats and groups are all giving their support towards a new occupation … the new location has been identified thanks to the deep knowledge of residents, the plan … to have a demonstration ending with the occupation of the building in the upcoming days…. I spoke to [name of person] about what is going on, we were both amazed by the response of so many people at such time. 'We can do it, we are determined and organised' [name of person] told me smiling at the end of our chat. (Cesare's research diary, August 2013)

These diary notes concern the response of militants and neighbourhood residents to the eviction of Communia, a squatting initiative that emerged in the San Lorenzo neighbourhood in Rome in April 2013, by the police in mid-August, a time when most Italian cities get very quiet, people go away for summer holidays and political activism is usually on pause. Summer is often the preferred time for police to carry out evictions in order to avoid clashes. However, in recent years, several Italian squatting initiatives evicted during summer months have seen a strong response from activists and residents. The most dramatic occurred in central Rome in August 2017, when hundreds of squatters – mostly refugees – were violently evicted without a clear or coherent plan for their rehousing (Annunziata, 2020). Squatting is just one example of the alternative social projects over vacant spaces in post-crisis cities. In a previous article (O'Callaghan et al, 2018), we have drawn on the work of Povinelli (2011) to frame alternative social projects as all those experimenting with alternative human and post-human relations. In that article, and here, we emphasise the important role that urban vacant spaces have played in the experimental formation of alternative social projects. Urban vacant spaces can stand in contradistinction to the normative vision of neoliberal capitalist space (Doron, 2000; O'Callaghan, 2018), and are characterised by radical openness to prefigurative experiments producing alternative urban futures (Bresnihan and Byrne, 2015). However, such experiments are often short-lived, being subject to repossession by institutional and propertied interests. What makes it possible for alternative social projects engaged with the reappropriation of vacant spaces to resist institutional violence and eviction, reproducing themselves over time?

In this chapter, we address this question by emphasising the central role of (im)material infrastructures in the reproduction of these initiatives. We conceptualise this in two interdependent ways. First, (im)material infrastructures are made of people, personal relationships, shared practices and histories, and cultural and social capital, leading to the formation of embedded knowledge. Here, our conceptualisation builds on critical scholarship in urban studies, notably, the work of Abdumaliq Simone (for example, Simone, 2004) and Colin McFarlane and Jonathan Silver (2017). Examining everyday life in the inner city of Johannesburg, Simone (2004) extends the conceptualisation of infrastructure to people's everyday lives and activities; his idea of *people as infrastructures* points at the multiplicity of objects, spaces, people and practices that city residents engage with. McFarlane and Silver (2017: 463) define social infrastructure as the 'practice of connecting people and things in socio-material relations that sustain urban life. It is not just a context or a noun, but a verb: social infrastructure is made and held stable through work and changing ways of connecting. It is a connective tissue, often unpredictable'. Second, extending this conceptualisation, we argue that urban vacant spaces form an integral resource to produce social infrastructures. They do so in their capacity to function both as physical spaces that enable contentious actions and experiments in commoning, and as sites that transgress normative views of urbanisation and potentially open up alternative futures. However, crucially, as we discuss in this chapter, vacant spaces have to be *made into an (im)material infrastructure* to be shared in common through the actions of activists and social movements that articulate a claim, a vision and an apparatus to reappropriate them.

Contributing to interdisciplinary literature on the reappropriation and reuse of vacant spaces in post-crisis cities, the chapter focuses on what makes the reinvention and reproduction of alternative social projects possible, rather than on their emergence or failure. Previous studies (including ours) have tended to focus on what has made the emergence of alternative projects possible, the subjects involved, institutional responses and public discourse around them, and their limits, successes and failure (for example, Martinez Lopez and García Bernardos, 2015; Di Feliciantonio, 2017a, 2017b; Bazzoli, 2018; Giubilaro, 2018; O'Callaghan et al, 2018; Di Feliciantonio and O'Callaghan, 2020). Little attention has been devoted to what sustains the reproduction of these spaces over time, even in cases of eviction or a general hostility from formal institutions. We mobilise our argument by working comparatively across two cities – Rome and Dublin – which have both seen reappropriation of urban vacant spaces as an important activist strategy in the post-crisis period.

Methodologically, the chapter builds on several research projects around urban vacant spaces that we have carried out since 2010 (individually and together) in the two cities. Data collection and analysis have included: policy analysis, media discourse analysis, a questionnaire, in-depth interviews and participant observation.

The chapter proceeds as follows. First, we introduce the context of alternative social projects in vacant spaces in the post-crisis period, before outlining our conceptualisation of (im)material infrastructures in terms of people and vacant spaces. We then examine (im)material infrastructures at work in our case-study cities. We conclude by offering some reflections on the role of (im)material infrastructures in shaping the emerging post-pandemic city.

Alternative social projects in urban vacant spaces

While urban vacant spaces have traditionally been associated with transgressive uses and practices (Colomb, 2012), in the current post-crisis moment, they seem to be at the core of political contention, their reappropriation challenging private property (O'Callaghan et al, 2018). According to Martinez Lopez (2019), initiatives around vacant spaces are part of urban social movements focused on 'urban commons'. In his view, these initiatives 'point to the redistribution of public resources…. Movements defending the urban commons set social barriers to the overwhelming commodification of life' (Martinez Lopez, 2019: 33). In the case of Communia in Rome, one of us (Di Feliciantonio, 2017a) has shown how the initiative's claims were multiple, being regrouped around the urban commons; at the same time, the reappropriation of a vacant building by an open community can be seen as a form of urban commoning.

The use of 'common' as a verb relies on the feminist critique of the commons (for example, Federici, 2011). In the fields of geography and urban studies, Amanda Huron (2018: 62) has conceptualised the specificity of urban commoning as 'the messy, everyday, necessarily compromised work of trying to build networks of survival in the midst of the high-pressure centrality of the urban. Urban commoning is not pure. It should in no way be romanticized. It is often … an act of desperation.' Two characteristics of the *urban* point to the uniqueness of the experience of urban commons/commoning: (1) the saturation of urban spaces, leading people to compete or share resources; and (2) in cities, strangers come together to work for common goals and objectives (Huron, 2015).

Huron's endeavour to highlight the specific character of the urban in the claim for the commons echoes recent geographical network approaches to the study of urban social movements, notably, the work of Nicholls (for example, Nicholls, 2008). In his perspective, the city works as a 'relational incubator' for social movements, 'facilitating complex relational exchanges that generate a diversity of useful resources for campaigns operating at a variety of spatial scales' (Nicholls, 2008: 842). Given the complexity and density of cities, they offer social movements the possibility to develop *strong ties* based on shared norms, trust, emotions and interpretive frameworks. Strong ties allow groups to address specialised issues effectively, as in the case of community-based groups. However, urban groups and initiatives are also connected through *weak ties*, that is, different groups pool their specialised resources for another cause. When these ties are kept and reinvented over time, they lead to the creation of what Nicholls (2008: 848) defines as 'cultures of resistance' embedded in urban spaces: 'these cultures not only provide insurgents with a coherent identity but they also give a profound sense of meaning to collective forms of resistance. These cultures are captured, produced and reproduced through symbolic products like the built environment.'

Recent work in geography and urban studies has expanded conceptualisations of infrastructure to include the immaterial and improvisatory relationality of people coming together to make cities function towards sustaining their livelihoods (McFarlane and Silver, 2017; Simone, 2018). Within this literature, various scholars have centred questions of the collective (if politically ambivalent) creation of alternative modes of urban inhabitation (Simone, 2018), as well as the reappropriation of waste materials in the eking out of livelihoods (Lawhon et al, 2018). Vasudevan (2015), in his analysis of global geographies of squatting, draws a relationship between such forms of experimentation in producing new 'lifeworlds' and the material resources that squatted spaces provide towards this task. Conceived in this way, vacant sites/buildings operate as contested waste spaces through which alternative projects of habitation can germinate and come into being (O'Callaghan et al, 2018).

Vacant space is not inert, however; indeed, it is a complex and temporally shifting phenomenon in cities. As Ferreri (this volume) also notes, politicising vacancy requires a performative strategy. In line with this, Noterman (2020) shows how strategies aimed at intervening to 'take back' or alternatively 'take over' vacant property often involve contested political goals and differential understandings of property. Our own examples also reflect the political work involved in making vacant property into a resource for (im)material infrastructure. First, this work involves the articulation of a *claim* made in relation to specific properties and expressing a specific dynamic contradiction between current vacancy, future plans (actual or perceived) and existing need not being met. Second, a *vision* for putting lives and infrastructure in common is produced through discursive practices that position justice and need – and therefore action – against speculative property interests. Finally, an *apparatus* for sustaining alternative social projects over vacant spaces is enabled by the (im)material infrastructures of social movement networks that provide practices, tactics and local knowledge. In the following section, we reflect on how a claim and a vision for vacant property have been articulated in Rome and Dublin.

Urban vacancy as infrastructure

As we have outlined already, vacant spaces can form an infrastructure for the creation of new lifeworlds (Di Feliciantonio and O'Callaghan, 2020). Moreover, vacancy has emerged as a key political antagonism in the post-crisis period. Across a range of cities, activist movements have mobilised a claim on vacant spaces against the neoliberal city, and produced a vision of these spaces as a resource for and a means of urban commoning. Thus, vacant spaces are never inert; rather, discursive and material work is involved in transforming them into an actionable infrastructure, that is, a resource by which urban commoning can be operationalised as a prefigurative strategy.

Our starting point for considering the politics and visibility of vacancy is the context of the post-crisis period. As is now widely documented, the 2008 global financial crisis (GFC) caused widespread economic collapse, as expressed though localised property bubbles, the expression and outcomes of which were geographically specific (Kitchin et al, 2014; Fields, 2018). Vacancy became a core site of political antagonism and governmental intervention across a range of contexts during this period. However, while analogous claims over vacancy can be seen, important differences in terms of the nature and type of vacancy, the discursive articulation of this challenge/ opportunity and (significantly for our discussion here) the embedded knowledge and experience of activist groups in occupation influence the reproduction of alternative social projects in these spaces. We turn now to questions of what it means to reappropriate vacant property in the context of post-crisis urbanisation.

In Rome, vacancy has been a recurrent characteristic of the city's growth and development, with land-rent speculation being the main driver of urban development since at least fascist times (Di Feliciantonio and Aalbers, 2018). The city has been epitomised by a persistent housing crisis due to the long-standing lack of investment in social housing. Following the GFC, austerity policies led to the proliferation of abandoned 'cultural spaces' (theatres, cinemas and so on) and public spaces (for example, parks and schools). In conjunction, the housing crisis, experienced mostly by migrants and younger people, has been exacerbated by: (1) the recession and declining prospects of homeownership; and (2) the increasing diffusion of Airbnb for short-term accommodation (Celata, 2017). In response to this situation, the city experienced a wave of new occupations, especially between 2010 and 2013. These occupations built on the strong legacy of autonomous politics from the 1970s, which had culturally, politically and socially embedded the practice of squatting in the city. The public discourse established by the new wave of occupations cast vacant buildings as a wasted resource that should rightfully be put to use for housing, work and social activities for dispossessed populations. The occupations concerned both publicly and privately owned buildings. In the case of public buildings, activists denounced their abandonment in a context where thousands of families were eligible for social housing but their needs were not met, and where workers in the cultural sectors experienced extreme precarity (Di Feliciantonio, 2016a, 2017a). In the case of private buildings, activists denounced their speculative character, as in the case of Communia (Di Feliciantonio, 2017a). However, since 2014, several of these occupations have been evicted, often violently, in the name of 'legality' and 'safety' concerns for those living there (Di Feliciantonio and O'Callaghan, 2020). Nevertheless, the city still hosts dozens of squats that claim the right of access to housing, cultural, social and work spaces, and reject neoliberal and post-political discourse around 'legality'.

In Dublin, vacancy became visible and politicised following the GFC for a number of interlocking reasons. Ireland was severely impacted by the GFC, manifested specifically by an extraordinary property crash, leaving a landscape of vacant and unfinished developments (Kitchin et al, 2014). Vacancy became a central feature of public discourse about, and policy responses to, the crisis (O'Callaghan et al, 2018). In Dublin, this also gave rise to wider discussions concerning the persistence of large pockets of vacant land, a residual outcome of speculation during the boom. The dearth of development activity, combined with a set of bottom-up initiatives to reuse vacant spaces (Bresnihan and Byrne, 2015), was later met with policy intervention focused on solving the problem of vacancy in the interim and long term (Moore-Cherry, 2016). For a time, a consensus around claims to temporary use was broadly achieved between policy actors, grass-roots groups and development interests. However, the recovery of Dublin's property market from 2013 and, in particular, the emergence of a new and pervasive housing and homelessness crisis further politicised the issue of vacancy and legitimated more contentious responses, including occupations (O'Callaghan et al, 2018). A set of new housing action groups, including the Irish Housing Network (see McArdle, this volume), made a claim that indicted vacancy as an outcome of property-led development, speculation and austerity urbanism (O'Callaghan et al, 2018). Taking inspiration from the Spanish Plataforma de los Afectados por la Hipoteca ('Platform for those affected by mortgage debt'; PAH), activists used occupations of vacant properties to provide homeless services in the context of a widening crisis. In doing so, this vision also implicated the failure of state policy in response to the crisis, which intensified property speculation and therefore housing dispossession. Within this context, therefore, reappropriating vacant property was articulated as a mechanism through which alternative modes of urban inhabitation could be struggled over.

As our case studies demonstrate, vacancy can become politically visible during particular moments and in context-specific ways. This is neither an a priori fact nor a generalised condition. Rather, vacancy is mobilised as an infrastructure through place-specific claims that position vacant spaces as a point of antagonism against the neoliberal city, and as a pivot upon which a vision for reclaiming the urban commons can be made. The centrality of vacancy to crisis narratives and responses in a number of countries gave rise to a range of broader discourses about the possibilities of vacant spaces. Coupled with this, new modes of dispossession, both stemming from the GFC and as a result of post-crisis property market dynamics (for example, Waldron, 2018), served to highlight the contradiction between buildings and land being left empty during a time of burgeoning housing need, and stimulated responses to 'take back' vacant property (Di Feliciantonio and O'Callaghan, 2020; Noterman, 2020). While our case studies are comparable in terms of the claims they make on post-crisis vacancy, however, context-specific factors heavily influence the ways in which alternative conceptualisations and projects over vacant spaces can be mobilised and sustained. We turn now to the apparatus of (im)material infrastructures.

Immaterial infrastructures at work

Given the widespread diffusion of squatting by both individuals without a formal political claim and organised groups reclaiming squatting as a key political practice (Di Feliciantonio, 2016a), Rome offers the possibility to understand the relationship between a new generation of initiatives reclaiming vacant spaces as 'urban commons' (Di Feliciantonio, 2017a) and an established 'culture of resistance' (Nicholls, 2008). In this respect, Communia represents a useful example: the people involved in the three occupations that took place in 2013 did not have a background in the autonomous movement that has played a central role in the history of squatting in Italy (Mudu, 2012). The most politically experienced among them had a background in a small anti-capitalist party (Sinistra Critica ['Critical Left']), while the political experience of the younger ones mostly came from the massive student mobilisations that took place in the country in 2008 and 2010 (Cini, 2017). Despite their lack of previous experience with squatting, and the long-standing contention among Italian leftist groups, Communia squatters got substantial support from neighbourhood residents and other social centres and groups. For instance, the identification of the vacant property to occupy in both the second and the third occupation came from someone engaged with another political initiative. In both cases, the building to be occupied was privately owned, the main aim being to denounce the speculative plans for the redevelopment of the traditionally lower- and middle-class neighbourhood of San Lorenzo. Against the increasing privatisation of space in the neighbourhood, centred around the student nightlife economy, activists reclaimed the *common* use of abandoned buildings, challenging plans for luxury real estate to be developed. As discussed by one of the members of the initiative:

> 'Communia is the result of a collective effort that goes beyond those who attend the weekly assembly or manage the space practically. So many people from different groups and spaces have contributed to what we are ... we learn from others, we teach others, we get from others, we give to others.... This is the beauty of being in Rome, maybe we fight each other, but we have shared roots and common trajectories ... this fucked-up city is our extraordinary heritage; I don't think there is another city in Europe with such a massive substratum of anti-systemic initiatives, spaces and people still enduring.' (M7G, personal interview, February 2014)[1]

This description by M7G highlights the importance of shared practices and histories to sustain both the formation and the survival of initiatives after eviction, as in the case of Communia. The sharing of practices and histories leads to the formation of an embedded, tacit knowledge diffused through members of different initiatives. Discussing the day of the third occupation of Communia in September 2013 after the violent eviction in August, a member of Communia explains: "People knew what to do, from how to open the gate to how to take care of electricity, how to organise the guard shifts, what would have happened in case the police had come" (P21, personal interview, March 2014). Asked whether all this had been discussed openly, she says: "Not everything in detail [was discussed], there is no need for that, there is a certain praxis with these things, you know what to do, the most important thing is to be aware of the people you can rely on, whom to call" (P21, personal interview, March 2014). Pushed to reflect on how this praxis is established, she further elaborates:

> 'You learn by helping someone in need, maybe another initiative threatened with eviction, during a demonstration ... We were all there in 2008, in 2010, so many things happened, despite all the problems and the conflicts, we shared so much, we created such big actions, you cannot cancel that, they stay with you ... no matter what, you know what to do in certain situations once you have experienced them.' (P21, personal interview, March 2014)

While M7G highlights the importance of the long-standing history of activism and the politics of occupation in the city, P21 acknowledges the central role of the student demonstrations of 2008/10 in the formation of a praxis and tacit, embedded knowledge shared by those involved with the occupations that emerged in Rome after the GFC. Activists from different initiatives often share cultural and social capital; several of them belong to the increasing young class of Italians with a high cultural capital (for example, a university degree) but low and precarious economic capital. It is no coincidence that the 2011–13 wave of occupations saw a strong presence of university students (Di Feliciantonio, 2016b), who usually start their engagement through day-to-day activities in occupied social centres that act as 'entry points' towards a more sustained engagement in the housing movement, as well as other networks and struggles. Everyday or mundane activities within social centres lead to the formation of strong personal and relational bonds built around care and support. In the case of Communia, these bonds are often framed as some sort of 'politics of love' (Wilkinson, 2009; Di Feliciantonio, 2018), as exemplified by the following words of one of the 'leaders': "I love my comrades and I feel like I get back the same amount of love that I give … we share a horizon, something concerning one or some of us gets to concern everyone, being here means being with others, sharing with them, loving them" (VY5, personal interview, February 2014). These words echo Huron's (2018) analysis of commoning as built around care and mutual aid; however, as seen in this subsection, the (im)material infrastructures Communia relies on also include shared practices, cultural and social capital, and embedded knowledge. This demonstrates the importance of long-term cultures of resistance to the mobilisation of vacant spaces as an (im)material infrastructure.

While Rome has a long-standing history of autonomous politics that has favoured the creation of (im)material infrastructures, Dublin has a weak tradition, with historical engagement having been mostly around social housing (Hearne et al, 2018). As discussed by M: "We are extremely young [in organisation] and we lack solid references for practices, campaigns and strategies … Our primary aim is to try to rebuild awareness and consensus because they have been completely lost. The neoliberal myth crushed the Left" (M, personal interview, June 2016). Nevertheless, in recent years, housing activism has grown and transformed substantially in the city. The post-crash period also saw the emergence of a small ecology of independent social centres and squatted spaces. While these served as incubators of activist and alternative cultures (Bresnihan and Byrne, 2015), the rapid foreclosure of many due to the return of Dublin's property market has also stimulated group formation. Emerging out of a deep property crash, from 2014, Dublin has experienced a resurgent market and associated housing crisis. The combination of the collapse in construction output, a decimation of the social housing budget and the entry of new institutional players led to a crisis of affordability in the private rental sector, driving thousands into homelessness (Hearne, 2020). The inadequate state response and reliance on market actors led to significant rent increases. Figures from the Residential Tenancies Board (RTB) show average rents in Dublin increased by approximately 65 per cent between 2010 and 2019.[2] Meanwhile, those accessing homeless services increased by 130 per cent between July 2014 and December 2016 (Waldron et al, 2019). Characterised by a focus on new forms of family homelessness, the state response was the creation of a new disciplinary regime of 'emergency accommodation' that saw homeless families housed on a temporary basis in hotels/B&Bs and, later, purpose-built 'family hubs' (Hearne, 2020). The new wave of housing activism in Dublin emerged in direct response to this burgeoning homelessness crisis, taking these dynamics as its point of political contention. Emblematic of this approach is the Irish Housing Network (IHN), an umbrella group from a range of local housing action groups, who have used occupation of vacant property as a strategy to politicise housing and homelessness.

The occupation of the Bolt Hostel (see the chapter by McArdle, this volume), a vacant former homeless hostel taken over by activists in July 2015 to house homeless individuals on a nightly basis, is illustrative of how vacancy forms a resource to experiment in producing (im)material infrastructures. In Dublin, as elsewhere, vacancy was identified as a resource that could be put to work towards building an urban commons (Bresnihan and Byrne, 2015; Di Feliciantonio and O'Callaghan, 2020). While operationalised by housing activist groups intent on politicising the housing system as a whole, the key contradiction immediately identified was that of homelessness, and its most visible face: rough sleeping. The Bolt Hostel was an action that combined a somewhat uneasy marriage of autonomous strategies (taking over a space to provide shelter and care) with political invocations for the state to act to resolve the homelessness crisis and wider housing policy/market failure. Thus, it simultaneously made claims on the rights of groups to utilise the resource of vacancy to meet their needs and on the state's duty to facilitate this provision. The vision for taking over vacant property, composed of care, direct action and bottom-up mobilisation, was directly inspired by the PAH. As M noted:

> 'The PAH is a great source of inspiration, we [IHN] look at them so much … They were able to impose a new discourse, they got on the streets, blocked evictions, you need massive organisation to do that … We are a small group, we are growing but we need to create consensus around what we do.' (M, personal interview, June 2016)

As the quote suggests, the action was a means of experimenting with strategy to build capacity and consensus around a wider housing movement. This is reflected in the organisational teams-based approach the IHN used. One of the activists describes the organisational approach: "We set up a cases team who were processing people who wanted to come and stay there who were homeless … an actions team who were taking care of the building … a media team who were taking care of actually getting media attention and … a legal team" (Q, personal interview, April 2016). In operating on multiple fronts and with limited organisational experience and capacity, the consensus from those involved was that the effectiveness of the action was mixed, with most viewing it as a partial success. The action raised media and public awareness of a contradiction between vacancy and growing homelessness, and provided a template for similar direct actions that could be learned from and modified by the IHN and other groups. However, those involved also suggest that they were unprepared for the level of social care and public health issues faced by staging the action as an intervention in service provision. Likewise, they were under-resourced when Dublin City Council took legal proceedings against two of the activists on grounds of trespass, ultimately influencing the IHN's decision to leave the occupation.

These experiments have extended beyond the Bolt Hostel to incrementally build infrastructures of care and political strategies pursuing housing justice and the urban commons. While the experimental strategies translated and advanced into further actions, including Apollo House and Take Back the City, the apparatus for building political subjectivity through care is reflected more widely in everyday movement politics. An example of this is through the weekly support groups run by a number of area-based groups. These aim to challenge and transform the disciplining subjectivities created through a neoliberal housing system and punitive system of emergency accommodation. Like the assemblies of the PAH well examined by scholars (Di Feliciantonio, 2017c), these support groups aim to remove the stigma of homelessness by participation in a collective space to share. They aim to socialise the homelessness crisis as a collective issue, and empower those who take part to be 'part of the solution' by getting involved. The emphasis here is also on emotional and mental health aspects of housing difficulty, and providing a means for social reproduction, for example, in the form of communal kitchen and family days. This enables the cultivation of activists but, more broadly, reshapes the narrative about housing and homelessness, and challenges the creation of a new disciplinary regime of 'social cleansing' emergent through the 'emergency'.

As such, alternative projects over vacant space in Dublin developed in an experimental capacity along with the nascent formation of radical and autonomous groups and networks. Dublin, therefore, offers the opportunity to understand how (im)material infrastructures can be produced at the intersection between experimental and performative strategies for politicising vacancy and the creation of political subjectivity through the articulation of practices of care through everyday personal and emotional bonds.

Coda: (im)material infrastructures in the post-pandemic city

At the time of completing the revisions for this chapter (July 2020), it is clear that a new economic and financial crisis is going to hit the global economy because of COVID-19; we can expect a new wave of rising vacancy rates across cities around the globe. At the same time, millions of people are at risk of losing their jobs (where they have not already), which could imply increasing evictions and foreclosures, therefore leading to increasing homelessness rates and housing precarity. What is the post-pandemic city going to look like? Is it going to alleviate or exacerbate exclusion and social inequalities? This is impossible to predict, as its configuration will depend upon multiple factors and processes, including the resistance brought by social movements to the violence of neoliberalism and their ability to shape public debate and institutional agendas.

In this chapter, we have shown how the reappropriation of urban vacant spaces by social movements in post-crisis cities represents a form of urban commoning against neoliberal and austerity urbanism. We have argued that vacant spaces themselves are part of the (im)material infrastructures functioning as *apparatus* for the reproduction of alternative social projects over time and against institutional repression. Beyond vacant spaces, these (im)material infrastructures include people, personal relationships, shared practices and histories, embedded knowledge, and cultural and social capital. This *apparatus* will be at the forefront of grass-roots efforts to promote social justice in the post-pandemic city, favouring the creation of solidarities among those affected by the new urban reality. However, the changes in everyday life determined by the pandemic – for example, social distancing and the reduction of physical presence – pose a serious challenge to the reproduction of these (im)material infrastructures given that they tend to rely on the physical occupation of spaces by activists and their 'being there' with one another. At the same time, formal institutions could exploit the current situation to repress alternative social projects in the name of public safety. Against these challenges, social movements and critical urban scholars need to expand their creative imagination, experiment with new practices of coming together and carry on their generative, alternative world-making effort.

Acknowledgement

This research was funded by the Irish Research Council (REPRO/2015/118).

Notes

[1] In order to guarantee anonymity, research participants in Rome were assigned a code made of letters and/or numbers to identify themselves in the research. Participants in Dublin were assigned a letter.

[2] RTB (2019) 'RTB average monthly rent report by number of bedrooms, property type, location and year', CSO Statbank, RIA02.

References

Annunziata, S. (2020) 'Displacement and discrimination: "evictability" of refugees in Revanchist Rome', *ACME: An International Journal for Critical Geographies*, 19(1): 377–84.

Bazzoli, N. (2018) 'Lottare Per La Casa Nel Quartiere Che Cambia Volto. Il Potenziale Politico Dei Commons Urbani', *ACME: An International Journal for Critical Geographies*, 17(2): 269–91.

Bresnihan, P. and Byrne, M. (2015) 'Escape into the city: everyday practices of commoning and the production of urban space in Dublin', *Antipode*, 47(1): 36–54.

Celata, F. (2017) *La 'Airbnbficazione' delle città: gli effetti a Roma tra centro e periferia*, Rome: Dipartimento di Metodi e Modelli per l'Economia, il Territorio e la Finanza. Available at: https://web.uniroma1.it/memotef/sites/default/files/Celata_Airbnbificazione_Roma_2017_0.pdf (accessed 9 July 2020).

Cini, L. (2017) 'Italian students as a political actor. The policy impact of the recent student mobilizations in the field of higher education', *PArtecipazione e COnflitto*, 10(1): 306–32.

Colomb, C. (2012) 'Pushing the urban frontier: temporary uses of space, city marketing, and the creative city discourse in 2000s Berlin', *Journal of Urban Affairs*, 34(2): 131–52.

Di Feliciantonio, C. (2016a) 'Subjectification in times of indebtedness and neoliberal/austerity urbanism', *Antipode*, 48(5): 1206–27.

Di Feliciantonio, C. (2016b) 'Student migrants and squatting in Rome in times of austerity and material constraints', in P. Mudu and S. Chattopadhyay (eds) *Migrations, Squatting and Radical Autonomy*, London: Routledge, pp 93–8.

Di Feliciantonio, C. (2017a) 'Spaces of the expelled as spaces of the urban common? Analysing the re-emergence of squatting initiatives in Rome', *International Journal of Urban and Regional Research*, 41(5): 708–25.

Di Feliciantonio, C. (2017b) 'The reactions of neighbourhoods to the eviction of squatters in Rome: an account of the making of precarious investor subjects', *European Urban and Regional Studies*, 24(4): 352–67.

Di Feliciantonio, C. (2017c) 'Social movements and alternative housing models. Practicing the "politics of possibilities" in Spain', *Housing, Theory & Society*, 34(1): 38–56.

Di Feliciantonio, C. (2018) 'L'amore alla guida degli spazi di messa in commune?', *ACME: An International Journal for Critical Geographies*, 17(2): 454–79.

Di Feliciantonio, C. and Aalbers, M.B. (2018) 'The pre-histories of neoliberal housing policies in Italy and Spain and their reification in times of crisis', *Housing Policy Debate*, 28(1): 135–51.

Di Feliciantonio, C. and O'Callaghan, C. (2020) 'Struggles over property in the "post-political" era: notes on the political from Rome and Dublin', *Environment and Planning C*, 38(2): 195–213.

Doron, G.M. (2000) 'The dead zone and the architecture of transgression', *City*, 4(2): 247–63.

Federici, S. (2011) 'Feminism and the politics of the commons', *The Commoner: A Web Journal for Other Values*, 24 January.

Fields, D. (2018) 'Constructing a new asset class: property-led financial accumulation after the crisis', *Economic Geography*, 94(2): 118–40.

Giubilaro, C. (2018) 'Undoing Commons. Diritto alla Città, Attivismo Culturale e Pratiche di (Un-)Commoning nel Sud d'Italia', *ACME: An International Journal for Critical Geographies*, 17(2): 325–47.

Hearne, R. (2020) *Housing Shock: The Irish Housing Crisis and How to Solve It*, Bristol: Policy Press.

Hearne, R., O'Callaghan, C., Di Feliciantonio, C. and Kitchin, R. (2018) 'The relational articulation of housing crisis and activism in post-crash Dublin, Ireland', in N. Gray (ed) *Rent and its Discontents: A Century of Housing Struggle*, London: Rowman & Littlefield, pp 153–67.

Huron, A. (2015) 'Working with strangers in saturated space: reclaiming and maintaining the urban commons', *Antipode*, 47(4): 963–79.

Huron, A. (2018) *Carving Out the Commons: Tenant Organizing and Housing Cooperatives in Washington*, Minneapolis, MN: University of Minnesota Press.

Kitchin, R., O'Callaghan, C. and Gleeson, J. (2014) 'The new ruins of Ireland? Unfinished estates in the post-Celtic Tiger era', *International Journal of Urban and Regional Research*, 38(3): 1069–80.

Lawhon, M., Millington, N. and Stokes, K. (2018) 'A labour question for the 21st century: perpetuating the work ethic in the absence of jobs in South Africa's waste sector', *Journal of Southern African Studies*, 44(6): 1115–31.

Martinez Lopez, M.A. (2019) 'Framing urban movements, contesting global capitalism and liberal democracy', in N.M. Yip, M.A. Martinez Lopez and X. Sun (eds) *Contested Cities and Urban Activism*, Singapore: Palgrave Macmillan, pp 25–45.

Martinez Lopez, M.A. and García Bernardos, A. (2015) 'Ocupar Las Plazas, Liberar Edificios', *ACME: An International Journal for Critical Geographies*, 14(1): 157–84.

McFarlane, C. and Silver, J. (2017) 'Navigating the city: dialectics of everyday urbanism', *Transactions of the Institute of British Geographers*, 42(3): 458–71.

Moore-Cherry, N. (2016) 'Re-thinking the post-crash city: vacant space, temporary use and new urban imaginaries?', *Irish Geography*, 48(1): 6–12.

Mudu, P. (2012) 'At the intersection of anarchists and autonomists: Autogestioni and Centri Sociali', *ACME: An International E-journal for Critical Geographies*, 11(3): 413–38.

Nicholls, W. (2008) 'The urban question revisited: the importance of cities for social movements', *International Journal of Urban and Regional Research*, 32(4): 841–59.

Noterman, E. (2020) 'Taking back vacant property', *Urban Geography*, online first, DOI: 10.1080/02723638.2020.1743519.

O'Callaghan, C. (2018) 'Planetary urbanization in ruins: provisional theory and Ireland's crisis', *Environment and Planning D: Society and Space*, 36(3): 420–38.

O'Callaghan, C., Di Feliciantonio, C. and Byrne, M. (2018) 'Governing urban vacancy in post-crash Dublin: contested property and alternative social projects', *Urban Geography*, 39(6): 868–91.

Povinelli, E. (2011) *Economies of Abandonment: Social Belonging and Endurance in Late Liberalism*, Durham: Duke University Press.

Simone, A. (2004) 'People as infrastructure: intersecting fragments in Johannesburg', *Public Culture*, 16(3): 407–29.

Simone, A. (2018) 'The urban majority and provisional recompositions in Yangon: The 2016 Antipode RGS-IBG Lecture', *Antipode*, 50(1): 23–40.

Vasudevan, A. (2015) 'The autonomous city: towards a critical geography of occupation', *Progress in Human Geography*, 39(3): 316–37.

Waldron, R. (2018) 'Capitalizing on the state: the political economy of real estate investment trusts and the "resolution" of the crisis', *Geoforum*, 90: 206–18.

Waldron, R., O'Donoghue-Hynes, B. and Redmond, D. (2019) 'Emergency homeless shelter use in the Dublin region 2012–2016: utilizing a cluster analysis of administrative data', *Cities*, 94: 143–52.

Wilkinson, E. (2009) 'The emotions least relevant to politics? Queering autonomous activism', *Emotion, Space and Society*, 2(1): 36–43.

13

Tracing the role of material and immaterial infrastructures in imagining diverse urban futures: Dublin's Bolt Hostel and Apollo House

Rachel McArdle

Introduction

This chapter focuses on the rise of radical actions as a response to the extreme austerity implemented by the Irish government after the global financial crisis of 2008. Globally, the presence and visibility of vacant spaces in urban sites contributed to their use by activists to imagine alternative futures (DeSilvey and Edensor, 2013; Németh and Langhorst, 2014; Ziehl and Oßwald, 2015). There has been an increase in using occupation-based practices as strategies to claim space and achieve political goals (Vasudevan, 2015, 2017; Wood, 2017). After the financial crisis, Ireland's landscape was littered with vacant buildings and ghost estates – the 'new ruins of Ireland' (Kitchin et al, 2014). These ruins were physical reminders of 'everything that had gone wrong with Ireland' (Hosford, 2017). As Hearne et al (2018: 154) insightfully argue, 'activism has been shaped by, and has acted as a response to, the main characteristics of each period and the different crises generated by them'. Ireland faced a 'tsunami of austerity' (Hearne, 2014: 18), resulting in a housing and homelessness crisis, with over 9,000 homeless people in April 2020 (Focus Ireland, 2020). As a response, there was an increase in movements in Ireland that used housing and occupation as strategies for political action (see also the chapter by Di Feliciantonio and O'Callaghan, this volume).

In the post-crisis period, vacant spaces and the urban landscape in Dublin were resources that helped politicise urban actors and supported activist interventions (Di Feliciantonio and O'Callaghan,

2020). At that time, many diverse groups emerged at the grass-roots level and combined to form a politicised housing movement. The Irish Housing Network (IHN) is the most salient example of this; in this chapter, I analyse two examples of their projects. The first is the Bolt Hostel (BH) in 2015, which was an occupation by activists of a former homeless shelter in Dublin's North inner city, which lay vacant at the time of occupation. The activists worked on fixing up the shelter to highlight the incongruity of increasing homelessness at the same time as widespread vacancy, opening it as an unsanctioned homeless hostel in July 2015. The activists left after just a few weeks in August 2015 due to legal action brought by Dublin City Council. In December 2016, activists took over a former Department of Social Protection building in the centre of Dublin, and this occupation, Apollo House (AH), lasted slightly longer into mid-January 2017. Both were organised by activists from the IHN and had similar goals: to highlight the homelessness crisis; and to attempt to illustrate a solution via bottom-up direct action. Unlike BH, though, AH was organised as a collaboration between housing activists, the trade unions Mandate and Unite, and prominent artists/musicians, such as Glen Hansard. I use these two examples to demonstrate that vacant sites were used by activists as a resource to articulate their political goals. Therefore, these ruins play an important role in the activist landscape of Dublin. I illustrate this by connecting the two examples through their '(im)material infrastructures' (see the chapter by Di Feliciantonio and O'Callaghan, this volume). BH and AH are connected spatially and temporally, and the logic of occupation (Vasudevan, 2015) endures beyond the time frame of these two projects, and influences future occupations.

In the next section, I define my use of the concept of material and immaterial infrastructures, which focuses on the intangible connections between people, places and spaces. Then, I investigate the infrastructures of BH and AH. I argue that the material and immaterial infrastructures of BH contributed to AH, through the choice of building (Pruijt, 2013), the volunteer network (de Moor, 2016) and the creation of urban commons (Bresnihan and Byrne, 2015). This research forms part of a larger project (2013–18)[1] focusing on 'Liquid Urbanisms'[2] in Dublin and employs a flexible activist case-study approach based on the methods of in-depth ethnographic participant observation at AH and social media analysis of the two case studies from 2015 to 2018. In addition, semi-structured interviews with BH and AH volunteers and a volunteer survey were conducted by both myself and the IHN research team.

Material and immaterial infrastructures of radical spaces

Vasudevan (2015, 2017) argues that squatting as a practice produces new lifeworlds and that even if the individual squats, social centres and occupations do not last, the idea of occupation endures. Occupation is a 'critical process that prefigures and materialises the social order which it seeks to enact' (Vasudevan, 2015: 316). The idea of claiming space persists beyond the time frame of the practices themselves, and allows activists and scholars to imagine how the city can be remade. Vasudevan insightfully demonstrates that radical practices offer a politics of infrastructure. Vacant spaces can aid processes of politicisation; therefore, vacancy itself is a resource that radical politics can be mapped onto. Till (2005) and Anderson (2010) both highlight the traces that remain in place as material or non-material remnants left in place by cultural life. Scholars can examine these 'traces', which combine as infrastructure. Thus, material and immaterial infrastructures act as resources that can influence the politicisation of activists, in a similar way to how vacant spaces ignite political imaginations.

Further, Simone's (2004: 407–8) concept of people as 'infrastructure' – the 'ability of residents to engage complex combinations of objects, spaces, persons and practices' – describes how people mobilise various spatial, residential, economic and transactional contexts in producing city life. For Simone, people engage with the resources they have available at different scales. People learn how to work within these contexts through 'traces of past collaboration and an implicit willingness to interact with one another in ways that draw on multiple social positions' (Simone, 2004: 408). People uncover how to use the resources and possibilities available to them, which are mobile, provisional and unevenly distributed, based on prior working relationships and acknowledging power differences. Building on this concept, Di Feliciantonio and O'Callaghan (this volume) outline how bonds and connections can be made that are not linked to the physicality of places, but embedded in the creation of projects.

I argue that although alternative projects and spaces may not survive, the material and immaterial infrastructures of these projects – such as physical objects, symbolic presences, people, connections, lived experiences and memories – do remain, and new lifeworlds can be created as a result. Radical spaces generally have an ambiguous, if not a negative, relationship with legality; squats, autonomous social centres, protests and direct actions are often closed relatively quickly. Yet, when places or centres close and new ones open, those legacies are often passed on to new and existing members by those involved in previous occupations through collective rituals, objects and organisational history. By focusing on the experiential everyday rhythms of the peoples and places involved in these alternative forms of urban life, scholars learn more about their timespaces and urban politics. The material and immaterial infrastructures, combined with vacant spaces, act as resources that are used by activists in innovative ways. This influences the imaginary of what cities can be, and may lead to alternative futures being created. I use the concept to demonstrate how cities are more than simple agglomerations of buildings, and I claim that material and immaterial infrastructures enable scholars to focus on how interactions between people can have a significant impact on place and cities.

BH and AH

BH and AH were both created by the IHN. The IHN is an umbrella organisation that formed in May 2015, encompassing around 21 grass-roots housing activist groups that share a common goal of tackling the housing crisis by combating both housing precarity and homelessness. These member groups include organisations based on a ranged of axes, for example: location (for example, in North Dublin, the North Dublin Bay Housing Crisis Committee); at-risk populations or those more likely to be negatively affected by austerity and thus more vulnerable to housing insecurity (for example, Single Parents Acting for the Rights of our Kids [SPARK]); or national groups trying to end the housing crisis (such as Homeless Fightback). Many of these groups were already formed when the IHN was established. The IHN has eight basic principles, including that housing is a right, regardless of income, and that the individuals most affected by housing issues should be the driving force behind the movement (Irish Housing Network, 2017). The IHN emerged in the post-crisis period and used occupation as a strategy to draw attention to the housing crisis.

BH was an illegal occupation of a former homeless hostel, created with the explicit goal of providing temporary emergency accommodation for homeless people. BH was open for three weeks in July 2015 and housed homeless people on an ad hoc basis, though the IHN admit that this did not happen on the scale they had hoped (Kavanagh, 2016). The IHN publicised BH on social media and many tradespeople got involved during the three weeks to make the building habitable. As public support grew for BH, Dublin City

Council started a dialogue with the IHN to ascertain their demands. The IHN stated that it wanted the building to be used to house homeless people or, if this was unacceptable, for another building to be found (Farrell, 2015). According to activists, Dublin City Council tentatively agreed to a possible partnership in the future. However, after a fire inspection, Dublin City Council declared the building a health-and-safety hazard, and threatened to bring an injunction order against members of the IHN on the grounds of illegal trespass. The IHN left BH in August 2015.

AH was another takeover of a building in private ownership. While the building had previously housed the Department of Social Protection, at the time of the occupation, the vacant AH was controlled by the National Assets Management Agency (NAMA) as part of a property portfolio and has since been sold on to another financial actor. The property itself has since been demolished. From December 2016 to January 2017, the building was occupied by activists. The IHN worked with the trade unions Mandate and UNITE, as well as artists, including Glen Hansard, Jim Sheridan and Damien Dempsey – a collaboration known as Home Sweet Home (HSH). HSH successfully housed over 40 people a night for almost 30 days, provided for many more outside the facility in terms of non-housing resources and succeeded in securing six-month beds for 76 people (Holland, 2017; Irish Housing Network, 2017). The aim of AH was similar to BH: to provide temporary accommodation while highlighting the levels of homelessness that existed. AH had bedrooms, bathrooms, dormitories and shared spaces such as a kitchen and lounge, as well as storage space for all the donations received. According to the activists, this design reflected the way a homeless shelter would ideally be organised. In January 2017, HSH agreed to leave AH after Dublin City Council conceded to demands to declare a national housing emergency, house all the current residents of AH and create new facilities for homeless people. Only the second aim was achieved. AH reignited conversations about homelessness and the housing crisis in a much broader way than BH. BH and AH are linked through their rhythmic temporalities. Both were short-term occupations of space and yet had a lasting impact on the activist landscape of Dublin. Through this, we can expand our ideas of urban temporalities. BH and AH have rhythms that are different to the normative, neoliberal rhythms of capitalist processes. Paying attention to these alternative rhythmic temporalities allows deeper insight into cities. The strategies deployed by BH were developed for AH; therefore, the material and immaterial infrastructures of BH had a meaningful impact on AH.

Material infrastructure: vacant buildings

The IHN specifically chose the BH building to make a symbolic statement, and this process was repeated for AH a year later. Both buildings were linked with the Irish social protection system. For BH, the IHN took over a former Dublin City Council hostel for homeless people that closed in 2011 and was empty for more than three years when the IHN began their occupation in 2015. In December 2016, AH was occupied, a building managed at the time by NAMA. NAMA was a symbol of the bank bailout and the austerity budgets that followed, so by occupying this building, the IHN were 'taking back' a building that was figuratively controlled by a semi-public body.

For BH, choosing a former Dublin City Council hostel was intended to 'show … up Dublin City Council. We take a building ourselves, put it in good condition, fix it up, show that it can be done, even with very limited resources like ours' (Agnew, 2015). The IHN wanted to highlight a solution to a homelessness crisis that saw 5,000 people homeless at the time, with 90,000 on housing waiting lists (Costelloe, 2015). A clear lineage between BH and AH was the careful choice of building for an occupation. The AH building was "not exactly owned by NAMA, but NAMA owned the loans against it, they were secured. So, in essence, the taxpayers owned it" (AH interviewee, 2017). Similar to the strategic selection of BH, the choice to occupy AH was deliberate, including "the fact as well it was on top of the old social welfare office. That was a nice little poetic irony" (AH interviewee, 2017). The occupation of this building drew attention to the level of vacancy and underutilised space in Dublin. Overall, the very choice of the BH building in July 2015 impacted the activists a year later when choosing the AH building in December 2016. Vacant buildings were chosen to support political goals and therefore acted as catalysts for the IHN.

Using the material infrastructure as mobilisation: the volunteer network

When BH opened in July 2015, volunteer tradesmen very quickly became involved to bring the building to a safe standard for low cost: 'the IHN hadn't a cent to put into the Bolt, everything was donated' (Conlon, 2015). The result was that with volunteers, the IHN: 'made a building that [was] disused [and] vacant for over 3 years liveable, they decorated the rooms, got furniture for the rooms, electricity worked throughout the building, there was running water throughout the building, working showers with hot water, cookers and they helped house homeless people' (Conlon, 2015). The IHN brought the successful lessons of the original project, BH, to the later project, AH. The IHN credit the success of AH (O'Sullivan, 2016; Holland, 2017; McCarthy, 2017) to their network, which had been built up since its foundation in May 2015 and through BH in July 2015 (*Broadsheet*, 2017). AH was created by a network of supporters and activists, some of whom became involved through their volunteer work with BH, though AH was a much bigger project, with the added collaboration with HSH.

In a similar way to BH, once the word spread about the occupation, people started to volunteer to work at, and offer resources to, AH. AH relied on donated goods and money (Holland, 2017), and included people who were not members of the core HSH groups. Overall, 4,000 people signed up to volunteer (Holland, 2017). The direct action of occupying, renovating and volunteering for the projects also brought people together in solidarity. These actions, such as fixing a bathroom or painting a wall, are material practices that have a greater impact in giving people a sense of purpose and uniting them. According to one BH member: 'We have learned hard tasks can be achieved by people when they come together and fight and struggle for it', and 'the Bolt brought people together in struggle against the state' (Holland, 2017). Another commentator wrote that BH stood as an 'emblem of resistance in the face of the worst housing crises Ireland has seen in decades' (Costelloe, 2015).

Through BH and then AH, people felt a sense of empowerment that often built on or led to a politicisation of activists (Di Feliciantonio, 2016), as the following quotes illustrate:

> '[I]t just kind of exploded, loads of people wanted to take part and like myself just said, "I'll come down and lend a hand", and it was massive within a couple of days.' (AH interviewee, 2017)

> 'I think the legacy is that anything is really possible when ordinary people come together and care about each other.' (AH interviewee, 2017)

> 'Friends who weren't necessarily political beforehand – it definitely helped politicise them in some way.' (AH interviewee, 2017)

Other volunteers who had more previous experience of activism mentioned their involvement in the water charges movement, with one mentioning how the movement was not *just* about water (AH interviewee, 2017), which signifies that this involvement, and the later work with AH, was a broader contestation against austerity urbanism in Dublin.

There were many differences between BH and AH, in particular, the celebrity endorsement and later financial critique of AH (Mannix Flynn, cited in Ní Aodha, 2017). Nevertheless, AH was built using the infrastructure that the IHN created with BH through the choice of building and the volunteer network. As Lynch (2017) convincingly claims: '[T]he occupation of Apollo House did not come out the blue, but grew out of years of experience of similar occupations and resistance…. Strong social movements such as this do not materialize out of thin air.' The quote indicates how members of the IHN, through BH and AH, were politicised through the practice of occupation as a form of resistance to the housing problem. This growth of housing movements as a response to the post-crisis period is also seen worldwide at this time (Martínez López, 2020). For example, Thurber and Fraser (2016) outline tenant organising in the US and argue that any material achievements gained were rooted in the epistemological work done by tenants. For the authors, 'it is a properly political act to relentlessly demand to be heard' (Thurber and Fraser, 2016: 60). Tracing the material and immaterial infrastructure of these projects allows scholars to better understand housing movements in the post-crisis period.

Immaterial infrastructures: prefiguring the future

Through BH and AH, members of the IHN and volunteers achieved material goals, but beyond that, the act of occupation 'opens up the possibility for a politics that can counter epistemological injustices, and imagine a present that could be otherwise' (Thurber and Fraser, 2016: 60). Bresnihan and Byrne (2015) propose a threefold explanation for an urban commons: owning in common, producing in common and organising in common. These are all applicable to BH and AH. First, the two buildings were owned in common, as volunteers took over vacant buildings that, though privately owned, were not in use (see also Caulkins, this volume). Second, the occupations were produced in common, by the IHN for BH and the HSH for AH. Decisions were made through consensus and horizontal governance. Finally, and related to the previous point, both spaces were organised in common, using whatever resources, volunteers, skills and supplies were available.

Through creating an alternative to the mainstream housing market and coming together collectively, BH and AH created not only material options for homeless people, but also an alternative imaginary for urban citizens. Urban commons are often created in moments of crisis (Huron, 2015; McGuirk, 2015; Di Feliciantonio, 2017). People began to envision what the city could look like if more projects like BH and AH were created. The IHN's intervention into 'Dublin's great enclosure' (Bresnihan and Byrne, 2015: 39) is even more significant in the context of 'the privatisation/financialisation of urban space and the commodification of urban life'. At the time, BH and AH created urban commons through 'creative ways to use the powers of collective labour for the common good' (Harvey, 2011: 107). These urban commons were not sustained beyond the time frame of occupations, but BH and AH still contributed to the utopian future of what the city could be.

This chapter began by considering vacant spaces as resources but the projects created within those vacant sites are also fundamental to the future of cities. For example, in 2018, BH and AH influenced a new movement, Take Back the City (TBTC), of which three groups (out of a total of seven) under the IHN umbrella were founding members.[3] TBTC took over vacant buildings in Dublin in August and September 2018. As they were threatened with eviction in one place, they moved and were supported by protestors. They followed this action by holding protests at the Department of Housing, Airbnb offices and the Residential Tenancies Board, institutions that the activists 'felt were enabling the [housing] crisis to continue' (McDermott, 2019). The protestors were directly inspired by BH and AH, as well as historical legacies. Although TBTC did not solidify into a sustained social movement, the occupation of vacant buildings and the protest against institutions related to housing provision still had hundreds of volunteers, and highlighted the acceptance of direct action as a legitimate response to the housing and homelessness crisis. Thus, BH and AH have normalised direct action as a useful practice for activists and contributed to the imaginary of what Dublin can be in the future.

Conclusion

BH and AH fuelled political imaginations in the city and influenced the later TBTC. In this chapter, the material influences of choosing vacant buildings were discussed, followed by how this impacted the immaterial infrastructure of people through the volunteer network. The final section looked at how material and immaterial infrastructures allow scholars to envision the traces and connections between these projects, and to prefigure and imagine a more equitable Dublin.

Internationally, occupation as a tool for political change has increased since the 2008 crash (Vasudevan, 2015; Wood, 2017). Wood (2017) reminds us of how the visible symptoms of the crisis acted as catalysts for action, and vacant spaces are often a catalyst in these occupations (Martinez López, 2013; Priemus, 2015). In the vacant landscape of post-crisis Dublin, the new urban ruins have contributed to a politicisation of urban actors. As part of the urban landscape, vacant buildings were emblematic of the post-crisis neoliberal period in Dublin. Levels of vacancy are often discussed regarding the financial and economic processes that have led to their creation, but I argue that these vacant spaces have a significant role on activists' imaginations. De Moor (2016) outlined how research focuses not on the everyday practices and internal decision-making of squats, but rather on the relation of the squats to external authorities. By investigating how activists are using vacant spaces from the intimate and connected experiences of activists, we can learn more about the local scale (Wood, 2017) and how the very spatiality of cities affects our responses to them. This is part of 'an urban politics that is grounded in the concrete, in the embodied experience of inhabiting the city' (Wood, 2017: 19).

The focus of post-crisis cities has often been on the political and economic situation within these places. This chapter has instead centred on the lived and experiential nature of radical spaces in Dublin, Ireland, a perspective that yields new insights in understanding how people are adapting and responding to the post-austerity period. By paying attention to the responses to these crises, scholars should acknowledge the role these sites play as resources for activists. I agree with Wood (2017: 11) that 'we must ground this work in the concrete life of the inhabited city'. The production of material and immaterial infrastructures is rooted in the intangible connections and networks that urban actors have, based on traces built up through engagements in the city. Rather than focusing on the 'increasingly claustrophobic spatialities of financialization' (Simone, 2019: 68), material and immaterial infrastructures, combined with the urban vacant landscape, allow activists and scholars to imagine alternatives to what the city is and what we would like it to be.

Notes

[1] My PhD research was funded by the John and Pat Hume Scholarship at Maynooth University (2014–16) and the Irish Research Council Government of Ireland PhD Scholarship (2016–18).

[2] 'Liquid Urbanisms' is a meta-concept that embodies the range of experiential timespaces in the city, with types and tributaries. The three types are: creative urbanisms, community-based urbanisms and autonomous urbanisms. The four tributaries include: networks and places; timespaces and rhythms; values and urban commons; and political beliefs and institutional relationships. BH and AH are examples of autonomous urbanisms.

[3] Dublin Central Housing Action, the Blanchardstown Housing Action Community and the North Dublin Bay Housing Crisis Community.

References

Agnew, R. (2015) 'Bolt Hostel: call of the wasteland', *Totally Dublin*, 31 July. Available at: www.totallydublin.ie/more/features-more/bolt-call-of-the-wasteland/ (accessed 28 May 2018).

Anderson, J. (2010) *Understanding Cultural Geography: Places and Traces*, London and New York, NY: Routledge.

Bresnihan, P. and Byrne, M. (2015) 'Escape into the city: everyday practices of commoning and the production of urban space in Dublin: escape into the city', *Antipode*, 47(1): 36–54.

Broadsheet (2017) 'Homes Sweet Homes'. Available at: www.broadsheet. ie/2017/02/24/homes-sweet-homes/ (accessed 28 November 2017).

Conlon, J. (2015) 'The reality of homelessness, the fight for decent housing and lessons from the Bolt Hostel', *Workers Solidarity Movement*, 24 August. Available at: www.wsm.ie/c/reality-homelessness-dublin-bolt-hostel-history (accessed 29 May 2018).

Costelloe, N. (2015) 'VIDEO: Dublin hostel renovated for homeless families in need', *Irish Examiner*, 21 July. Available at: www. irishexaminer.com/video/lifestyle/video-dublin-hostel-renovated-for-homeless-families-in-need-343571.html (accessed 29 May 2018).

De Moor, J. (2016) 'Practicing openness: investigating the role of everyday decision making in the production of squatted space', *International Journal of Urban and Regional Research*, 40(2): 410–24.

DeSilvey, C. and Edensor, T. (2013) 'Reckoning with ruins', *Progress in Human Geography*, 37(4): 465–85.

Di Feliciantonio, C. (2016) 'Subjectification in times of indebtedness and neoliberal/austerity urbanism', *Antipode*, 48(5): 1206–27.

Di Feliciantonio, C. (2017) 'Spaces of the expelled as spaces of the urban commons? Analysing the re-emergence of squatting initiatives in Rome', *International Journal of Urban and Regional Research*, 41(5): 708–25.

Di Feliciantonio, C. and O'Callaghan, C. (2020) 'Struggles over property in the "post-political" era: notes on the *political* from Rome and Dublin', *Environment and Planning C: Politics and Space*, 38(2): 195–213.

Farrell, S. (2015) 'The Bolt Hostel story', *Trade Union Left Forum*, 24 July. Available at: www.tuleftforum.com/the-bolt-hostel-story/ (accessed 28 November 2017).

Focus Ireland (2020) *About Homelessness*, Dublin: Focus Ireland. Available at: www.focusireland.ie/resource-hub/about-homelessness/ (accessed 23 June 2020).

Harvey, D. (2011) *A Brief History of Neoliberalism*, Oxford: Oxford University Press.

Hearne, R. (2014) 'Achieving a right to the city in practice: reflections on community struggles in Dublin', *Human Geography*, 3(1): 14–25.

Hearne, R., O' Callaghan, C., Di Feliciantonio, C. and Kitchin, R. (2018) 'The relational articulation of housing crisis and activism in post-crash Dublin, Ireland', in N. Gray (ed) *Rent and Its Discontents: A Century of Housing Struggle*, Lanham: Rowman & Littlefield, pp 153–67.

Holland, K. (2017) 'What exactly did the Apollo House occupation achieve?', *The Irish Times*, 13 January. Available at: www.irishtimes.com/news/social-affairs/what-exactly-did-the-apollo-house-occupation-achieve-1.2935129 (accessed 28 November 2017).

Hosford, P. (2017) 'Ghost estates are disappearing, but what's actually happening with them?', *The Journal*, 2 April. Available at: www.thejournal.ie/ghost-estates-whats-happening-3308561-Apr2017/ (accessed 17 March 2020).

Huron, A. (2015) 'Working with strangers in saturated space: reclaiming and maintaining the urban commons', *Antipode*, 47(4): 963–79.

Irish Housing Network (2017) *Irish Housing Network – A Radical Network Dedicated to the Right to Decent Housing for All*, Dublin: Irish Housing Network. Available at: http://irishhousingnetwork.org/ (accessed 12 September 2018).

Kavanagh, C. (2016) 'What's going on now with the Bolt Hostel?', *Dublin Inquirer*, 17 August. Available at: www.dublininquirer.com/2016/08/16/follow-up-whats-going-on-now-with-the-bolt-hostel/ (accessed 28 November 2017).

Kitchin, R., O'Callaghan, C. and Gleeson, J. (2014) 'The new ruins of Ireland? Unfinished estates in the post-Celtic Tiger era: debates and developments', *International Journal of Urban and Regional Research*, 38(3): 1069–80.

Lynch, T. (2017) 'Organizing against the Irish housing emergency', *ROAR Magazine*, 20 February. Available at: https://roarmag.org/essays/ireland-housing-crisis/ (accessed 17 April 2020).

Martinez López, M.A. (2013) 'The squatters' movement in Europe: a durable struggle for social autonomy in urban politics', *Antipode*, 45(4): 866–87.

Martínez López, M.A. (2020) *Squatters in the Capitalist City: Housing, Justice, and Urban Politics*, New York, NY: Routledge.

McCarthy, B. (2017) 'Speaking out for the homeless at Dublin's Apollo House', *Al Jazeera*, 3 January. Available at: www.aljazeera.com/indepth/features/2017/01/speaking-homeless-dublin-apollo-house-170103094842868.html (accessed 28 November 2017).

McDermott, S. (2019) '"It had fantastic resonance": a year after taking over Dublin's vacant buildings, Take Back the City disbands', *The Journal*, 18 April. Available at: www.thejournal.ie/take-back-the-city-housing-movement-ireland-4769573-Aug2019/ (accessed 15 June 2020).

McGuirk, J. (2015) 'Urban commons have radical potential – it's not just about community gardens', *The Guardian*, 15 June. Available at: www.theguardian.com/cities/2015/jun/15/urban-common-radical-community-gardens (accessed 10 November 2018).

Németh, J., and Langhorst, J. (2014) 'Rethinking urban transformation: temporary uses for vacant land', *Cities*, 40: 143–50.

Ní Aodha, G.N (2017) 'Mannix Flynn: "Apollo House completely failed"', *The Journal*, 25 February. Available at: www.thejournal.ie/mannix-flynn-late-late-show-3258478-Feb2017/ (accessed 12 November 2018).

O'Sullivan, D. (2016) 'Activists take over city block to house Irish homeless', *CNN*, 19 December. Available at: www.cnn.com/2016/12/19/world/ireland-dublin-building-homeless/index.html (accessed 28 November 2017).

Priemus, H. (2015) 'Squatters in the city: new occupation of vacant offices', *International Journal of Housing Policy*, 15(1): 84–92.

Pruijt, H. (2013) 'The logic of urban squatting: the logic of urban squatting in Europe', *International Journal of Urban and Regional Research*, 37(1): 19–45.

Simone, A.M. (2004) 'People as infrastructure: intersecting fragments in Johannesburg', *Public Culture,* 16(3): 407–29.

Simone, A.M. (2019) *Improvised Lives: Rhythms of Endurance in an Urban South*, Cambridge and Medford, MA: Polity.

Thurber, A. and Fraser, J. (2016) 'Disrupting the order of things: public housing tenant organizing for material, political and epistemological justice', *Cities*, 57: 55–61.

Till, K.E. (2005) *The New Berlin: Memory, Politics, Place*, Minneapolis, MN: University of Minnesota Press.

Vasudevan, A. (2015) 'The autonomous city: towards a critical geography of occupation', *Progress in Human Geography*, 39(3): 316–37.

Vasudevan, A. (2017) *The Autonomous City: A History of Urban Squatting*, London and New York, NY: Verso.

Wood, P.B. (2017) *Citizenship, Activism and the City: The Invisible and the Impossible*, London and New York, NY: Routledge.

Ziehl, O. and Oßwald, S. (2015) 'Practices in second hand spaces: producing value from vacancy', *Ephemera*, 15(1): 262–77.

Conclusion: Centring vacancy – towards a research agenda

Cian O'Callaghan and Cesare Di Feliciantonio

Introduction

In the conclusion, we reflect on what we can learn from the chapters in this book about working critically and productively with ruins and urban vacancy as a lens to interrogate wider urban challenges. The genesis for this collection started with a workshop held at Trinity College Dublin in March 2017. While seeking to draw together a wide range of voices and approaches on the topic, our starting point was the ways in which the 2008 global financial crisis had made vacancy more visible and politicised across a range of different contexts. That crisis constituted a juncture that was expressed in the 'new ruins' that represented the collapse of a particular manifestation of financialised capitalism. 'New ruins' provided a concept to grapple with the political, economic and cultural fallout of the crisis, and to expand our theoretical lexicon. In the post-crisis period, vacant spaces presented a set of possibilities for dealing with the legacies of the previous era of growth and decline, becoming a vehicle to narrate the crisis (O'Callaghan et al, 2014), while also proposing alternative urban futures based on the commons (Bresnihan and Byrne, 2015). Since that time, a number of changes have occurred: the reassertion of neoliberal policy responses; the rolling out of new forms of financialisation; the increased pressure on urban real estate markets due to tourism and platform capitalism; the foreclosure and aggressive eviction of alternative projects/spaces; and the emergence of a regime to govern vacancy. While the possibilities presented by vacancy in the post-crisis juncture have been eroded, as a conceptual category and a site of policy, market and grass-roots intervention, urban vacant spaces remain significant.

As this book demonstrates, a growing body of work seeks to understand vacancy as being at the intersection of a range of emergent urban problems. If our political and conceptual understandings of the possibilities of vacancy in the post-crisis period were naive, unpacking more fully the dynamic role that vacancy plays in the city can provide a lens to address pressing questions. It is perhaps too early to assess what ways vacancy will present a challenge and an opportunity in the post-COVID-19 city. However, with the prospect of looming recession and the logistical challenges of social distancing putting strain on the economy, we can imagine increased vacant retail and commercial spaces, while mainstreaming homeworking will impact the supply and demand of office space. The collapse in tourism and international students has already led some cities, such as Lisbon, to redress the balance between short-term lets and long-term housing unaffordability by moving towards a 'standard' rent. Similarly, with burgeoning precarity, we can expect interventions and reappropriations of vacant spaces, albeit in a form that is yet to come.

With this task in mind, it is essential that we build on the repertoire of knowledge gleaned from the post-crisis period of engagement and scholarly interest on ruins and vacant spaces. This book speaks to such a task by synthesising a range of approaches that closely interrogate the material and discursive processes that go into the production of vacant space.

Drawing Lefebvre into dialogue with ruin studies, Gordillo (2014) provides a useful framework for thinking about different forms of vacant space as socially produced. His dialectic between 'ruin' and 'rubble' casts vacant sites/buildings as contested spaces wherein elite actors attempt to produce what Lefebvre (1991 [1974]) calls 'abstract space' (see also O'Callaghan, 2018). By attending to the ruins and vacant spaces as sites of discursive struggle, lively encounter, capitalist enclosure and political contention, the chapters in this volume illuminate a set of processes that go into producing vacancy in a range of manifestations. As we argued in the Introduction, and as illustrated throughout the different sections of the book, (exceptional) ruins and (ordinary) vacant spaces operate on a continuum; moreover, we can employ the conceptual tools of ruins studies to more deeply interrogate urban vacancy as an active and constitutive component of cities. In the remainder of this chapter, we briefly map out a research agenda based on two primary components: (1) to provide a more nuanced continuum between ruins and vacant space; and (2) to emphasise the processes and conceptual work involved in articulating three different manifestations (the ruin, vacancy as empty space and vacancy as resource for the commons).

The ruin

It is undeniable that *vacant spaces are made into ruins* through a confluence of actors and relations. Pohl's discussion of ruins as a 'fantasy' space gets to the heart of what makes modern ruins significant in representational and affective terms. By looking closely at Michigan Central Station, Pohl pieces together how ruins become sites of 'enjoyment' through their function as a hinge articulating specific narratives connecting the present to a world before the crisis. Specific vacant spaces become targeted to articulate this 'fantasy' and, through specific interventions, begin to resonate as ruins, thus serving an important cultural function in cities. As the chapters by Till and Jasper on Berlin highlight, however, the articulation of particular sites as ruins, and therefore as culturally significant, is a heavily contested, messy and ambivalent process. Till weaves these questions into the context of Berlin's history as a 'wounded city' (Till, 2012) marked by violence, as well as its contested property claims stemming from partition. Her analysis shows the complex negotiations between memory-work, urban development pressures, property restoration and 'dignity restitution'. Whereas the Jewish girls' school was forcibly made into a ruin by the violence of National Socialism, its recognition *as a ruin* and its subsequent renewal as a place restoring Jewish life within the city were the outcome of campaigning, temporary interventions and an accommodation with commercial property interests. As a counterpoint, Jasper's chapter shows how, despite many forms of intervention, wastelands have been progressively transformed into abstract space for redevelopment. The question of what becomes a ruin of cultural significance or, alternatively, can be erased by capitalist redevelopment requires a relational perspective on urban social space, as well as an approach that excavates hidden practices and forgotten histories of vacant spaces.

Focusing on the diverse temporalities of ruin, therefore, is an increasingly fertile avenue for research. Whereas scholarship on modern ruins privileges grand narratives of epochal change, the perspective of 'new ruins' allows us to access how ruins factor into the making of these epochal narratives and, moreover, how these are reversible or at least adaptable. Lee's chapter focuses on China's monumental 'ghost cities', but her argument could equally be applied to other post-crisis cities where a glut of housing oversupply was transformed into a ruin to act as a vehicle to mediate crisis. Across countries like Spain, Ireland and the US, these ruins of crisis have subsequently receded back into the landscape of business-as-usual development. However, their brief moment makes them all the more apposite to interrogating the making and unmaking of ruins. Thinking through and with these dynamics offers us a lens to view 'new ruins' as quotidian and evolving.

Vacancy as empty space

If ruins can become important cultural sites that make them highly visible within cities, property development interests often seek to do the opposite: to *render space as vacant* and, therefore, clear for redevelopment. As the chapters in Part II suggest, however, there is often significant work involved in this process. Vacant spaces are subject to all kinds of sanctioned and unsanctioned uses (Doron, 2000), which are held in abeyance by the dominance of capitalist urban imaginaries and the spectre of future development. In order to enable redevelopment, 'vacant' sites need to be discursively and materially cleared. The literature on property studies, gentrification and urban regeneration provides tools for conceptualising these processes, but a new sub-field on the political economy of vacancy has begun to emerge. By foregrounding empty lots as lived and contested spaces, McClintock's chapter shows how the neoliberal city is dependent on settler-colonial and racial-capitalist logics to render urban space *as vacant* in order to transition it towards particular types of desirable uses and users. As Gribat's chapter also shows, producing vacancy often involves promoting and encouraging temporary uses that can serve to erase existing uses and users, as well as condition particular trajectories of future redevelopment. The chapters by Gribat and by Caramaschi and Coppola both document the arsenal of different rationalities and strategies that 'resolve' vacancy in ways that fit with the grain of dominant urban development logics. While in L'Aquilla, temporary or emergency responses became permanent housing solutions, in Tangier (as Wagner's chapter shows), forms of ordinary daily use sustain the status quo by giving the appearance of activity where there is (partial) emptiness. In the extreme, then, is demolition, which clears the material and memory traces of previous uses. As Gribat's chapter shows, demolition requires a rationale (or problematisation) to be operationalised. Koscielniak's chapter adds another dimension to this research agenda by emphasising decline itself as part of the apparatus of uneven geographical development. Recognising the material and metabolic aspects of producing vacancy, his call to turn the tools of urban geographical research on demolition itself offers a crucial step change in our vocabularies of urban decline and regeneration. In sum, these cases show how different rationalities and strategies – primarily working with the grain of neoliberal market logics – make vacancy visible or invisible in order to pursue particular development agendas.

Vacancy as resource for the commons

In opposition to the *terra nullius* or abstract space that property interests seek to achieve, bottom-up reappropriations – aiming to performatively stage vacant sites/buildings as urban commons – suggest alternative ways of valuing vacant spaces. The set of high-profile occupations following the global financial crisis have become characteristic of new forms of what García-Lamarca (2017) calls 'insurgent activism'. Mobilising around housing and wider issues of precarity, these groups employ a diverse range of strategies and actions. Engagements with vacancy have formed a core concern. Although such engagements are often temporary – either by design or due to their eviction – they differ from other forms of temporary use in their explicit politicisation of vacancy. Such projects involve the establishment of new social relations. It comes as no surprise, then, to see an increasing number of scholarly analyses focusing on the process of subjectivation of those involved (for example, Di Feliciantonio, 2016, 2017; Karaliotas, 2017). Vacant sites/buildings are a significant component in this process. Moreover, as the chapters in this book suggest, vacancy is neither inert nor taken as given in such encounters. The chapters by Ferreri and Caulkins emphasise how politicising vacancy is an ambivalent and contested process. Whereas vacancy is often normatively considered in terms of a simple opposition between buildings/space either 'in use' or 'vacant long-term', these analyses show that vacancy is much more complicated to quantify and mobilise around. Official data on vacancy can over- or undercount residential or commercial units. This can be due to both inefficiencies in methodologies of data collection and the complexities of determining vacancy itself – more often than long-term vacancy, dynamic property markets produce short-term, intermittent or seasonal vacancy. As such, making claims on vacant buildings/sites for urban commoning involves contesting private property via alternative understandings of property rights (O'Callaghan et al, 2018; Noterman, 2020). Both Ferreri and Caulkins elaborate the contested logics at play in Barcelona and São Paulo when vacancy is mobilised to produce new property relations, emphasising the kinds of spatial, policy and legal entanglements that result. Di Feliciantonio and O'Callaghan, in their chapter, provide a framework for understanding the process by which activist groups articulate vacancy as a resource for 'world-making'. Prefiguring the kinds of social infrastructures formed within experimental occupations of vacant spaces, there must be a *claim, a vision and an apparatus* that transform – via a self-decreed expropriation – vacant sites/buildings into a resource for the commons. The work that is involved in this process relates to Lefebvre's (2003 [1970]) concept of *autogestion*. As Purcell (2014 149) suggests, '[a]ppropriation is thus closely linked to both de-alienation and *autogestion*, to inhabitants making the space of the city their own again.' As McArdle's chapter highlights, although appropriations and occupations may be temporary, the apparatus for mobilising alternative claims on vacant space contributes to new forms of praxis that survive individual actions.

Conclusion

To sum up, a research agenda focused on urban vacancy needs to trouble the stability of existing categorisations. To do so, as the chapters collected in this volume demonstrate, it has to document the processes at work in: making vacancy (in)visible; shaping cultural imaginaries around particular sites or, conversely, rendering others as 'empty' non-place; and how dominant understandings are challenged by bottom-up reappropriations. This involves many conceptual and methodological tools familiar to urban geographers, planners and others; however, by turning these on vacancy itself – as its own object of study – we enable them to do new critical work. As sites are increasingly cannibalised in the interests of financial capital and face new challenges in the post-pandemic context, it is within the interstices of vacancy that we can discover the capacity for urban transformation.

References

Bresnihan, P. and Byrne, M. (2015) 'Escape into the city: everyday practices of commoning and the production of urban space in Dublin', *Antipode*, 47(1): 36–54.

Di Feliciantonio, C. (2016) 'Subjectification in times of indebtedness and neoliberal/austerity urbanism', *Antipode*, 48(5): 1206–27.

Di Feliciantonio, C. (2017) 'Spaces of the expelled as spaces of the urban common? Analysing the re-emergence of squatting initiatives in Rome', *International Journal of Urban and Regional Research*, 41(5): 708–25.

Doron, G.M. (2000) 'The dead zone and the architecture of transgression', *City*, 4(2): 247–63.

García-Lamarca, M. (2017) 'From occupying plazas to recuperating housing: insurgent practices in Spain', *International Journal of Urban and Regional Research*, 41(1): 37–53.

Gordillo, G.R. (2014) *Rubble: The Afterlife of Destruction*, Durham: Duke University Press.

Karaliotas, L. (2017) 'Staging equality in Greek squares: hybrid spaces of political subjectification', *International Journal of Urban and Regional Research*, 41(1): 54–69.

Lefebvre, H. (1991 [1974]) *The Production of Space*, Oxford: Blackwell.

Lefebvre, H. (2003 [1970]) *The Urban Revolution* (trans R. Bononno), Minneapolis, MN, and London: University of Minnesota Press.

Noterman, E. (2020) 'Taking back vacant property', *Urban Geography*, online first, DOI: 10.1080/02723638.2020.1743519.

O'Callaghan, C. (2018) 'Planetary urbanization in ruins: provisional theory and Ireland's crisis', *Environment and Planning D: Society and Space*, 36(3): 420–38.

O'Callaghan, C., Boyle, M. and Kitchin, R. (2014) 'Post-politics, crisis, and Ireland's "ghost estates"', *Political Geography*, 42: 121–33.

O'Callaghan, C., Di Feliciantonio, C. and Byrne, M. (2018) 'Governing urban vacancy in post-crash Dublin: contested property and alternative social projects', *Urban Geography*, 39(6): 868–91.

Purcell, M. (2014) 'Possible worlds: Henri Lefebvre and the right to the city', *Journal of Urban Affairs*, 36(1): 141–54.

Till, K.E. (2012) 'Wounded cities: memory-work and a place-based ethics of care', *Political Geography*, 31(1): 3–14.

Index

Page numbers in *italic* type refer to figures and photographs; those in **bold** type refer to tables. References to endnotes show both the page number and the note number (231n3).

A

abandonment 5–6, 86n7, 125, 204
  and absent ownership 168–9, 170
  and ghost cities 79–80, 81
  and post-disaster redevelopment 130, *131*, 138, 139, 140
Academy of Science, Berlin 43
activism, political 12, 181–93, 197–208, 211–24, 247–8
  and artistic initiatives 230, 233
  Barcelona 181, 184, 188–9, *190*, *191*, *192*, 193n7
  and empowerment 223, 235
  and eviction 190, 193n7, 204, 211, 216, 219–20
  and financialisation of housing 182, 237
  and global financial crisis 182, 234
  and homelessness 232, 237
  Ireland 217, 220–3, 229–30, 238
  and Jewish girls' school, Berlin 41, 48
  and neoliberalism 182, 217, 220, 222, 223, 238
  and residents' participation 204–5, 207
  Rome 211, 216, 218–20
  São Paulo 204, 206–7
  and social function of property 13, 182, 200–1, 202, 203–4, 207
  and urban agriculture 100–1, 103
  and vacant housing 181–93, 193n7, 204, 206–7
  and vacant space/land 215, 229–35, 238
  and volunteers 61, 234–6, 237
  and wastelands, Berlin 54, 55, 67
  see also social movements; social projects, alternative; squatting/ occupation
Acuerdo Ciutadano, Barcelona 185
Adamo Group 150, 152, 153, 154, 156
AEG electric company 58, 59
affluence 96, 97
agriculture, urban 10, 91–104
  and activism 100–1, 103
  and appropriation/ reappropriation 95–6, 103
  and capitalism 92, 95–6, 102, 103
  and capitalist urbanisation 93, 94, 102

  and commons 92, 93, 102, 103
  and displacement/ dispossession 102, 103
  and entrepreneurship 91, 93, 95
  and gentrification 96, 99–101, 102
  and green cities 10, 92, 93, 95, 101
  and Indigenous people 92, 97–8, 99, 102, 103, 104n1
  and land use 93, 94
  and race issues 10, 92, 98, 101, 102, 103, 245
  and reclamation 98, 102, 103
  and settler colonialism 10, 97–102, 103, 198
  and sustainability 92, 95–6, 97, 101
  and use value 93, 97, 102
  and wastelands 91, 99–100
Airbnb 216, 237
Akers, J. 157
AKT Peerless 149–50, 152, 153, 154
alcohol consumption 205
'Altergrowth' project 110
Alternative Liste: Für Demokratie und Umweltschutz environmental party 60
amenities, social and civic 76, 78, 133
American dream 26, 97
Anderson, J. 231
Andreucci, D. 148
antagonism, political 11–12
anti-Semitism 9, 35, 36, 43
Apollo House, Dublin 13, 222, 230, 232, 233, 235, 236, 237
Apostolopoulou, E. and Adams, W.M. 65
appropriation/reappropriation 13, 38, 54, 82, 189, 248
  and infrastructures 212–14, 215, 217, 223
  and urban agriculture 95–6, 103
Arendt, Hannah 9, 35, 36, 41–6, 48
Argent Securities 151
art galleries, international 41
artistic initiatives 198
  Halle/Saale, East Germany 115, *116*, 117–18
  and infrastructures 230, 233, 236
  and wastelands, Berlin 54, 59, 63

Asmus, Ullrich 60
Atuahene, B. 36
Audin, J. 84
'Auditorium Elements and *Origins of Totalitarianism*' installation (Hefti, Hofer and Oettli) 44–5
austerity measures 2, 109, 146
  and infrastructures 216, 217, 223, 229, 234, 236
autogestion 205–6, 248
Azienda Territoriale per l'Edilizia Residenziale (ATER) 137

B

backfilling 11, 149–50, 152, 153, 154–6, 157
Backfill Material Programme 149
back-to-the-city movement 147, 198
Badiou, A. 22
Barcelona 12–13, 184–92, 193n3, 247
Barcelona en Comú (BnC) 184
Barcelona Housing Obsevatory (O-HB) 184, 185
Beer, Alexander 42
Behrens, Alfred 53
Behrens, Peter 58
Benjamin, W. 4
Berlin 37, 40–1, 245
  activism 41, 48, 55
  artistic initiatives 9, 35, 41–6, 48, 54, 59, 63
  and biotopes/biodiversity/ ecology 53–8, 60–1, 63–7
  gentrification 47, 62–3
  parks/leisure spaces 58, 59, 61, 62, 66
  see also Jewish life and culture; wastelands
Berliner Stadtbahnbilder film 53
'Bertolt Brecht' grammar school, Berlin 35
biotope, urban 53, 54, 55, 60–1, 63, 64–5, 66
Bloc Llavors, Barcelona 190, *191*
Board of Third Sector Organisations, Catalonia 185
Bolt Hostel, Dublin 13, 221, 230, 232–3, 234–5, 236, 237
Brazil 200, 208
  see also São Paulo, Brazil
Bresnihan, P. and Byrne, M. 236
buildings, vacants *see* housing, vacant

C

Candidatura d'Unitat Popular (CUP) 184
capitalism 4–5, 29–30, 67, 81, 148, 233, 243

racial 10, 92, 98, 102, 103, 245
  and urban agriculture 92, 95–6, 102, 103
Caramaschi, Sara 10–11, 125–41, 245
care, ethics of 39
Carpenters Estate, London 181
Cartesian notion of empty space 198
CASE, 'sustainable and eco-commpatible anti-seismic complexes' 127, *128*, 134–5, 136, 139
castration 23, 24
Catalonia 183, 189
Caulkins, Matthew 13, 197–208, 247
celebrity endorsement 230, 233
Celtic Tiger era, Ireland 86n7
cens d'habitatge buits 184, 186
census 2010, Brazil 201
census 2011, Spain 183, 184, 186
Charta für das Berliner Stadtgrün 65
China 75–6, 245
  see also 'ghost cities', Chinese; Ordos Kangbashi, Inner Mongolia
Choy, T. 64
Citibank 201
cities, empty 1–3
  see also 'ghost cities', Chinese; housing, vacant
cities, green 10, 92, 93, 95, 101
cities, post-crisis 6, 14n1, 22–4, 147, 238
cities, wounded 36–8, 39, 245
City Statute, São Paulo 200
civic society 26, 66, 120
Cochrane, A. 113
colonialism, settler 10, 97–102, 103, 198, 245
commercial property market 63–4
commodification 155, 213
commons, urban 12, 247–8
  and infrastructures 13, 213–15, 218, 220, 221, 236–7
  and urban agriculture 92, 93, 102, 103
  and vacant housing 182, 189
Communia initiative, San Lorenzo 211, 213–14, 216, 218–20
communities/neighbourhoods 100–1, 146, 147, 218, 220, 231–2, 235
CONFABV 185
Conference on Jewish Material Claims Against Germany (Claims Conference) 37, 42, 46
Connolly, C. 1
conservation/conservation areas 53, 55, 64, 65, 66, 113, 117
consierges *see* guardianship

Constitution, Brazil 200, 203–4, 207
construction, cyclical 81
Coppola, Alessandro 10–11, 125–41, 245
cortiços 201
Coulthard, G.S. 102
'Council of 11' 112
Cover, R. 199–200
COVID-19 pandemic 1–2, 73–4, 85, 223–4, 244
Crowne Plaza, Ordos 85
Cultural and Art Centre, Kangbashi 82, *83*
culture 198
  Berlin 40–1, 55, 58, 59, 63
  cultural heritage 117, 128, 133, 245
  cultural initiatives 115, 117
  Jewish life and culture 9, 36, 43, 46, 47, 245
Curtis Street, Detroit 153

D

data collection 12–13, 55, 183–4, 186, 192, 201, 247
death drive 8, 27–8
decay 21, 26, 27
decentralisation 75, 133
dehumanisation 97, 98
deindustrialisation 3, 58
Delaney, D. 200
democracy 45, 46
demolition 11, 114–15, 116, 119, 120, 145–57, 245
De Moor, J. 238
Departamento da Função Social da Propriedade (DFSP) 202, 203, 206
Department of Housing, Dublin 237
Department of Social Protection, Dublin 233, 234
dereliction *see* demolition
DeSilvey, C. and Edensor, T. 3, 35, 81
Desimini, J. 3
de Soto, H. 206
Detroit, Michigan 8, 11, 21–31, 99, 145–57
  and backfilling 149–50, 152, 153, 154–5, 157
  and environmental issues 149–50, 154
  and gentrification 146, 147
  and HHF 149, 150–2, **153**, 155, 156, 157
  and homeownership 147, 150–1
  and land use 147, 148, 154, 155, 156, 157
  and land value 147, 148, 157

Michigan Central Station 8, 25–6, 28, 29, 30–1, 245
  and mortgages 145, 147, 150–1, 152
  redevelopment 29–30, 99, 146–7, 149, 155, 156–7
  and rentiership 148, 157
Detroit Blight Removal Task Force (DBRTF) 145
Detroit Building Authority (DBA) 150
Detroit City Council 150, 156
Detroit Demolition Programme (DDP) 145, 148, 149–50, 151, 152, 154, 156
Detroit Land Bank Authority (DLBA) 147, 150, 151, 153
Detroit Planning and Development Department 151
Deutsche Bahn AG 64, 66
D'habitatge buit a habitatge social working group 185
Di Feliciantonio, Cesare 1–15, 204, 211–24, 231, 243–8
difference, social 97
Diggable City report 93, 99–100
dignity restoration 36, 38–9, 40, 47–8
Dikeç, M. 113
Dillon, B. 4, 27
Dillon, L. 99
Di Palma, V. 67
dirt 149, 154
disadvantage, social 139, 140
disasters, natural 125, 126, 127
'Discovery Day Open Glaucha' event 117
discrimination 40
displacement/dispossession 98, 102, 103, 190, 192, 193n7, 218
DMC group 155–6
Dolar, M. 24, 25
Donald, S.H. and Lindner, C. *83*
donations 233, 234–6
Doron, G.M. 170
Dublin 13, 217, 220–3, 229–38
  Apollo House 13, 222, 230, 232, 233, 235, 236, 237
  Bolt Hostel 13, 221, 230, 232–3, 234–5, 236, 237
  and emergency housing 221–2, 232–3
  homelessness 217, 221–2, 223, 230, 233
  and housing crisis 221, 232, 233, 237
  and neoliberalism 220, 222, 238
  and squatting/occupation 217, 230
Dublin City Council 222, 230, 232–3
Dudow, Slátan 59
Duggan, Mike 26, 145, 150

E

ecology 9, 55–8, 60, 61, 64
Ehemalige Jüdische Mädschenschule
    Berlin 47
empowerment 233, 235
enjoyment 8, 26–8, 245
entrances, single 204
entrepreneurship 91, 93, 95, 147
environmental issues 95–6, 149–50,
    154
    see also biotope, urban;
        ecology; wastelands
Europa Risorse fund 127, *128*
everyday life 200, 212, 220, 232
eviction 190, 193n7, 204, 211, 216,
    219–20, 243
exclusion 140, 146, 182
experience, lived 82–4, 85–6
exploitation 98, 154, 172

F

fantasy 24–5, 26, 28, 30–1, 244–5
Farkas, Brian 146, 152
favelas 201, 206
Federal Republic of Germany
    (FRG) 37
Ferguson Street, Detroit 153
Ferreri, Mara 12, 181–93, 215, 247
film production 53, 59
financialisation of housing 54, 65, 175,
    182, 183, 188, 237, 243
Focus E15 181
Ford Motor Company 25–6, 29,
    30, 147
Forkert, K. 41
Forouhar, Parastou 45
Foucault, M. 110
Frente Luta e Moradia 202
Freud, S. 27–8
Fuchs, Michael 46
Fullilove, M.T. 37
Funken, P. 42, 46
Future World, Ordos Kangbashi 80

G

Galster, G.C. 25–6
García-Lamarca, M. 247
gardens 93–6, 97
Genghis Khan Square, Ordos
    Kangbashi 78–9
genocide 37, 44, 97–8
gentrification 98, 198–9
    Berlin 47, 62–3
    Detroit 146, 147
    and urban agriculture 96, 99–101,
        102
    and vacant space/land 6, 62

German Democratic Republic
    (GDR) 38, 109, 111
Germany *see* Berlin; Halle/Saale, East
    Germany; wastelands
'ghost cities', Chinese 4, 9, 73–86, 245
    and abandonment 79–80, 81
    and lived experience 82–4, 85–6
    local government 76, 77, 80, 81
    residents in 82–4, 85–6
    and urbanisation 75, 76–8, 84
ghost estates, Ireland 21, 183
Gilbert, Dan 29, 145, 147
Glaucha, Halle/Saale 110, 113,
    116–18, 119
global financial crisis 2008 (GFC) 4–5,
    21, 109, 145, 243
    and activism 182, 234
    and infrastructures 216, 217, 229, 234
    and vacant housing 182, 183–4
    and vacant space/land 6, 216, 217
'Global War on Terror' 44, 46
Gobi Desert 76
Google Earth 150
Gordillo, G.R. 5, 244
graffiti 188
Great Recession 145
green corridors 58, 60, 66
Gribat, Nina 10, 11, 109–21, 245
Griessmühle club 63
Grüne Mitte plan 60
guardianship 6, 11, 164, 171–2,
    173–4, 175

H

habitats 56–7, 58, 60, 64, 66
Halle/Saale, East Germany 10, 109–21
    artistic initiatives 115, 116, 117–18
    Glaucha 110, 113, 116–18, 119
    and ISEK 113, 115, 116, 121n3
    Neustadt 110, 111, 112, 113–16, 119
    population figures 109, 121n1
    problematisation 110, 113, 115, 116,
        117, 119
    Stadtumbau Ost programme 113–16,
        117, 119, 120, 121n4
    and state subsidisation 117, 119, 120
Hammet, Beate 47
'Hannah Arendt *Denkraum*' exhibition,
    Berlin 9, 35, 41–6, 48
Hard, G. 64
Hardest Hit Funds (HHF) 149, 150–2,
    153, 155, 156, 157
Harvey, D. 154
health, mental and social 223
Hearne, R. 229
histories 5, 8, 9
Hocking, Scott 30

homelessness 13, 59, 197, 229–38
  and activism 232, 237
  Dublin 217, 221–2, 223, 230, 233
  and infrastructures 223, 229, 230,
    232, 233, 237
  Ireland 229, 234
  and vacant housing 189, 190, 192,
    193n7, 197
Home Sweet Home (HSH) 233,
  235, 236
Hotel Neustadt 115
housing, emergency 11, 189, 221–2,
  232–3, 245
housing, excess 86n7, 112–16,
  118, 119
housing, high-rise 114, 115
housing, luxury 62, 218–19
housing, private 129
housing, public see housing, social
housing, social 181, 216, 220
  and post-disaster redevelopment 130,
    135, 136–8, 139
  and vacant housing 120, 121, 184–5,
    187, 202, 204–6
housing, temporary 126, 127–35, 204,
  233, 245
housing, vacant 10, 13, 109–21,
  181–93
  and activism 181–2
    Barcelona 181, 184, 188–9, 190,
      191, 192, 193n7
    and eviction 190, 193n7, 204
    São Paulo 204, 206–7
    and squatting/occupation 188–9,
      192–3, 206
  as a catalyst for action 165, 234, 238
  and commons 182, 189
  and conservation/conservation
    areas 113, 117
  and data collection 12–13, 181–93,
    201
  and demolition 114–15, 116, 119,
    120, 245
  and displacement/dispossession 190,
    192, 193n7
  and excess housing 112–16, 118,
    119
  and financialisation of housing 182,
    183, 188
  and global financial crisis 182, 183–4
  and homelessness 189, 190, 192,
    193n7, 197
  and investment in property 117, 188,
    189–90, 191
  and oversupply of housing 119,
    125–6, 128, 130, 131, 141,
    183, 245

and post-disaster redevelopment
    125–6, 128, 130, 131, 133, 136,
    138, 141
  and problematisation 110, 113, 115,
    116, 117, 119
  and property ownership 112, 114,
    117, 119, 185, 186–7, 207
  and public housing companies 112,
    114, 119, 121n2
  and real estate investment trusts
    (REITS) 185, 189–91
  and refurbishment 186, 187, 189, 191
  and restructuring 113, 119, 121
  and rightsizing 114, 116, 119
  and social housing 120, 121, 184–5,
    187, 202, 204–6
  and socially productve use 197, 199,
    200, 203, 244
  and social movements 185, 206–7,
    215
  Spain 181–2, 183–4
  and symbolic value 113, 115,
    116, 119
  and taxation 187, 203
  and temporary use 117, 119
  and tourism 186, 187, 188, 190, 191
  and urban change 116–18, 119
  and urban vacancy 109–21, 183, 192
  see also Barcelona; 'ghost cities',
    Chinese; Halle/Saale, East
    Germany; São Paulo, Brazil
housing as capital 164, 169, 175
housing associations 120
housing crisis
  Dublin 221, 232, 233, 237
  and infrastructures 216, 221, 232, 237
  Spain 12, 183, 190
  and wastelands 59, 66
housing insecurity 148, 232
housing market 134, 186, 193n3
housing policy, GDR 111
housing politics 205–7
housing rights 187, 232
housing stock 114, 120, 183–4, 186
housing vouchers 127, 128
Huron, A. 214, 220
Huyssen, A. 46

I

impacts, social and
  environmental 65, 95–6
imperialism, European 165–6
Indigenous lands and people 92, 97–8,
  99, 102, 103, 104n1
inequality, social 40, 120–1, 135, 189
  elites, propertied 10, 165
  low-income people 94, 106, 121, 147
infrastructure, social 212

infrastructures, (im)material 13, 218–23, 229–38, 247
  and activism 211, 215, 217, 218–23, 229–35, 238
  and alternative social projects 212, 213–15
  and appropriation/reappropriation 212–14, 215, 217, 223
  and artistic initiatives 230, 233, 236
  and austerity measures 216, 217, 223, 229, 234, 236
  and commons 13, 213–15, 218, 220, 221, 236–7
  and cultures of resistance 214, 218, 220
  Dublin 217, 220–3, 230, 232–3, 238
  and emergency housing 221–2, 232–3
  and global financial crisis 216, 217, 229, 234
  and homelessness 223, 229, 230, 232, 233, 237
  and housing crisis 216, 221, 232, 237
  and neoliberalism 220, 222, 223, 238
  and ownership 216, 218, 233
  Rome 216–17, 218–20
  and social movements 213–14, 215, 217, 220–4, 236, 237
  and speculation 215, 216, 217
  and squatting/occupation 211–12, 215–20, 229–30, 231, 234–6, 238
inhabitants, local 199
innovation 185, 200, 206
Integriertes Stadtentwicklungskonzept (ISEK) policy document 113, 115, 116, 121n3
International Building Exhibition Urban Renewal Saxony-Anhalt (IBA) 117, 120, 121n7
investment 77–8
  and demolition 147, 148
  São Paulo 198, 202
  and vacant housing 117, 188, 189–90, 191
Ireland 21, 86n7, 183, 229
  see also Dublin
Irish Housing Network (IHN) 217, 221–2, 230, 232–3, 234–5, 236, 237
Izair Skender 151

J

Jacobs, J. 173
Jasper, Sandra 9, 53–67, 245
Jewish Community of Berlin (JCB) 42, 46, 47

Jewish girls' school, Berlin 35, 42–3, 46–7, 245
Jewish Heritage Europe 47
Jewish life and culture 9, 36, 43, 46, 47, 245
  and race issues 35, 39, 48
Jews, Moroccan 166
Jofa-Atelier film studios 59
Johannisthal airport, Berlin 61
justice, social 223–4, 236
justice, social and ecological 61–2
justice, spatial and restorative 9, 35, 36, 38–40, 46, 48

K

Katzir, Ram 'Milk Teeth' sculpture 42, *43*, 44
King, T.L. 98
Kitchin, R. 4, 21
Kolorado initiative 115
Koscielniak, Michael R.J. 11, 145–57, 245
Kuhle Wampe oder Wem gehört die Welt film 59
Kunst-Werk Institute for Contemporary Art (KW) 41–2

L

labour, forced 59
Lacanian psychoanalytic theory 8, 22–6, 28, 29–30
Lachmund, J. 61
Landau, R. 166
land contracts 147
land prices 206
landscape design 53
land use 39, 64
  and demolition 147, 148, 154, 155, 156, 157
  and urban agriculture 93, 94
  see also vacant space/land
land value 147, 148, 157, 203
L'Aquilla, Italy 10–11, 125–41, 245
  see also redevelopment, post-disaster
law/legality 231–2
  Brazilian law 202–3, 207, 208
Lee, Christina 9, 73–86, 245
Lefebvre, H. 199, 244, 248
LGBTQ events, Berlin 63
lifeworlds 13, 215, 231
'Liquid Urbanisms' 230, 239n2
Lisbon 244
lived experience 81, 84, 199, 203–4, 207, 238
lizards 56, 64
Llei pel Dret a l'Habitatge de Catalunya 187

local government 76, 77, 80, 81, 135–6
location of housing 205–6
logics, spatio-legal 13, 197–208
  logic of public
    administration 201, 202–3
  market logic 201, 202
  and productivity 197, 198–9, 200,
    201, 203
  see also squatting/occupation
loss 8, 21–31
  and enjoyment 8, 26–8, 245
  and fantasy 24–5, 26, 28, 30–
    1, 244–5
  and remainders 4, 8, 22, 24–6
Lynch, T. 236
Lyons, S. 27, 31

M

M7G interview 219, 220
Macaulay, R. 21, 26–7
maintenance 139, **152**, 169
MAP, 'provisional habitation
  module' 127, *128*
market potential 81, 93, 96, 146,
  197, 202
Martin, D. 81
Mauerweg, Berlin 66
McArdle, Rachel 13, 229–38, 248
McClintock, Nathan 10, 11,
  91–104, 245
McFarlane, C. 2, 212
McGowan, T. 29–30
McKittrick, K. 97
memorials 38, 39, 47
memory 30, 41, 46, 245
Michigan Central Station, Detroit 8,
  25–6, 28, 29, 30–1, 245
Michigan Central Station Preservation
  Society 26
Michigan State Housing Development
  Authority (MSHDA) 151, 152
migrants/migration 75, 135
  and absent ownership 166–7,
    169–70, 172–3, 175
Minha Casa Minha Vida
  programme 206
mining industry 76, 77, 78
M interview 222
mobility, circulatory 163–4, 168–70,
  173–4
mobility, population 129
modernisation 75, 117
Montreal, Canada 91, 92, 94, 95,
  101, 104n1
mortgages 145, 147, 150–1, 152
Motor City Mapping 145
Movimento Moradia Luta e Justiça
  (MMLJ) 201, 204–5

Müggelsee, lake 59
MUSP ('provisional school use
  module') 136

N

National Assets Management Agency
  (NAMA) 233, 234
National Demolition Association
  (NDA) 146
National Forum for Urban
  Reform 200
National Socialism 9, 35, 37–8, 42, 59
Natur-Park Südgelände,
  Schöneberg 53, 61
neglect 30, 147
neoliberalism 1, 3, 6, 96, 243, 245
  and activism 182, 217, 220, 222,
    223, 238
Neustadt, Halle/Saale 110, 111, 112,
  113–16, 119
Newham, East London 181
New Synagogue, Berlin 39
New York High Line model 62
Nicholls, W. 214
Niederschöneweide, Berlin 63
nightlife 63, 218
'nomos' 199–200
non-governmental organisations
  (NGOs) 135
non-human life 54, 55, 57–8, 64, 67
nostalgia 26, 30
Noterman, E. 215

O

Oberschöneweide, Berlin 63
obsolescence 80–1, 136, 139
O'Callaghan, Cian 1–15, 35, 211–24,
  231, 243–8
occupancy rates 80
offsetting 64, 65
Ökokonto strategy 65
Omplim els buits programme 185
Ordos Kangbashi, Inner Mongolia 9,
  76, 77–80, 81, 82, 84–5
Ordos Library, Ordos Kangbashi 78
Ordos Museum, Ordos Kangbashi 78,
  81, 86n4
Otherness 97–8
oversupply of housing 119, 125–6,
  128, 130, *131*, 141, 183, 245
  see also 'ghost cities', Chinese
ownership 13, 77, 92, 137
  and demolition 147, 150–1, 153
  and social class 10, 164, 165,
    169, 175
  and spatio-legal logics 203, 207
  and vacant housing 112, 119, 185,
    186, 187, 207

see also housing, social; property
    development; property rights;
    squatting/occupation
ownership, absent 11, 163–75
  and abandonment 168–9, 170
  and guardianship 6, 11, 164, 171–2,
    173–4, 175
  and housing as capital 164, 169, 175
  and migrants/migration 166–7,
    169–70, 172–3, 175
  and mobility 163–4, 168–70, 173–4
  and second homes 11, 167,
    169, 173–4
  and squatters 172, 174
  and tourism 166, 167
  and vacancy management 171–4, 175
ownership, private
  and demolition 147, 150–1
  and post-disaster
    redevelopment 133, 134
  and squatting/occupation 216,
    218, 233
  and vacant housing 114, 117,
    119, 186–7
ownership, public 133, 185, 187, 216

P

P21 interview 219, 220
Paperson, L. 100
Park am Gleisdreieck,
    Kreuzberg 53, 62
parking 171–2
parks/leisure spaces 58, 59, 60, 61,
    62, 66
Partido dos Trabalhadores (PT) 194,
    203, 206
'Petrification/Versteinerung'
    installation 43–4
Pettino area, L'Aquila 137
Pisos Buits programme, Barcelona 185
planning, urban 54, 59, 60, 65, 120,
    137, 140, 141
Plataforma de los Afectados por la
    Hipoteca (PAH), Spain 181, 184,
    217, 222
Pohl, Lucas 8, 21–31, 244–5
policing of squatters in vacant
    buildings 205
political economy 9
  see also agriculture, urban; demolition;
    Halle/Saale, East Germany;
    ownership, absent; redevelopment,
    post-disaster
population density 2, 79, 109, 121n1,
    128, 167
Portland, Oregon 92, 93, 94, 95, 96,
    99–100, 101, 104n1

post-crisis period 243
  post-crisis cities 6, 14n1, 22–4,
    147, 238
  post-crisis objects 24, 25
  post-crisis properties 11, 145–57,
    168–9, 238, 245, 247
Postkult initiative 117–18
Povinelli, E. 212
Prestes Maia, São Paulo 201, 204,
    207, 208
problematisation 110, 113, 115, 116,
    117, 119
productivity, social and economic 197,
    198–9, 200, 201, 203
profitability 11, 66, 78, 96, 115, 146,
    173, 190–1
Prohabit website 205
property development 41, 55, 66, 94,
    167, 199, 245
  see also redevelopment, post-disaster
property rights 13, 36–8, 138, 204, 247
property studies 2, 7, 246
psychoanalysis, Lacanian 8, 22–6, 28,
    29–30
psychogeography 9, 82
public housing companies 112, 114,
    119, 121n2
public-private partnerships 167
public services 135, 136
Purcell, M. 248

Q

quality of construction 81
Quest, Richard 73–4

R

race issues 147
  and Jewish life and culture 35, 39, 48
  and urban agriculture 10, 92, 98,
    101, 102, 103, 245
railway zones, abandoned *see* wastelands
real estate investment trusts
    (REITS) 185, 189–91
reclamation 98, 102, 103
record keeping 152–3, 156
Redell Salter 151
redevelopment 5–6, 198–9, 218–19,
    245, 246
  Detroit 29–30, 99, 146–7, 149,
    155, 156–7
redevelopment, post-disaster 10–11,
    125–41
  and abandonment 130, *131*, 138,
    139, 140
  and disadvantage 139, 140
  and oversupply of housing 125–6,
    128, 130, *131*, 141

and private ownership 133, 134
and reconstruction 126, 127–8,
   132–3, 134
and social housing 130, 135, 136–8,
   139
and state support 136, 137, 139, 140
and students 129, 135, 138, 142n2
and temporary housing 126, 127–
   35, 245
and urban planning 137, 140, 141
and vacant housing 125–6, 128, 130,
   131, 133, 136, 138, 141
refurbishment 186, 187, 189, 191
regeneration, urban 6, 40–1, 62–3
*Registre d'habitatges buits o amb ocupants
   sense títol habilitant* 185
regulations, stratification of 138
remainders 4, 8, 22, 24–6, 35
'remittance houses' 169–70
rental agents 172
rented property 135, 173, 244
rent gap 96, 147, 198
rentiership 148, 157
rent increases 63, 221
REO Nationwide Inc 151
reparation payments 37, 38
resettlement 100–1
Residential Tenancies Board,
   Dublin 221, 237
residents in ghost cities 82–4, 85–6
residents' participation 204–5, 207
resistance, cultures of 214, 218, 220
restructuring, with/without
   priority 113, 119, 121
reunification of Germany 37, 40, 61,
   111–12, 116, 119
rightsizing 114, 116, 119, 140
Robinson, M. 81
Rome 13, 211, 216, 219–20
Roseler, Martha, 'Reading Hannah
   Arendt (Politically)' 45
Roy, A. 204
rubble 5, 244
ruination 3–5, 21, 125–41, 169
   see also redevelopment, post-disaster
ruin lust/ruin porn 26–7
ruins 3, 35, 244–5
   ancient/classical 4, 21, 30–1
   and decay 4, 21, 26, 27
   modern 4–5, 21–2, 25, 81, 130,
      131, 245
   post-disaster 10–11, 125–41
   pre-earthquake 130, *131*
   see also agriculture, urban; housing,
      vacant; Jewish girls' school,
      Berlin; Ordos Kangbashi, Inner
      Mongolia; wastelands

S

Safransky, S. 98–9, 183
sanctions 187
San Francisco 99
San Lorenzo, Rome 218
São Paulo, Brazil 197, 198, 200–2,
   203–7, 247
S. Bates Street, Birmingham 156
Schneider, Greg 47
Schöneweide railway yard 55–9,
   63–4, 66
second homes 11, 167, 169, 173–4
segregation, social 120–1
self-determination 44, 103
Seymour, E. 157
Shepard, W. 75
Siegmund, Judith 44
Simone, A. 212, 231
slums 167, 201
Smith, N. 98, 198
social class 10, 147, 164, 165, 169, 175
social function of property 13, 182,
   200–1, 202, 203–4, 207
social movements 200, 215, 236, 237
   and alternative social projects 213,
      214, 220–4
   and cultures of resistance 214,
      218, 220
   and data collection 182, 184, 185,
      186, 192
   and squatting/occupation 188–9,
      217, 229–30
   see also social projects, alternative
social projects, alternative 13, 211–
   20, 223–4
   Take Back the City (TBTC)
      movement 222, 237
   and urban change 116–18, 119
   and vacant space/land 213–15,
      216, 231–5
social relationships 103, 247
soil testing 150
Soja, E. 40
Sorace, C. and Hurst, W. 75
source washing 154, 156
space, conceived and lived 199
space, public 59, 60, 62, 65, 100–1,
   133, 216
Spain 181–2, 183–4
   see also Barcelona
Spanish people 167
Special Office for the Reconstruction,
   L'Aquilla *131*, 133
speculation 11, 77, 156, 197, 215,
   216, 217
sprawl, urban 129

squatting/occupation 181–93,
197–208, 211–24, 229–38
and absent ownership 172, 174
and alternative social projects 211–12,
215, 216–20
Apollo House 13, 222, 230, 232,
233, 235, 236, 237
Bolt Hostel 13, 221, 230, 232–3,
234–5, 236, 237
Communia initiative 211, 213–14,
216, 218–20
Prestes Maia 201, 204, 207, 208
and social movements 188–9, 217,
229–30
Stadtumbau Ost programme 113–16,
117, 119, 120, 121n4
state support 136, 137, 139, 140
Stone Crest Income & Investment
Opportunity Fund 1 151
stories, intergenerational transmission
of 37
Stout Street, Detroit 150–3, 156
students 117, 129, 135, 138, 142n2,
220, 244
subjectivity 31, 222
subsidisation, state 117, 119, 120, 134,
168, 173
Südgelände railway yard, Berlin 61
Sukopp, Herbert 60
support groups 222–3
surveillance 173–4
sustainability 92, 95–6, 97, 101
symbolic statements 234
symbolic value 113, 115, 116, 119
symbols of prosperity 78

T

Take Back the City (TBTC)
movement 222, 237
Tangier, Morocco 11, 163–4, 165–
7, 245
see also guardianship;
ownership, absent
Tangier International Zone
management 166
taxation 77–8, 94, 147, 167, 187, 203
technicians, nomospheric 200
Tempelhofer Feld, Berlin 62–3, 66
tenants 120, 121, 134, 137, 190
Terra nullius 97, 98, 247
Thurber, A. and Fraser, J. 236
Till, Karen E. 9, 35–48, 54, 231, 245
time 85–6
Torrens, Maria Rovira 184
totalitarianism 42, 45, 46
tourism 216, 243, 244
and absent ownership 166, 167

and vacant housing 186, 187, 188,
190, 191
trade 167
trade unions 230, 233
Trigg, D. 21
Tronto, J.C. 38–9

U

underoccupation 130, *131*, 138, 139
unemployment 59, 223
United Nations Convention to Combat
Desertification 85
United States 44, 45, 150
universities 135
unremarkableness 200
urban change 54, 116–18, 119
urban development 6, 10, 65, 76, 80,
91–104, 216
urbanisation 1, 9–14
and ghost cities 75, 76–8, 84
and urban agriculture 93, 94, 102
urbanisation, capitalist 4, 93, 94, 102
urbanisation, shadow 11
urbanism, austerity 109, 223, 239
urbanism, settler 97–102
urban political economy 2, 3, 7
urban shrinkage 109, 121n7
urbs nullius 99, 103
use, socially productive 197, 199, 200,
203, 244
use, temporary 6, 12, 42, 93, 117, 119
use value 93, 97, 102, 146

V

vacancy *see* housing, vacant; vacant
space/land
vacancy, cyclical 163, 164
vacancy management 171–4, 175
vacant space/land 5–6, 7, 244, 245
and alternative social projects 212,
213–15, 216, 231–5
and entrepreneurship 91, 93, 95, 147
and gentrification 6, 62
and global financial crisis 2008
(GFC) 6, 216, 217
see also demolition; wastelands
value, symbolic 113, 115, 116, 119
value grabbing 148, 155, 157
Vancouver, Canada 92, 94, 100,
101, 104n1
vandalism 135
Vasudevan, A. 54, 207, 214, 231
Vauras Investment 190
Vergara, C.J. 28
Villes sans Bidonvilles initiative 167
violence 98
state 35, 36–7, 38, 39–40, 48

'Vocation - Job Graft. Labour Work
      Action' course 44
volunteers 61, 95, 234–6, 237
Vonovia, real estate company 63

W

Wagner, Lauren 11, 163–75, 245
Wagner, Martin 59
waiting lists 205, 234
Wang, Laura 84–5
'waste' 24
wastelands 117, 217
   Berlin 9, 53–67, 245
      and activism 54, 55, 67
      and artistic initiatives 54, 63
      and biotopes/biodiversity/
         ecology 53, 54, 55–8, 60–1, 63,
         64–5, 66
      and conservation/conservation
         areas 53, 55, 64, 65, 66
      and green corridors 58, 60, 66
      and housing crisis 59, 66
      and leisure space 58, 59, 60, 61, 62,
         65, 66
      and non-human life 54, 55, 57–8,
         64, 67
   and offsetting 64, 65
   Schöneweide railway yard 55–9,
      63–4, 66
   and urban planning 54, 59, 60, 65
   and urban agriculture 91, 99–100
water charges movement 236
Wayne County Sheriff and
      Treasurer 151
weapon production 59
webcams 173
welfare, social 205, 234
wife beaters 205
Wilhelminian period, Germany 116
Wilson, J. and Bayón, M. 31
Wood, P.B. 238
World Jewish Congress 37
World War II 37, 59

Y

Yin, D. 81, 82

Z

ZfZK 115, 121n6
Zionist Federation of Germany 43